EUROPE'S ADVANTAGE

EUROPE'S ADVANTAGE

Banks and Small Firms in Britain, France, Germany, and Italy since 1918

FRANCESCA CARNEVALI

OXFORD

UNIVERSITY PRESS

OXFORD
UNIVERSITY PRESS

Great Clarendon Street, Oxford OX2 6DP

Oxford University Press is a department of the University of Oxford.
It furthers the University's objective of excellence in research, scholarship,
and education by publishing worldwide in

Oxford New York

Auckland Cape Town Dar es Salaam Hong Kong Karachi
Kuala Lumpur Madrid Melbourne Mexico City Nairobi
New Delhi Shanghai Taipei Toronto

With offices in

Argentina Austria Brazil Chile Czech Republic France Greece
Guatemala Hungary Italy Japan Poland Portugal Singapore
South Korea Switzerland Thailand Turkey Ukraine Vietnam

Oxford is a registered trade mark of Oxford University Press
in the UK and in certain other countries

Published in the United States
by Oxford University Press Inc., New York

British Library Cataloguing in Publication Data

Data available

Library of Congress Cataloging in Publication Data

Data available

Typeset by SPI Publisher Services, Pondicherry, India
Printed in Great Britain
on acid-free paper by
Biddles, Kings Lynn, Norfolk

ISBN 0-19-925739-6   978-0-19-925739-3

1 3 5 7 9 10 8 6 4 2

To Ann Fuller and Luciano Carnevali,
with love and gratitude

ACKNOWLEDGEMENTS

This work has been a long time in the making and has benefited from the help of many people. Margaret Ackrill, Forrest Capie, Michael Collins, Phil Cottrell, Nick Crafts, Leslie Hannah, Lucy Newton, Patrick O'Brian, Duncan Ross, Giulio Sapelli, Katherine Watson, and Adam Tooze provided much of the early inspiration. Jessie Campbell at Barclays Bank Archives and Edwin Green at HSBC helped enormously with the primary research. Jonathan Zeitlin made this project possible by believing in it and providing me with a fresh perspective. Over the years Sue Bowden, Peter Cain, Giuseppe Conti, Gerd Hardach, Michel Lescure, Peter Scott, and Jim Tomlinson have helped me with valuable advice and insights, while David Musson and Matthew Derbyshire at OUP have given me more than just excellent editorial support. Friends and colleagues have listened to the details of comparative banking with endless patience and good humour. For all their help I particularly wish to thank John Bourne, John Breuily, Paolo Di Martino, Tony Gandy, Simon Kitson, Sabine Lee, Scott Lucas, Noelle Plack, Anna Spadavecchia, and Chris Wickham. Monica Borg, Rosemary Clarke, Clara Covini, Danielle Fuller, Elaine Fulton, Deborah Jewison, Helen Laville, and Gordon Lynch gave me the support to finish this book during the last difficult months. I cannot thank them enough. Andrew Priest lived with this book for almost as long as I did and gave me endless encouragement and practical help. Finally, I wish to dedicate this book to my parents, whose love made it possible.

CONTENTS

LIST OF ARCHIVES, ABBREVIATIONS, AND PARLIAMENTARY PAPERS

ABCC	Association of British Chambers of Commerce
ABI	Associazione Bancaria Italiana
ACMA	Anonima Costruzioni Macchine Automatiche
BBA	Barclays Bank Archives
BDI	Bund der Industriellen
BEA	Bank of England Archives
BIDC	Bankers Industrial Development Company
CARIPLO	Cassa di Risparmio delle Provincie Lombarde
CGA	Credit Guarantee Association
CGPME	Confédération Génerale des Petites et Moyennes Enterprises
CIC	Crédit Industriel et Commercial
CIT	Chambers of Craft Industries and Trade
CNC	Conseil National du Crédit
CNPF	Conseil National du Patronat Français
DC	Democrazia Cristiana
DG Kasse	Deutsche Genossenschaftskasse
DQP	Diversified Quality Production
DSGV	Deutscher Sparkassen und Giroverband
EAG	Economist Advisory Group
EEC	European Economic Community
EIA	Engineering Industries Association
EMS	European Monetary System
ERM	Exchange Rate Mechanism
FBI	Federation of British Industry
FRG	Federal Republic of Germany
GET	Groupe d'Étude de la Tannerie
HBOS	Halifax and Bank of Scotland
ICFC	Industrial and Commercial Finance Corporation
ICS	Istituti di Credito Speciale
IMI	Istituto per la Mobillizzazione Industriale
IRC	Industrial Reorganization Corporation
KWG	Reichskreitwesengesetz
LAMAS	Large-scale Mechanical Automation Systems
LCB	Local Clearing Bank
MBA	Midland Bank Archives
NA	National Archives
NUM	National Union of Manufacturers

PCI   Partito Comunista Italiano
PP   Parliamentary Papers
RPM   Resale Price Maintenance
SARA   Special Areas Reconstruction Association
SCM   Sociétés de Caution Mutuelle
TFR   Tanneries Françaises Réunies
VDG   Verein Deutscher Werkzeugmaschinenfabriken e.V.

PP 1918, Committee on Bank Amalgamations, Cmd. 9052 (Colwyn Committee)

PP 1931, Committee on Finance and Industry, Cmd. 3897 (Macmillan Committee)

PP 1959, Committee on the Working of the Monetary System, Cmd. 827 (Radcliffe Committee)

PP 1971, Committee of Enquiry on Small Firms, Cmd. 4811 (Bolton Committee)

LIST OF TABLES

1

Introduction

On 18 March 1918 Mr Thomas Bertram Johnston, a Bristol businessman, sat in front of a group of men in a room at the Treasury to relate his concerns over the disappearance of local banks. The man chairing the meeting was Lord Colwyn and among those present were some of the most distinguished bankers and businessmen of the time. What came to be known as the Committee on Bank Amalgamations sat for four days listening to witnesses, Mr Johnston one of twenty-one. He described a provincial business community where local banks, businessmen, local politicians, and the professional middle classes worked together to ensure the economic prosperity of the city. He told the men in the room of a number of cases where local businesses had seen the long-term support of their bank disappear, once this bank had been taken over by one of the London banks. He came to London armed with a proposal: a plan to create a state-sponsored Industrial Bank to supply local needs with local funds.[1] The men in the room duly noted Mr Johnston's concerns and plan but nothing came of his scheme. When the committee published its report Mr Johnston was likely to have wondered at the day wasted travelling to London, for the committee recommended that bank amalgamations be allowed to continue, as 'large banks are good for traders, and particularly for large traders'.[2] In its deliberations the needs of provincial, small, and medium-sized firms were forgotten. The long-term implications of this for the structure of British economy and society were far-reaching, such as the loss of competitiveness experienced in the 1970s and 1980s.

This book is the story of why during the twentieth century Britain developed into the economy with the most concentrated industrial structure in Europe and what part its banks played in this development. It is not, however, intended to be about industrial finance, or if it is, it is so only indirectly. Nor does it answer the extensively debated question 'Did British banks fail industry?',[3] although the readers might find enough evidence to reach their own conclusion. It is, instead, a book about how economic structures are created and modified not by unseen market forces but by politicians, businessmen, and other social groups. In this sense economic outcomes are the result not of natural laws but of collective political control and judgement; in Polanyi's terms the economy is embedded in society.[4]

Britain is compared with France, Germany, and Italy because these countries present a spectrum of possibilities, a range of counterfactual cases that show why banks have behaved differently and small firms have fared better. These three countries have been chosen because not only their economic structures different from Britain's but they are also different from each other. They share similarities, however, in terms of the environment that fostered small firms and this allows the identification of patterns and regularities. These are used to compare the experience of these countries with that of Britain where the environment was different. In terms of industrial and banking concentration Britain and Italy are at the opposite ends of the spectrum, while France's case is closer to Britain's and Germany is placed somewhere between France and Italy.[5] The comparison throws into sharp relief how the structure of economies is the result of design and deliberation. This book's contention is that the differences between the economies of Britain, France, Italy, and Germany are the result of the interplay between social, economic, and political groups and of the victories and defeats of different groups at different times. Each choice made by each group generated consequences which in turn gave shape to a unique blend of industrialization in each country that allowed it to respond differently to the challenges of systemic change. In this context the study of the relationship between banks and small firms is particularly illuminating. The story of this relationship shows clearly that the British economy became the most concentrated in Europe through the interaction of different political and social groups with the state and its agencies. The industrial structures of Germany, France, and Italy were the result of the same dialectical process. Hence, the comparison between these four countries shows how the differences in their banking and industrial structures were also the result of the state's attitude towards small firms.

In Britain, as in the other three countries, the role of the state has been to arrange a constant series of compromises between interest groups to avoid conflict.[6] In terms of the economy this has meant that throughout the twentieth century different economic and social groups, and central and local governments, have clashed over the shape of modernization. This clash led to compromise solutions and deviations from a perceived 'ideal type' of development. An example of this is the adaptation of American methods of production after the Second World War.[7] The following chapters show why in Britain small firms came out as losers in this conflict and in France, Germany, and Italy as winners (to different extents) .

WHY SMALL FIRMS MATTER

In this book small firms are considered as part of local economies. These can be defined simply and loosely as spaces where most local savings found their way to local financial intermediaries and then back into the local economy. A definition as fluid as this allows us to apply the term 'local economy' to a city such as Solingen, to an industrial district such as the Potteries, to a locality such as the Choletais, to a region such as Piemonte. Like Russian dolls, most of these spaces can be 'unpacked' to reveal more local economies within them, making any attempt at a precise definition rather pointless. Instead, what matters here is that in these spaces savers, consumers, and producers had interchangeable roles, could broadly identify each other, and were joined by a common interest in their 'local economy'. The banks within this space were local by virtue of their own involvement in the economic well-being of the area.

It follows, therefore, that we need to consider the actors in these spaces not just as economic beings but also as social ones. From this perspective we can see banks as social institutions whose activities at a local level might not have been strictly efficient in economic terms. Nevertheless, they provided their localities with the resources to develop competitive solutions. The fact that sectors in some countries have been more success-ful than in others in responding to growing world market pressures in the 1970s and 1980s suggests that this can be related 'to different mixes of markets, hierarchies, informal networks, associative self-regulation, and state intervention in the management and control of transactions inside and across sectoral boundaries', as Hollingsworth and Boyer have written.[8]

The idea that economic 'efficiency' comes in many forms was analysed extensively by Michael Piore and Charles Sabel when they launched the flexible specialization manifesto in 1984. Flexible specialization was in-tended as a strategy of permanent innovation, accommodation to cease-less change, rather than as an effort to control it; a strategy based on flexible, multi-use equipment, skilled workers, and cooperative arrange-ments between firms. Since the publication of *The Second Industrial Divide* flexible specialization has become a byword for a viable, modern alterna-tive to mass production.[9] A year later *Past and Present* published another contribution to the debate, by Sabel again but this time with Jonathan Zeitlin.[10] These two works brought together the disparate efforts of his-torians, sociologists, economists, and political scientists to show that alternative methods to those of mass production not only flourished during the Second Industrial Revolution but were also the solution to the economic crisis that engulfed the world in the 1970s. These works were published at a time when the crisis of mass production seemed terminal and small firms and industrial districts could provide not just different ways of making goods but also a different model of capitalism, based on cooperation rather than competition. The premise behind these studies was that mass production was not the automatic outcome of increased levels of mechanization, nor was it the unique path to technical progress. Instead, mass production was the result of the interplay between social and political forces where some groups won and others lost. Therefore the intellectual hegemony of mass production as the dominant model for growth over the best part of the twentieth century was one outcome out of many, not the only possible one.

By the mid-1980s Piore and Sabel could write that continental European countries were reacting more rapidly to the crisis of mass production and consumption thanks to the permanence of craft elements in their economies. The aim of their book was to show up the weaknesses of the 'American system of production' and this could be done more sharply by not including Britain in the picture as it was considered to have followed the 'American way' too closely. Hence Britain was excluded from the historical narrative generated by flexible specialization. Where Britain was part of this narrative it was for the purpose of analysing the rapid decline of its manufacturing sector in the 1970s and 1980s. This decline was attributed to the failure to adapt its productive structures to the new climate of international competition. Competitiveness could only be recaptured by adapting productive structures to fragmented markets and slow and uncertain growth in world trade. Britain's industrial decline was the consequence of industrial structures that had grown too rigid because of concentration.[11] Flexibility and the ability to respond to fast-changing consumer demand had been lost, together with the country's small firms.

More than a decade later the grounds of the debate had shifted. The research that had gone on in the meantime had sought to chart the fortunes of small firms, regional economies, and industrial districts while at the same time observing the reaction of large firms to changing market conditions. Large firms had not disappeared but had adapted instead, becoming more flexible and more adept at coping and influencing changes in demand, while industrial districts had shown their own limits and rigidities.[12] This showed the risk of substituting one paradigm for another. Ten years on, Sabel and Zeitlin concluded that progress did not lead to the consolidation of one particular form of industrial organization but that 'constantly shifting background conditions ... can produce abrupt redefinitions of the appropriate way to organise economic activity'.[13]

If we accept that the dominance of mass production was only one possible outcome then we must accept that trajectories could have been different and that over time decisions were taken by economic and social groups (workers, firm owners, institutions) that led to that outcome. Piore and Sabel explain how each country adopted mass production methods at the beginning of the twentieth century because its elites perceived the commercial and military potential of the mass production economy as indispensable to national survival, in the face of the USA's rise to economy dominance.[14] These countries, however, might have followed technological trajectories that looked similar but the manufacturing sector in each country adapted to the mass production model in different ways. As a result each country maintained combinations of large and small firms and centralized and regional economies in variant proportions.

The temporal focus of this book is on the interwar period and on the 1950s and 1960s (although where necessary reference is made to earlier and later periods). The reason for this focus is that it is not possible to understand the resurgence of small firms from the 1970s onwards without an understanding of the forces that promoted (or hindered) their growth in the years after the Second World War. The diffusion of mass production and consumption from America to Europe during the 1950s and 1960s did not exclude small firms. In each of the four countries studied here small firms had to be accommodated as part of governments' involvement with the economy. The configuration of this accommodation was part of the exceptionally high growth rates enjoyed by these countries. Moreover, in each country small firms faced the turbulence of the interwar years protected (or harmed) by different institutional arrangements. These institutional arrangements were those that allowed small firms to contribute to the post-war economic 'miracle'. The following chapters show how in Germany, France, and Italy small firms, far from occupying a marginal place in the process of modernization, were central to the growth experienced by these economies.

Table 1.1 shows that by the early 1990s Britain's industrial structure was less concentrated than Germany's. What this table cannot show, however, is that this has been the result of a process of concentration in Germany[15] rather than an increase in the share of small and medium-sized firms in Britain (those employing fewer than 250 people). For most

Table 1.1. Italy, Germany, France, and Britain: distribution of employment by size of 'industrial enterprise' (as defined by Eurostat) in 1990s (%)

Number employed	Italy (1991)	Germany (1992)	France (1992)	Britain (1993)
< 250	71.4	37.5[a]	47.0	44.5
1–9	23.3	7.4	8.1	7.2
10–49	29.2	14.3	17.7	15.6
50–249	18.9	15.8[b]	21.2	21.7
250 >	28.6	62.5[c]	53.0	55.5

[a] Less than 200
[b] Between 50 and 199 employed
[c] More than 200

Source: Eurostat, 1996.

of the twentieth century there has been a steady decline in the weight
of small and medium-sized firms in the British economy (as shown in
Table 6.1) and it is only since the late 1970s that there has been a revival
in their number. The rise and fall of small firms in Britain is analysed in
Chapters 2 and 6 but what Table 1.1 highlights is how in the 1990s small
and medium-sized firms still provided a substantial share of employment
in the four largest economies in Europe.

The literature on the topic of small firms has emphasized the fact that
an industrial system comprising a distribution of small, medium, and
large firms allows a more favourable distribution of economic power in
society. In the long run excessive industrial concentration has unfavour-
able and destabilizing effects as it reduces competition. Small firms can
foster social mobility and reduce social conflict while being a source of
economic regeneration and creating market turbulence, thus providing an
additional dimension to competition.[16] Moreover, small firms make at
least two further important contributions to the economy in general, and
industrial markets in particular. First, small firms play a considerable role
in the process of technological change.[17] And if small firms are not
considered in isolation but as units that operate together to create a
'system of innovation'[18] then the understanding of the potential of small
firms for innovation can be furthered. Within the system innovation is not
only a cumulative process activated by one firm but stems also from the
input from other firms, suppliers, users, and institutions such as universities, science parks, and research centres. The various elements of the
system contribute to the process of innovation by introducing different
and complementary knowledge concerning specific technologies involved in different moments of the cumulative process that will eventually lead to innovation.[19] Second, small firms have generated in recent
years the largest share of new jobs.[20]

The claim here is not that all small firms in all sectors are dynamic and
innovative. In some sectors, like car manufacturing or oil refining, economies of scale require large-scale operations, but small firms can still
occupy niche markets that are too small for large-scale producers and
are characterized by demand not satisfied by mass-produced goods, for
example Sinclair calculators, or Aston Martin automobiles. Typically
though, small firms will have a more dynamic role in those sectors,
characterized by high rates of product innovation, competition on the
basis of performance maximization rather than price, loose entrepreneurial organization, and the use of general purpose manufacturing technology with relatively skilled labour.[21]

One of the most interesting things to emerge from recent research
on small firms in Britain is that the most rapid growth in employment
has taken place among the very smallest firms, particularly those with five
or less employees. Once established, small firms grow rapidly but soon

find a ceiling which they find difficult to get beyond. This ceiling appears once they have employed eight to ten people. Very few firms grow beyond this point and the mortality rate of firms in this group is very high.[22] The implications of this for the whole economy are serious because only those firms that grow can provide long-term employment prospects.[23] Moreover, high mortality rates reduce the innovative impact that small firms can have, as identified by the Committee of Inquiry on Small Firms (Bolton Committee) in 1971.[24] The origins and nature of the barriers to the growth of small and medium-sized firms show clearly that these are also the result of political and social forces, rather than just the outcome of pressures from the market. Chapter 2 details how the lack of adequate sources of external capital was identified in 1931 as one of the barriers to the growth of small firms in Britain by the parliamentary committee set up to investigate industry and finance in Britain.[25] Since then there have been a number of studies into the failure of the financial system to provide the relatively small sums of capital that small firms need to grow.[26]

BANKS AND SMALL FIRMS

A firm will need finance for different purposes depending on what life stage it is in. A new firm will need start-up finance, even in the case of a business that begins its operations in a basement or garage, to buy equipment and working capital to buy supplies, as customers do not pay immediately. In this case the two most common sources of finance will be private, either from the owners, their family and friends, or redundancy money. The other source tends to be the owner's bank and takes the form of an increased overdraft or loan, secured by a house or other personal assets. During the normal course of events a small firm's biggest problem will be cash flow, as wages and suppliers have to be paid regularly, while customers do not pay at the moment of purchase. If normal shortages of cash coincide with another short-term problem, like an illness or a temporary downturn in demand, the only possible source of finance is the bank.

The following stage is expansion, which might take the shape of a move to larger premises and/or the purchase of new or different machinery, for product or process innovation. There are two different interpretations of the innovative process that suggest differences in the type of capital required by small firms for innovation. Following the Schumpeterian concept of innovation technological change is something momentous that needs a considerable investment in capital. The Rosenbergian view of innovation instead interprets innovation as a cumulative process and is more concerned with the liquidity of the firm at the moment of the decision to innovate. This will determine the extension and the articulation of the first steps towards change.[27] In both cases the most probable source of finance is a bank loan or in some cases a venture capital institution that will take a share of equity.

All this brings us to the relationship between small firms and banks. If liquidity is the issue for innovation (or survival) then a small firm might decide to innovate if it can negotiate an extension of its overdraft and, most importantly, if it knows that this will not be withdrawn during a bad general economic phase.

In 2002 the Competition Commission identified the problems of small firms as arising from the price fixing arrangements of the four banks that control 90 per cent of the lending to small firms, Barclays, Royal Bank (owner of NatWest), HSBC, and Lloyds TSB. Banks have been quick to refute such accusations, pointing instead at the number of services offered to small firms and to the fact that they are more costly to assess. In all fairness to them the report did conclude that 'there is little evidence that demand for appropriate debt finance is not being met'.[28] This conclusion was based on the finding that

of those firms whose application for a term loan has been rejected, about 40 per cent were on the basis of a bad business plan or excessive outstanding debt . . . The remaining 60 per cent had insufficient collateral or were refused because they were just starting up and had no track record. . . . It may be that at the margin some viable projects do not get debt funds.[29]

Chapter 6 shows that this is exactly the same conclusion reached thirty years earlier by the Committee of Enquiry on Small Firms (Bolton Committee). In other words the recurring problem faced by small firms and banks is one of transaction costs and information asymmetries.

The implications of banking concentration for the development of small firms have been neglected mainly because of neoclassical assumptions about the perfection of capital markets, with all firms, lenders, and borrowers having equal access to finance and information.[30] These (unrealistic) assumptions have led to a dismissal of institutional constraints as one of the factors that can be used to explain the existence of unsatisfied borrowers. Moreover, firms have been treated as homogeneous entities, without considering the importance of differences in size and location. However, a historical and comparative analysis of the activity of banks in different countries shows that institutional arrangements do matter and affect banks' lending practices. The reason for this is that capital markets are not perfect because of the existence of information asymmetries. This book's contention is that information asymmetries are the core of the problem of the supply of finance to small firms and ultimately of the existence of barriers to their growth. In Britain these information asymmetries are the result of the concentrated nature of British banking that, as this book shows, has its origins in the 1920s.

BANKS AND INFORMATION ASYMMETRIES

In theory, banks, as profit maximizers, aim to engage in transactions which involve the lowest marginal cost possible relative to the price charged. Transaction costs connected to the business of lending money concern, in the first instance, the cost of gathering information about clients and their business to minimize the risk of default. After the loan has been granted the bank incurs other costs, such as monitoring, to minimize the risk of moral hazard and, in some cases, the necessity to enforce contracts.[31] Bank lending is one of the cases where problems of asymmetric information are more likely to occur as borrowers possess much more information about themselves than the lender. Gathering information to reduce asymmetry is a time and human resources consuming activity and these costs can be reduced by imposing on customers the necessity to fulfil some formal requirement concerning, for example, their balance sheets and performance record. Not having much collateral and a limited cash flow, small firms might experience more difficulties in securing loans, or extensions of overdrafts, than large firms do, especially in the case of investments for innovation.[32] Information asymmetries can be reduced by additional knowledge of a more informal nature, about the trustworthiness of an applicant, and the prospects of the business. For a bank, however, the cost of acquiring information on the small firm beyond that which is formalized (such as collateral, cash flow, and track record) might be too high in relation to the returns.[33] This high cost could lead to the transaction (the loan) not taking place. Or if it did take place, the cost for the small firm could be very high (they might be charged higher interest rates than those commanded by large firms, for example). The effect of this mechanism might become perverse in the sense that it either increases the firm's capital costs, or, by restricting actual supply, makes it less innovative, in both cases making it less competitive.[34]

In assessing non-formalized information, however, not all financial institutions have the same cost function. Those banks whose decision-making centres are physically closer to the small firms can assess local knowledge more cheaply than those banks which use a branch network to transmit information from the periphery to the centre.[35] The mechanism of assessment of creditworthiness relies on the collection of reliable information. Within regional economic networks there are participants who can provide a bank with information additional to that formalized in an application form by the firm. These informants could be organizations that are clients both of the bank and the firm asking for a loan, associations such as the local Chamber of Commerce, or other local financial institutions. The regional economy is singular compared to other business networks as the welfare of the individual participants depends on the welfare of the whole community. Therefore, there is little incentive not to cooperate as withholding information or providing faulty information would reduce the welfare of the individual by reducing that of the community. Furthermore, as all the participants are locked together within the same economy and society, opportunistic behaviour is likely to be punished in the future. This mechanism of cooperation allows local banks to gain access to good quality information about the reputation of a firm and its activity. The information provided by these sources is particularly effective in the case of new firms searching for start-up capital as in their case the main asset of the firm is the reputation of the entrepreneurs. By belonging to a regional network these people are known to those with whom they have dealt in the past and thus can easily become known to the bank.

Transaction costs are also determined by the monitoring of customers to minimize risk. Banks generally gain knowledge of their customers' activity through long-standing business contacts and these allow contracts to become simplified over time, as the same customer approaches the same bank every time a loan is needed. These contacts and the knowledge derived from them make monitoring simpler, more effective, and cheaper. If the social element is introduced in the analysis of the relationship between banks and firms then the transactions that take place between them can be defined as idiosyncratic, a highly individual exchange. When seller and buyer are connected by the characteristics of the product they are exchanging, as in the case of a loan granted on the basis of knowledge that goes beyond what is quantified by a balance sheet, the governance structure used to limit opportunism is that based on relational contracting. This is a contract where the relation existing between buyer and seller allows for monitoring without increasing transaction costs.[36] Moreover, the social network that exists within a local economy creates ties that make monitoring easier, as the firm's reputation, and thus its ability to enter contracts with future suppliers and customers, is at stake. For the same reason contracts will be respected and enforcement will not be necessary. Inside the local economy the welfare of the community depends largely on individuals not taking undue risks, thus peer-monitoring mechanisms can mitigate moral hazard.[37]

This theoretical framework is necessary to explain why a banking system made of national banks with a branch network cannot efficiently supply the needs of regional economies, generating a fringe of unsatisfied borrowers. Without local banks investment information is trapped in local networks. During the twentieth century the persistence of local banks in continental Europe has been a consequence of the pressure that the periphery has put on the state to halt financial agglomeration. The existence of information asymmetries has justified a close relationship between banks and small firms and the promotion by the state of public and semi-public local banks. However, as Daniel Verdier trenchantly writes: 'local banks can only exist if the potential victims of financial agglomeration enjoy enough political power'.[38] Chapter 2 explores the political forces that promoted banking concentration in Britain, at the expense of local banks, including Mr Thomas Johnston's.

NOTES

1 National Archives, T1/12267, Committee on Bank Amalgamations, Minutes of evidence, 18/03/1918, 66–70.
2 PP 1918, *Report of the Treasury Committee on Bank Amalgamation*, Cmd 9052, point 6b.
3 Readers interested in this debate can start from Collins and Baker, *Commercial Banks* and the bibliography in Chapter 1 therein.
4 Polanyi, *The Great Transformation*.
5 Bagnasco and Sabel, *Small and Medium-Sized Enterprises*, 3.
6 Middlemas, *Politics in Industrial Society*, 13.
7 Zeitlin and Herrigel, *Americanization*; Djelic, *Exporting the American Model*.
8 Hollingsworth *et al.*, *Governing Capitalist Economies*, 9–10.
9 Piore and Sabel, *The Second Industrial Divide*, 17.
10 Sabel and Zeitlin, 'Historical Alternatives'.
11 Hirst and Zeitlin, *Reversing Industrial Decline*; Hirst and Zeitlin, 'Flexible specialisation'.
12 Bagnasco and Sabel, *Small and Medium-Sized Enterprises*.
13 Sabel and Zeitlin, *World of Possibilities*, 2.
14 Piore and Sabel, *The Second Industrial Divide*, 163.
15 Fritsch, 'The Role of Small Firms in West Germany'.
16 Beesley and Hamilton, 'Small Firms' Seedbed Role and the Concept of Turbulence'.
17 Nelson and Winter, *An Evolutionary Theory of Economic Change*; Winter, 'Schumpeterian Competition'. The most comprehensive study of small firms' innovation activity can be found in the University of Sussex SPRU study published in Rothwell and Zegveld, *Innovation and the Small and Medium-Sized Firm*.
18 Malerba, *Sistemi innovativi*, 13.
19 Ibid.
20 For the first analysis of the role played by small and medium-sized firms in generating employment see: Birch, *The Job Generation Process*; more recently Storey and Johnson, *Job Generation* and Storey, *Understanding the Small Business Sector*; Robson, 'Self-employment in the UK Regions'.
21 Sabel and Piore, *The Second Industrial Divide*.
22 Dunne and Hughes, 'Age, Size, Growth and Survival: UK Companies in the 1980s'; Hart and Oulton, 'Growth and Size of Firms'.
23 Storey, *Understanding the Small Business Sector*.
24 PP 1971, Committee of Enquiry on Small Firms, *Research Report No. 6*, Cmd 4811.
25 PP 1931, Committee on Finance and Industry, *Final Report*, Cmd 3282.

26 For a selection of the recent literature on the subject see Hughes and Storey,
    Finance and the Small Firm; Hughes, 'Finance for SMEs: A UK Perspective';
    Binks and Ennew, 'The Relationship between UK Banks and their Small
    Business Customers'; Lund and Wright, 'The Financing of Small Firms in
    the United Kingdom'; Small Business Research Trust, 'Business Finance'.
27 Amendola and Gaffard, *The Innovative Choice*.
28 Competition Commission, *Report on the Supply of Banking Services by Clearing
    Banks to Small and Medium-Sized Enterprises*, vol. 1, 6–7.
29 Ibid., vol. 5, 168.
30 Modigliani and Miller, 'The Cost of Capital'.
31 Goodhart, *Money, Information and Uncertainty*, 2.
32 Binks, 'Finance for Expansion in the Small Firm'.
33 Barber, Metcalfe, and Porteous, *The Barriers to Growth in Small Firms*, 39.
34 Stiglitz and Weiss, 'Credit Rationing in Markets with Imperfect Competition',
    395.
35 The mechanism of information exchange within a regional network is ana-
    lysed in the Italian case in Carnevali, 'Between Markets and Networks'.
36 Williamson, 'Transaction Cost Economics', 240–5.
37 Arnott and Stiglitz, 'Moral Hazard and Non-market Institutions', 179.
38 Verdier, *Moving Money*, 15–20.

PART I

BRITAIN, GERMANY, FRANCE, AND ITALY BEFORE 1939

2

Banking Cartels and Industrial Concentration in Britain

During the nineteenth century the market power of British banks had been widely dispersed. The banking system comprised hundreds of small, local banks, whose fortunes were closely tied to the local economy. These banks concentrated on short-term credit but in many cases also provided medium- and long-term loans for local businesses.[1] In 1826 banks were given permission to issue shares to the general public, thus local businessmen frequently became involved in establishing joint-stock banks while also being the banks' most active borrowers. By 1875 there were 122 joint-stock banks but still 236 private banks in England and Wales and eleven banks in Scotland.[2] Few banks had large branch networks and the distribution of assets and lending was equally simple with the main source of funds being deposits collected locally and most lending taking the form of short-term credits such as bill discounts. Businesses used bank loans as a source of short-term funds or to make up for unexpected contingencies. As Phillip Cottrell has pointed out, banks, finance, and customers were matched in terms of size and scale in that the small-scale family firm dealt with the local bank and regional banks made larger advances to the bigger industrial concerns.[3]

This symbiotic relationship, however, was not to last. In 1825 there had been more than 600 banks in England and Wales—local businesses with few, if any branches. By 1913 the average number of branches per bank had increased to 156. This process of expansion had taken place thanks to relentless amalgamation. Between 1870 and 1921, 264 mergers took place, the peak of merger activity coinciding with the banking crises of 1878 and 1890. As a result 370 domestic banks disappeared.[4] In addition to this, increasing stress was being given to banking liquidity following a series of financial crises (the first one in 1866, followed by the City of Glasgow Bank crash in 1878, and the Baring crisis of 1890). This meant a shift to larger holdings of government securities and a decline in the ratio of bank assets in the form of non-bank private sector financing.[5] By the culmination of the process in 1920 five banks (Midlands, Barclays, Lloyds, Westminster, and National Provincial) accounted for 80 per cent of English bank deposits. These were fully national banks, with a head office in London and a branch system extending all over the country.[6] Cottrell has pointed out that of the many reasons behind this rise in concentration, the main one was to use territorial expansion, in terms of number of branches, to compete for deposits and increase liquidity.[7]

The incentives to amalgamate and take over other banks were many. Extensive branch networks allowed surpluses from certain areas to be transferred to areas requiring credit, credit risk could be diffused over a larger area, and operations could be standardized, thus reducing costs. The existence of the clearing system based in London meant that provincial banks had to maintain an agent in London, thus incurring higher costs than London banks. In other words the institutional regulation of the business of banking created an incentive for banks to move their head office to London away from the regions. Amalgamation allowed provincial banks to obtain a place in the Clearing House by absorbing a London bank which was already a member (as Midlands and Lloyds did) and private banks to join forces against joint-stock ones (as in the case of Barclays). The process of amalgamation is well represented by the case of the Midland bank. Between 1913 and 1918 it amalgamated the Sheffield and Hallamshire, the Lincoln and Lindsey, the Metropolitan Bank, and the London Joint-Stock Bank, thus becoming the largest bank in the world.[8]

By the end of this process of amalgamation, the nature of British banking had changed dramatically compared with the mid-Victorian period. Local and regional banks had virtually disappeared and the dominant type of commercial bank was a joint-stock limited concern based in London with a branch network encompassing the metropolis and provinces. Lending policies were affected as the activity of the branches was regulated by managers based in London, and local knowledge and contacts became less important.[9] Businessmen seeking loans in the post-First World War period had to negotiate loans with branch managers of a national concern[10] and this led to growing concern in Edwardian England over the perceived lack of bank support for industrial enterprise. This was attributed to the disappearance of provincial banks and the rise of branch banking, with branch managers being granted very little discretion as to the size of loans and the security required.[11] Structural change brought about by mergers, with the dominance of London-based branch banks and the decline of small local banks, also changed the overall asset structure of the system. The provincial banks held a much higher proportion of their assets in the form of credits to the non-bank private sector than the London banks did. After a merger, the combined London and provincial banks held significantly less of their assets in non-bank private sector credits than the absorbed provincial bank had.[12] Though mergers and increasing levels of liquidity made English (and Scottish) banks much more stable than their continental counterparts, they also became more conservative and less supportive of the private business sector.[13] As the banks grew in scale their interests changed, moving away from traditional commercial banking business. To diversify earning assets banks increased their foreign banking operations (especially acceptances) in line with the structural changes that were taking place in the economy with the growth of international trade and British foreign investments.[14] The banks' strategy is hardly surprising if one considers that most directors of the English joint-stock banks had their main business interest outside their banks. Their connections with private mercantile and financial firms meant that the main role of the joint-stock banks was to provide these firms with cash credit to support these firms' international financial operations.[15]

THE 1918 COMMITTEE ON BANK AMALGAMATIONS

The decision taken in 1918 by the Midland bank to take over the London Joint-Stock Bank generated a large public outcry expressing concerns about a strong money trust and of monopolistic behaviour.[16] In response to this the Treasury set up a committee to explore the impact of bank amalgamations (known as the Colwyn Committee, from the name of its chairman). The remit of the committee was to consider whether amalgamations between banks might negatively affect industrial and commercial interests and whether legislation should be introduced to prohibit, or regulate, such amalgamations. After listening to twenty-one expert witnesses the committee presented a report in May 1918 in which they pointed out the various advantages of establishing large commercial banks, such as economies of scale and the spreading of risk.

Nonetheless, the committee agreed that the amalgamation of large banks would create a cartel that was undesirable both from a political and financial point of view. Thus the committee recommended that all further amalgamations should be made dependent on the joint approval of the Treasury and Board of Trade.[17] This recommendation, however, was never turned into practice and was replaced by a private understanding between the banks and the government which allowed the continued absorption of small banks but did not permit the merging of any of the larger banks. In fact mergers were restricted to banks whose geographical coverage did not overlap.[18] After 1918 the five larger banks (Midland, Barclays, Lloyds, Westminster, and National Provincial) continued their expansion through the amalgamation of a number of provincial and Scottish banks.[19] By 1920 when the merger wave peaked the leading British clearing banks were larger in absolute terms than their American and German counterparts.[20] Mergers continued to take place throughout the interwar years. In 1924 the Midland took over the North of Scotland and Town and County Bank. In the same year the Royal Bank of Scotland took over a small private bank, Drummond's, followed by William Deacons in 1929, and Glyn Mills in 1939. In 1928 Martins merged with the Lancashire and Yorkshire Bank and in 1929 the District merged with the Manchester and County.

One could argue, however, that the committee's investigation had come too late. By the spring of 1918 the structure of British banking was already more concentrated than that of its main industrial competitors, the USA and Germany. Given the numerous benefits of eliminating competition, it is very unlikely that the bankers' quest for size would stop. The Colwyn Committee was set up by government in response to the public's fear of a small and powerful oligopoly. What the committee had to do was to 'manufacture' a rationale for banking concentration, to allay these fears. The rationale presented was that:

large banks are better for traders, and particularly for large traders, than small banks because, with their large resources, they can safely make individual advances on a more generous scale. And ... banks must keep pace with the growth in size of business houses ... to enable them to deal with the demands of the after-the-war trade both at home and abroad'.[21]

What follows is an analysis of the evidence used by the committee to come to this conclusion. The remit of the committee was to consider whether amalgamations might be damaging to industrial and mercantile interests. It is interesting to note, however, that of the twenty-one expert witnesses called only one manufacturer and one merchant were asked to present their evidence. Except for Sidney Webb and Thomas Goodwin who represented the Co-op Wholesale Society, all the other witnesses were connected in some way to banking and financial concerns, and only two of these represented provincial banks, the Liverpool and the District banks. The composition of the committee itself also largely excluded the voice of manufacturing interests.[22] In other words, financial interests set up the committee and shaped the direction of its investigation. Bankers were asked by bankers whether bank amalgamations should be allowed to continue. It is hardly surprising that the only voices unequivocally raised against further amalgamations were those of the lone manufacturer, Thomas Bertram Johnston, chairman and managing director of the Bristol Pottery Company, and of Thomas Goodwin, while everybody else spoke in favour. It is important, however, to consider in some detail the arguments put forward as they shine a powerful light over the nature of the concerns that motivated the players at this time.

As the evidence presented by the witnesses unfolded it became clear that commercial and merchant bankers intended amalgamations to be the takeover of the smaller banks by the larger ones since this was seen as the way of gaining the advantages of size in terms of deposits and lending capacity. This uncontentious point was shared by the other witnesses connected with the world of finance, the proviso always being that the government should intervene to avoid the creation of an oligopoly that would reduce competition. Size, however, was presented as important for another reason as well. Overwhelmingly, the rhetoric used by the bankers to win their argument involved the threat represented by the size of German banks and businesses. Sir Edward Holden, chairman of the Midland, echoed most of the other bankers when he explained to the Committee that if Britain was to continue competing on world markets it needed big banks that could compete against Germany's.[23] The minutes of the evidence contain numerous references to the power of the big German banks and of the need for British banks and businesses to stand up to them through emulation. The witnesses spoke in the spring of 1918, when the outcome of the war was still far from certain and it is likely that this sentiment carried a lot of weight with the members of the committee.

Of the 'big five', three banks spoke to the committee and claimed that their willingness and capacity to lend to small traders was undiminished by amalgamations, as the existence of local directors ensured that local knowledge was not wasted. The banks, however, made it clear that they expected the post-war world to be led by big business and if Britain was to retain its position as a world power it could only do so if its economy was assisted by big banks. The chairman of the Midland declared: 'There ought to be a sufficient number of powerful banks to ensure free competition amongst themselves, but with this limitation each of the banks ought to be made as powerful as possible.'[24] However, Thomas Bertram Johnston, the sole manufacturer called as a witness, argued exactly the opposite, claiming that amalgamations and the takeover of local banks were bitterly resented. The examples presented by Johnston (involving his own and other Bristol businesses, including a colliery) showed how the support to local manufacturing ceased once local banks were taken over. The picture he presented of Bristol was one of a town where banks, businessmen, local officials, and the professional middle classes cooperated to ensure the economic prosperity of the city and maintain social stability through employment. Though Johnston recognized that amalgamations in banking and industry were essential if the UK was to compete against Germany, his concerns were very clearly local. In his view big banks lacked the local knowledge and the commitment and involvement in the local economy to replace local banks.[25] The statement made by Drummond Fraser, managing director of the District Bank, Manchester's biggest bank, confirmed Johnston's words with many examples of the importance for banks of local knowledge and of the links between local banks and local customers. In his view, the takeover by London banks damaged this relationship and generated strong local feelings against amalgamations.[26] Provincial banks, however, were not united in their views as Hope Simpson, general manager of the Bank of Liverpool, supported further amalgamations as a way to gain an office in London and compete against the bigger banks.[27]

In the four days it took the Committee to listen to the twenty-one witnesses, evidence was presented as to why bank amalgamations should be allowed to continue. This evidence, however, was inevitably biased in favour of the banks as it came from representatives of the financial world. On the strength of this evidence the committee reported to the public that banking concentration was an inevitable necessity, as businesses were seen as getting bigger and their demands more pressing. To this end big banks should be allowed to take over the smaller ones. The statement of the one manufacturer that local banks were essential for provincial econ-omies went unheard because it did not coincide with the 'view of the world' formulated by the committee. Furthermore, listening to Johnston would have meant legislation to protect provincial banks, when not even they wanted to remain local. The bankers' wish was granted and British banking continued to be the most concentrated in the world.

However, the structure of British industry, and of German banking for that matter, was not really like those described by the committee and its witnesses. The relationship between industry and banks in Germany was known to bankers and economists at the time not to be restricted to the large combines and the Berlin banks. Regional banks were known to play a part in fostering the development of industry in those regions charac-terized by small-scale production. In Solingen (Sheffield's main competi-tor) production was organized using a system of outworkers who could purchase their homes thanks to *Landesbank* mortgages and use their savings to buy electric motors and grinding machinery. According to a contemporary observer, home ownership and low interest rates guaran-teed by the municipality fostered ambition and hard work in these indus-trial workers.[28] However, it was mostly the big Berlin banks that attracted the attention of contemporaries, for their connections with the steel and coal industries, those enduring symbols of industrial might.[29] Moreover, on the eve of the First World War Britain was still a country of small and medium-sized firms. It had some large industrial combines, the bigger ones in textiles, tobacco, brewing, and soap but these were smaller than the American and German ones, and were very much the exception.[30] In other words, the rationale presented by the Colwyn Committee to justify further banking amalgamations was a partial one and only marginally connected with the world of manufacturing. In 1918 British industry was far from being concentrated in the same way as the banking sector was as the formation of large commercial banks came well before the general rise of the manufacturing firms.[31]

The first census to record the number of firms and their size distribution was the one taken in 1924. At this date it was estimated that there were about 200,000 manufacturing firms employing fewer than ten people and these employed 8.5 per cent of the working population and contrib-uted 7.5 per cent of net output. In 1930 these figures had increased to

9.6 per cent and 8 per cent respectively.[32] The figures in the 1924 census relating to size distribution of firms are for 'industry', including non-manufacturing firms. The figures for the 1930 census instead also show the size distribution for 'factory trades' but consider the size of establishments (not enterprises).

Table 2.1 shows how substantial, even by 1930, was the small firm sector, both in terms of employment and net output, even just taking into account only those firms employing less than 100 people and without knowing anything about the contribution made by firms employing fewer than ten people. In fact, the industrial concentration process of the inter-war period affected only some sectors.

CONCENTRATION IN INDUSTRY?

In the 1870s and 1880s competition in the manufacturing sector was still very strong, with most industries populated by mostly small firms, and consumers enjoying an increasing choice of goods from an expanding geographical area. However, by the end of the century, changes in the nature of demand, as urbanization increased and technical and financial innovations took place, gave firms strong incentives to merge to increase their size. Between 1888 and 1914 on average at least sixty-seven firms disappeared in mergers every year and in the three years of most intense merger activity, between 1898 and 1900, as many as 650 firms were absorbed in 198 separate mergers.[33] These were the years that saw the creation of the great combines in the textile, tobacco, brewing, and soap industries, to mention but a few. The textile finishing combines, such as Bradford Dyers Association, for example, accounted for 80 per cent of their respective markets, while tobacco and cement groups controlled between 60 and 80 per cent of their markets.[34] As a result of this intense merger activity, the structure of British manufacturing on the eve of the First World War was very different from what it had been three or four

Table 2.1. Britain: employment and net output by size of manufacturing establishment, 1930 (%)

Size of firm	Net output	Per cent employed
11–99	23	24
100–199	14	15
200–499	21	23
500+	42	38

Source: *Census of Production*, 1935, part V, p. 23.

decades earlier. However, many of these pre-war large firms were in the staple industries, whose markets were already declining. Among the largest firms in 1905 there were only three chemical firms, and only one of them, Brunner Mond, was in a growing sector of the industry, while there was only one electrical engineering firm and none in car manufacture. On the eve of the First World War the new industries were poorly represented in the top fifty largest companies and contemporaries saw the slowdown of the economy as the result of the absence of large firms in these new industries, populated instead by a multitude of small and medium-sized firms.

The process of concentration of industry continued in the interwar years as the share of manufacturing output of the 100 largest enterprises increased from 16 per cent in 1909 to 24 per cent in 1935.[35] During the interwar years, marked by slumping demand, overproduction, and unemployment, amalgamations could deliver 'the enhancement of profits by the elimination of competition' as *The Economist* trenchantly put it in 1924.[36] The Federation of British Industry (FBI) heralded concentration, resulting from the combination of manufacturers, as leading to greater efficiency of production and reduction of waste. Competition was condemned as the evil manifestation of unrestricted individualism, leading to excessive price reduction and the deterioration of quality.[37] The rejection of market forces stemmed from the economic depression that marked these years. The experience of the depression made many question the ability of the market economy to deliver growth and consider whether the economy would be better managed, at a macro level with Keynesian tools, and at a micro level by 'rationalizing' the industrial structure. The rationalization movement united bankers, politicians, and trade unionists in the belief that competition was not able to resolve the problems of overproduction and underconsumption. The depression seemed to show that the world had become too complicated for the invisible hand of the market to be able to allocate resources and men should therefore devise a 'rational' system of industrial regulation.[38]

Rationalization was not without its opponents. The National Confederation of Employers Association, made up mostly of small and medium-sized firms, blamed the trade unions for monopolizing wage negotiations and making wages rigid, and government intervention and the expanding public sector for distorting the functioning of the private enterprise system. These opponents also pointed out that the growth of the combines was the cause of the problem as it created price inflexibility, preventing readjustment of supply and demand (a point made sixty years later by Piore and Sabel in their 1984 critique of mass production, *The Second Industrial Divide*). For large businesses, however, the cost of confrontation with the unions, which led to the General Strike in 1926, and the social cost of reducing public expenditure made rationalization seem like a preferable alternative. Governments of the time quietly acquiesced and a predominantly laissez-faire Parliament refused to oppose business lobby interests. The problems of the British economy could be solved, or so it was believed, by reducing costs via mergers, scale economies, and capacity reduction without using cuts in wages. Rationalization promised salvation without social confrontation, something that the British government wanted to avoid at all cost.[39] While on the continent small firms were able to find a voice and enough public and government support to gain concessions to safeguard them against the various dangers of 'rationalization', small firms in Britain were unable to do so. This is hardly surprising in a climate where the elimination of small firms was seen as 'inevitable' by economists such as Alfred Marshall.[40] By then contemporaries had become aware that Britain was lagging behind the USA and Germany and became inclined to think that the problem resided in the small-scale firms in the new industrial sectors. Sir Philip Dawson, MP, who knew Germany well, in his 1926 book *Germany's Industrial Revival* considered how German industry had overcome the difficulties of the war and the loss of world markets by setting up combines in cooperation with the banks.[41] The advantages of size in reducing production and labour costs and the ability of German staple industries to achieve this was the theme of many of the books published during and after the war.[42]

When in power the post-war Conservative governments' attitude towards rationalization and concentration did not move from the traditional rhetoric of laissez-faire. Nevertheless, a group of radical 'young Tories', such as Robert Boothby and Harold Macmillan rejected competition as a form of unrestricted individualism and sought to replace the competitive dynamics of the market with cooperation between business organizations. Corporativism was the solution to competitive chaos and the role of the state was to aid such development through provision of both financial assistance and statutory powers to promoters of industrial amalgamations.[43] The Labour party (when not in power) were not able to convince the government to accept their proposal for the investigation of monopolies. In fact, by adopting Keynes' ideas on demand management the Labour party also 'adopted' large firms and concentration, as it would be easier to control a few larger firms than many small ones. At the same time conflict between the Consumers' Council and the Cooperative Wholesale Society split the consumers' movement, ensuring that there was no weighty opposition to the rationalization movement.[44] The trade unions obviously preferred large firms as labour could be organized more easily.

While mergers were not actively promoted by the various interwar governments, they were not opposed. The government's position became clear in 1929 with the publication of the *Final Report* of the Balfour Committee on British industrial condition. The *Report* gave wide publicity to the need to rationalize the structure of British industry, along the lines of American and German big business. Rationalization, however, was also not to be left to market forces but could 'be performed more steadily and rationally and with less suffering through the mechanism of consolidation or agreement than by the unaided play of competition'.[45] With no opposition by the government, and no effective opposition from any other group, the incentives to develop large-scale organizations were many, not least the opportunities for personal gain offered by the stock market. The development in the stock market promised the owners of large firms the opportunity to turn their paper assets into ready cash as promoters inflated the *ex ante* expectations of the benefits to be derived from the economies of scale and monopoly power that would follow mergers. Given the government's reluctance to intervene directly in the finance of rationalization, it was unlikely that without the growth of the stock market this would have taken place on the scale that it did. The reluctance of the commercial banks to lend to small firms for capital investments, and the high cost of a public issue, meant that for these firms the only way to expand was to be acquired by a quoted company, further accentuating the concentration of assets in fewer and larger firms.[46] Those firms that were reluctant to merge or were too small to appeal to the stock market were 'helped' by the creation, on the Bank of England's initiative, of the Bankers' Industrial Development Company (BIDC) in 1929, a consortia of merchant banks whose aim was to re-equip, and where necessary amalgamate, companies in the staple industries facing financial difficulties. The banks provided capital to finance new investment and gained rights to a share in any future benefits of the merger. For the Bank of England, rationalization meant the creation of big amalgamations that would use the best elements of existing companies and reduce excess capacity. Amalgamations seemed to promise centralized management, economies of scale, increased market power, and therefore the mechanism that would reverse the decline of the economy. For the Bank, though, rather than merely offering involvement in the world of business, this was a political position in opposition to the threat of industrial nationalization by Labour government.[47]

The role played by the Bank in the muddled and not wholly successful rationalization of the steel industry shows the inability of bankers to act as entrepreneurs. The scale of the schemes devised by the BIDC and the need for long-term financial commitment required government guarantees and consent, but this ran counter to the ideological opposition of the Bank's governor, Montague Norman, to government intervention. At the same time the Bank's intervention in the staple industries (steel, cotton, shipbuilding),[48] meant that first the Labour government and then the National government after 1931 did not have to promote the reorganization of industry in any active way. In this respect the Bank became the government's intermediary.[49] The intervention of the Bank also moved the focus away from the clearing banks. These had (by the late 1920s) been blamed for most of the problems of British industry and the 'individualism run riot' of the Big Five had led the 1928 Conservative government, under pressure from industry and trade unions, to consider government loans to promote industrial reorganization.[50] Government and Bank were released from having to intervene by the activities of the BIDC.

CONCLUSION

Compared to the previous period, banking in Britain in the interwar period has been characterized as being concentrated and uncompetitive but stable. The creation of a banking cartel made bankers even more risk-adverse and carried costs in terms of agreements on interest rates and the price of services. Nevertheless, the economy, as a whole, could be said to have been benefited by a financial environment free of the crises that plagued continental European countries in this period. Despite the three economic recessions of the interwar period no bank failed. The only one in trouble, Williams Deacons, a small Manchester bank that had lent extensively to the cotton industry, was rescued by the Royal Bank of Scotland, after the Bank of England had promised the Royal to indemnify it against any loss.[51]

There is no doubt that one of the reasons why the system had become so concentrated by 1919 was that there was no opposition to this process. Banks merged because they could, and the comparison with what was happening in the other European countries shows that this comment is not as fatuous as it sounds. The structure evolved into a cartel because the central bank encouraged it so that it could more easily exercise its influence over a small number of bankers. Even though the Colwyn Committee on Bank Amalgamations expressed fears that a banking cartel might reduce competition, and although after 1919 no mergers were permitted without the approval of the Treasury Committee, mergers continued. The justification provided by the Committee was that big banks would serve the needs of the economy more effectively. However, though the commercial banks did lend to big industrial customers during the interwar period, they did so as 'powerful creditors . . . rarely controlling partners'.[52] The banks' liquidity increased and overall their advances decreased as a percentage of their total assets. This meant that once the Depression set in they were never in danger of suffering the fate of their European counterparts. The stability of the banking system may have provided protection for the real economy.[53] However, this stability was achieved at the expense of at least one sector of the economy: small firms. Provincial banks had dedicated a larger share of their assets as loans to local private customers, including credit provision for industry through the routine renewal of nominally short-term loans. As these banks were taken over, the preference for higher liquidity ratios of the London-based national banks reduced the supply of funds to industrial customers, especially the smaller, provincial ones.[54] Concentration created joint-stock banks with enormous resources and managerial structures closer to the interests of the City of London than to those of small provincial firms.[55]

In 1929 a parliamentary enquiry was set up under the chairmanship of Harold Macmillan to investigate the relationship between finance and industry. The committee reported in July 1931, stating that 'It has been represented to us that great difficulty is experienced by the smaller and medium-sized businesses in raising ... capital ... even when the security offered is perfectly sound'. Despite having identified a gap in the provision of finance to one sizeable sector of the economy the Macmillan Committee did not recommend any change in 'the character of present banking practices', because banks were thought, overall, to serve the needs of the economy well. Instead city institutions were asked to endeavour to provide relatively small domestic issues, of between £50,000 and £200,000.[56] Following the definition of what came to be known as the 'Macmillan gap' a number of initiatives were launched both in the private and public sector. Charterhouse Industrial Development Co. Ltd (connected to the insurers Prudential Assurance Co, Lloyds Bank, and the Midland), Credit for Industry (a subsidiary of the finance company United Dominion Trust, 50 per cent owned by the Bank of England), and Leadenhall Securities (created by the merchant bankers, Schroeder and Co.) were the main institutions that tried to provide small amounts of capital to the smaller firms. Their success, however, was very limited. Applications were assessed on criteria that ruled out most enterprises that were not well established.[57] The government also stepped in and the Special Areas Reconstruction Association Ltd (SARA), the Nuffield Trust, and the Treasury Fund were set up, between the mid- and late 1930s to fill the 'Macmillan gap' in Britain's depressed areas. These initiatives were criticized for behaving too much like the commercial banks, in terms of the interest rates charged and the security demanded. The funds at their disposal were too small in relation to the size of the problem mostly because they were created mainly as a token gesture, to show that financial institutions and the government were responding to political pressure.[58] The failure of these initiatives shows that the solution to the problems of small and medium-sized firms did not rest in the creation of new institutions.[59] The gap in the market had been created by the banks' rationing of credit to their smaller customers, as a direct consequence of the structural shift from local, provincial banking to national branch banking. This shift had been fully sanctioned by the state, despite evidence of its negative impact on one large sector of the economy. The climate of the interwar period, where most economic and political actors pushed for concentration marginalized small firms, most of which were in the consumer and new industries. The following chapters compare Britain's experience with that of Germany, France, and Italy where banking and banks were more segmented and diversified. Part II of the book will assess the impact of the financial gap on small firms' ability to innovate and grow to optimal size.

NOTES

1 Cottrell, *Industrial Finance*, 210; Collins and Baker, *Commercial Banks and Industrial Finance in England and Wales*.
2 Collins, *Banks and Industrial Finance in Britain 1800–1939*, 27; Checkland, *Scottish Banking*, 497.
3 Cottrell, Teichova, and Yuzawa, *Finance in the Age of the Corporate Economy*, 20.
4 Ibid., 21.
5 Goodhart, *The Business of Banking*, 167–91; Collins and Baker, *Commercial Banks and Industrial Finance*, 105; Checkland, *Scottish Banking*, 469–81.
6 Only three provincial banks were left, two based in the textile region of Lancashire while the third one was a northern Irish bank (agricultural). Despite this regional base these banks had head offices in London and belonged to the Committee of London Clearing Banks.
7 Cottrell, *Industrial Finance*, 197.
8 Collins, *Money and Banking in the UK*, 207. See also Capie and Rodrick-Bali, 'Concentration in British Banking 1830–1920'.
9 Cottrell, *Industrial Finance*, 197–8, 228, 236 passim; Matthisa, *The First Industrial Nation*, 387; Collins and Baker, *Commercial Banks and Industrial Finance*, 250–8.
10 For the hypothesis that these branch managers had less power than formerly independent bankers and that this might have meant that loans to industry could have been given a lower priority because they were riskier than other forms of investment see Cassis, 'British Finance: Success and Controversy' and also Ziegler, *Central Bank, Peripheral Industry: The Bank of England in the Provinces*. For a contemporary account see Truptil, *British Banks and the London Money Market*.
11 Cottrell, *Industrial Finance*, 236–7 and also Joseph, *Industrial Finance*.
12 Collins and Baker, *Commercial Banks and Industrial Finance*, 120–30.
13 Ibid., 105–6.
14 This was particularly true in the case of the Midland bank; see Holmes and Green, *Midland Bank*, 131–42. Barclays foreign department dates only from 1913 and its involvement in foreign financial markets developed fully after the First World War, see Ackrill and Hannah, *Barclays*, 79–85. For an overview of the link between the City of London, international trade, and foreign investments see Cain and Hopkins, *British Imperialism*, 161–80; for more detail see Truptil, *British Banks*, 125–6.
15 Cassis, 'Management and Strategy', 313.
16 Crick and Wandsworth, *A Hundred Years of Joint-Stock Banking*, 40–1.

17   Balogh, *Studies in Financial Organisation*, 10.
18   Cottrell and Anderson, *Money and Banking in England*, 316. See also National Archives (hereafter NA), T1/12267, Committee of Bank Amalgamations, Minutes of Evidence, 1918, 1–7.
19   In July 1918 Lloyds Bank took over the National Bank, in November 1919 Barclays took over the British Linen, and later in the month the Midland took over the Clydesdale Bank. Saville, *Bank of Scotland*, 524–5.
20   Ackrill and Hannah, *Barclays*, 72.
21   PP 1918, *Report of the Treasury Committee on Bank Amalgamation*, Cmd 9052, point 6b.
22   Apart from the chair, Lord Colwyn, and two industrialists, Sir Harry McGowan and Douglas Vickers, of the twelve members of the Committee, six were bankers, including Sir Richard Vassar-Smith, at the time chairman of Lloyds and president of the FBI, Sir John Purcell, chairman of the National Bank, and Captain Keswick, chairman of the Directors of the Hong Kong and Shanghai Banking Corporation, and, of course, Lord Cunliffe, the governor of the Bank of England. PP 1918, *Report of the Treasury Committee on Bank Amalgamation*, Cmd 9052.
23   NA, T1/12267, Committee of Bank Amalgamations, Minutes of Evidence, 1918, 166–7.
24   NA, T1/12267, Committee of Bank Amalgamations, Minutes of Evidence, 1918, 167.
25   NA, T1/12267, Committee of Bank Amalgamations, Minutes of Evidence, 1918, 66–70.
26   NA, T1/12267, Committee of Bank Amalgamations, Minutes of Evidence, 1918, 16–29.
27   NA, T1/12267, Committee of Bank Amalgamations, Minutes of Evidence, 1918, 368–9.
28   Stewart, *British and German Industrial Conditions*, 22–3.
29   H. S. Foxwell, the Scottish economist, who gave a favourable verdict in his statement to the committee on bank amalgamations, was a strong proponent of the German banking system. Foxwell, 'The Financing of Industry and Trade', 505; see also Mosely, 'The German Method of Banking' and also Joseph, *The Evolution of German Banking*.
30   Crouzet, *The Victorian Economy*, 81–4.
31   Cottrell, 'Finance and the Germination of the British Corporate Economy', 14.
32   Census of production, 1930, *Final Report*, Part V, 1935, 10–13. These figures, however, are very likely to underestimate as they were based on a sample of returns.
33   Hannah, *Rise of the Corporate Economy*, footnote 40, 21.
34   Ibid., 21–2.
35   Prais, 'A New Look at the Growth of Industrial Concentration', 283; Hannah's estimates are only slightly lower, *Rise of the Corporate Economy*, 180.
36   *The Economist*, 9 Feb. 1924, 241.
37   Ritschel, *The Politics of Planning*, 35.
38   For a full analysis of the movement see Hannah, *Rise of the Corporate Economy*, chapter 3.

39 Middlemas, *Politics in Industrial Society*, 178–80.
40 Marshall, *Industry and Trade*, 579–80.
41 Dawson, *Germany's Industrial Revival*.
42 Stewart, *British and German Industrial Conditions*; Meakin, *The New Industrial Revolution*.
43 Ritschel, *The Politics of Planning*, 39; see also Macmillan, *The Middle Way*.
44 Trentman, 'Bread, Milk and Democracy'.
45 PP 1931, Committee on Industry and Trade, *Final Report*, Cmd 3282, 179.
46 Hannah, *Rise of the Corporate Economy*, 66.
47 Tolliday, 'Steel and Rationalisation', 96.
48 Collins, *Banks and Industrial Finance in Britain*, 77–9.
49 Garside and Greaves, 'The Bank of England and Industrial Intervention'.
50 Middlemas, *Politics in Industrial Society*, 180.
51 Saville, *Bank of Scotland*, 543–4.
52 Tolliday, *Business, Banking and Politics*, 179. For the banks' involvement in industrial lending see also Ross, 'The Clearing Banks and the Finance of Industry'.
53 Capie, 'Commercial Banking in Britain', 395–413.
54 Collins and Baker, *Commercial Banks and Industrial Finance*, 178–201.
55 Cassis, 'Management and Strategy', 302.
56 PP 1931, Committee on Finance and Industry, *Report*, Cmd 3897, paras. 403–4.
57 Ross, 'The "Macmillan Gap" and the British Credit Market in the 1930s', 211–16; Thomas, *The Finance of British Industry 1918–76*, 119; Grant, *A Study in the Capital Market in Britain from 1919–1936*, 276–8.
58 Heim, 'Limits to Intervention: The Bank of England and Industrial Diversification in the Depressed Areas'.
59 Ross, 'The "Macmillan Gap"', 209.

3

Local Systems of Production in Germany

As shown in Chapter 2, one of the reasons given in 1918 by the Colwyn Committee on Bank Amalgamations to justify the concentration and centralization of banking was the need to face the competition of German banks. These were presented as the strong allies of Germany's giant combines, as almost the root of Germany's industrial might. This chapter establishes whether the assessment of the committee was accurate or whether it hid a more subtle picture.

SAVINGS AND COOPERATIVE BANKS:
THE UNTOLD STORY OF GERMAN BANKING

The story of German banking most familiar to historians outside Germany is that of the big Berlin banks. The rapid acceleration of German industrialization from the second half of the nineteenth century also meant an increase in the capital requirements of industry. These could no longer be satisfied, as they had been previously, by personal and familial networks. As the needs of industry grew these banks started consorting with other banks across regions, aided by legislation which from the mid-nineteenth century strengthened the private banks and also gave impetus to concentration among the joint-stock ones.[1] The big banks developed branching networks as a response to the expansion of the supra-regional networks of public savings banks and credit cooperatives to compete for savings.[2] These banks did not initiate the growth process but, as Jürgen Kocka has written, they 'acted like large flywheels; they did not initiate most changes, but, rather reflected and strengthened existing trends'.[3] This is the part of the picture that foreign contemporaries knew and feared. But there is another story, parallel to this, that of the savings banks and cooperative banks and their links with small firms. This is the other side of Germany's industrial and financial story.

Savings banks legislation was passed first in Prussia in 1816 and then in the other German states. This legislation gave cities the right to establish savings banks to encourage safe savings for depositors and pool capital locally. These savings were then invested in state bonds and loans to local governments to fund poor relief and infrastructure. In many places the local authority regularly depended on the savings bank to avoid high levels of taxation. Long-term commitments to public investment and low levels of taxation had a positive effect on the local economy, especially as it allowed the building sector (and connected industries) to expand.[4] By the mid-nineteenth century savings banks had become an important resource for local governments. As a consequence the banks' activities were placed under the administration of local government, who also created new banks. In 1836 there were 280 savings banks in the German states; by 1860 more than 800 had been established.[5] Germany's unification in 1871 provided added stimuli to the pace of industrialization, and the rapid growth of large-scale industry put pressure on the smaller firms to modernize. The demand for capital from small firms was rapidly overrunning the financial capabilities of the local savings banks. Savings banks were also being threatened by competition for savings from the cooperative banks and by the lack of a mechanism that would allow them to transfer money between themselves to extend their lending capacity. Hence in 1884 several regional associations of savings banks joined together to create a national association, the *Deutscher Sparkassenverband*. This gave the savings banks access to a larger pool of resources and a political voice that could be used to influence the government.

By 1900 the savings banks were administering accounts to the value of around 9 billion marks in some 15 million savings accounts and in 1913 there were more than 3,000 savings banks with about 7,000 branches administering deposits of around 20 billion marks with corresponding credits.[6] Of these, the total deposits of small-scale businesses in savings banks amounted to 6 billion marks in 1913, which would have made them the most important financial institution for craftsmen, shopkeepers, and small industrialists.[7]

The branch coverage of the savings banks was not uniform, with some regions like Württemberg with the highest density, one bank per 1,197 inhabitants, and Bavaria the lowest with one bank per 6,535 inhabitants, in 1905. The differences became smaller over time but were still marked at the beginning of the Second World War, demonstrating the decentralized nature of the savings bank movement.[8] Regional variations reflected the relative strengths of the different banking groups in different regions. The major commercial banks were concentrated in and around the Ruhr, where the large steel and coal concerns operated, and in most major cities. Where the big banks were weaker cooperative and savings banks were stronger, especially in sectors made mostly of small and medium-sized firms, such as machine tools, and in areas where the decentralized method of production dominated, such as Württemberg.

Savings banks' customers were overwhelmingly recruited from the working and the lower middle classes. For example, in 1920 in Prussia, which alone held over 60 per cent of all deposits in German savings banks, 57 out of every 100 inhabitants had a savings book, which in fact matched the average for the whole country. This was an impressive figure as it meant that almost every Prussian family made use of a savings account. In 1936, three quarters of all savings books were for small accounts, standing below 300 *Reichmarks;* these deposits, however, amounted to only 8.4 per cent of deposits, which means that there were some middle-class customers with much larger deposits. The amount of savings also varied regionally, with Bavaria lagging behind. Yet the fact that in some districts or regions there was a lower availability of savings did not reduce the availability of funds for investment thanks to the associational structure of the whole system and the establishment of giro offices. These solved any liquidity problems that might have arisen[9].

The size of the liabilities held by the savings banks is important because it gives an idea of the amount of resources that they had available to invest. The availability of such large quantities of local savings meant that the banks could refinance themselves by means of deposits, guaranteed by the local authority. By statute the banks had to invest their funds locally, and when seeking to invest the uncompromising principle was to invest safely and the local environment was thought to be the best place. Outside the industrial centres, however, the need for capital was relatively modest and often investment plans were limited to the mere replacement of equipment. Their main emphasis was on acquiring buildings and land, renovation and the financial settlement of inheritances. At the turn of the century, to a very large extent the savings banks invested money in loans connected with land, which always accounted for well over 50 per cent of the assets side in individual states. In Prussia these mortgage loans accounted for about 60 per cent of all loans; in Saxony and Hessen the volume of mortgage loans amounted to 80 per cent; in Baden and Württemberg to 70 per cent; and Bavaria to around 50 per cent. Securities such as bearer bonds came second, followed by local authority credit.[10] In 1909, the savings banks were given permission to employ up to 10 per cent of their savings deposits as commercial advances.[11]

For local governments, the loans made by savings banks to small craft firms had an important social and political role. A strong craft sector slowed down the proletarianization of the working class and industrial concentration. Proletarianization was feared because local governments thought that it would fan socialism, while the concentration of industry could give rise to strong private interests that could challenge local authority.[12] Nevertheless, in the early stage of Germany's industrialization savings banks played a limited role, although their ability to mobilize a large amount of working-class savings and channel these into regional and national capital markets had an important indirect effect on the economy. Moreover, mortgages had also an important impact as they were not purely for private investment. Hotels and department stores were financed by mortgages as were workshops and industrial plants.[13]

The savings banks played a decisive part in local economic development by supplying credit to large areas of the country where population was too scattered to accumulate enough savings to attract commercial banks. Their close ties with local government avoided the danger of a flight of capital from such areas to the major financial and industrial centres. Thus the savings banks acted as local levellers of capital. By financing the purchase of land for new buildings and plant they acquired the medium-sized industries as an important group of customers at a very early stage.[14]

The savings banks were not the only suppliers of funds to small firms. In 1852 the first credit cooperative was established by Hermann Schulze-Delitzsch with the aim of promoting the principles of self-help and mutual responsibility among workers. Cooperative banking held great appeal for the craft sector, whose existence was being threatened by the growth of industrial production, and by 1859 there were 80 commercial credit cooperatives spread across Germany, with more than 18,000 members.[15] Gerd Hardach writes of the rise of cooperative banking as a German peculiarity as it owes much to the traditional mentality of the German middle class; typical members were farmers, independent craftsmen, and shopkeepers who were reluctant to enter the capitalist market economy.[16] By the 1880s, the cooperative banks had established themselves in regions such as Saxony and in parts of the Rhine. By 1900 there were 112 cooperative banks in Württemberg alone. Cooperative bank members pooled money and borrowed as they needed. To avoid credit being limited by local availability of savings and to refinance their loans, the cooperative banks joined in regional associations and created regional clearing banks. The Imperial Cooperative Law of 1889 gave cooperative banks the ability to offer their clients the same services as the big commercial banks, such as short-term current accounts and acceptance credits, allowing them to become more like universal banks and meet the growing needs of the small firm sector. Their development was further aided by the decision taken by the Prussian government in 1895 to establish the *Preussenkasse*, a central bank for cooperatives, capitalized by the government. This bank subsidized the cooperative banks by holding deposits from the regional associations, for which it paid higher than market interest rates and refinancing their loans at below market rates.[17] The government took the decision to actively support the cooperative banks as a way of gaining farmers' and small firms' support by protecting them from the threat of proletarianization. By the First World War the cooperative banks were beginning to perform all of the banking functions that the great commercial banks in Germany provided, while being committed to the economic health of the industrial *Mittelstand*.[18]

At the same time, credit banking in these regions grew. Many private banks in Württemberg and the Rhineland grew by lending money to the bigger firms, normally those characterized by factory production.

The relationship between these private bankers and the factory owners resembled those between the cooperative banks and the small firms, but the sums were considerably larger.[19] This movement was paralleled in the countryside with the creation of rural credit cooperatives. In 1913 Germany had 17,000 rural credit cooperatives and they contributed much to the modernization and commercialization of German agriculture.[20]

Table 3.1 shows the size and range of the German banking system and how this did not experience concentration until 1929. The ability of the savings and cooperative banks to survive against the strength of the Berlin banks and continue supplying funds to the *Mittelstand* rested in their political voice, thanks to the national associations, and in the fact that the Prussian government was interested in preserving this sector of the economy as a force against the rise of an industrial proletariat which would strengthen the threat of socialism. Unlike the situation in Britain, one of the biggest developments in the consolidation of the structure of German banking was the savings banks' successful lobbying of the Imperial government in 1908. This granted them the power to implement transfer and checking accounts, to operate current accounts, and hold securities on deposit, making them more like universal banks. By creating the giro system, the savings banks achieved unity, because giro accounts required central clearing houses in the shape of regional giro clearing banks (*Girozentrale*). In 1918, regional savings associations created a central clearing bank, the *Deutsche Girozentrale* in Berlin. This solidified the associational structure of the savings banks and allowed individual banks to rely on cooperation with other banks in the association for their competitiveness.

Table 3.2 compares the assets of the various banking groups in 1913 and shows that the commercial banks, including the private banks, controlled less than one-third of the total assets of the banking system. Hardach has concluded that Germany's economic growth was not financed by the

Table 3.1.   Number of banks in Germany, 1913–38

Year	1913	1925	1929	1938
Commercial banks	352	402	296	199
Private banks	1,221	1,406	1,100	491
Savings banks	3,332	3,262	3,235	2,558
Cooperative banks[a]	18,557	20,977	21,499	19,076
Special banks	79	77	87	80
All banks	23,541	26,124	26,217	22,404

Note: [a] These figures include the very large number of rural credit cooperatives.
Source: Hardach, 1995, 273.

Table 3.2.   The structure of banking in Germany, 1913–38 (% of total assets)

	1913	1925	1929	1938
Commercial banks	31	49	33	15
Special banks	27	17	26	29
Savings banks	33	19	31	45
Cooperative banks	9	15	10	11

Source: Hardach, 1995, 274.

commercial banks but by savings banks, cooperative banks, and special banks, such as the mortgage banks. The savings and cooperative banks were successful because the commercial banks were conservative in their lending practices, preferring to concentrate on corporate finance, government lending, and wealthy individuals. Concentration in banking increased this trend and in the pre-war years contemporaries criticized the commercial banks for neglecting large sectors of the economy in favour of large industrial corporations.[21] Richard Tilly's research has also confirmed the bias of commercial banks in favour of big business and government loans.[22] For the big banks these customers meant higher profit margins and an easier evaluation of risk, compared to the higher cost of transactions with small business and agriculture. The divorce of the big banks from the smaller firms was the result of a historical process. At the beginning of the twentieth century, as the fixed-capital needs of large manufacturing firms became too big for the provincial credit banks, these firms started to look to the big Berlin banks for funds and the provincial banks had to find other customers. A number of large provincial banks started lending to small and medium-sized firms.[23] The bank mergers before the First World War, when the Berlin banks took over many provincial banks, did not disrupt this segmentation of the market as the provincial banks were able to keep their independence and banking practices. It was the effect of the war and inflation, which greatly reduced the reserves of the banks, that changed the situation as many more provincial banks were taken over by the big banks. With stabilization it became imperative for the commercial banks to reduce costs, and staff numbers were reduced and branches closed. To contain administrative costs the big banks concentrated their lending on large firms, since a small number of large accounts was easier to administer than many small ones.[24] The rapid rise of savings and cooperative banks shows that the financial mass market had great potential for growth that the commercial banks had failed to grasp. The savings and cooperative banks filled a gap, in the process capturing large segments of the market.[25]

As Table 3.2 on the structure of banking shows, the impact of hyperinflation on the banks was severe, although the commercial banks that concentrated on short-term business were equipped better to cope with currency depreciation. By shedding most of their small accounts, as the real value of most transactions became insignificant, the commercial banks were able to turn increasingly from traditional credit activities to stock-exchange and foreign-exchange speculation. The metropolitan banks and the large provincial banks continued to expand, mostly by taking over other banks, and between 1919 and 1923 the commercial banks took over more than 150 smaller banks. However, although the federal states had lifted restrictions on the lending of the savings banks to help the local economy, hyperinflation damaged the savings banks because of their heavy emphasis on long-term deposits. As peoples' propensity to save was sorely diminished by inflation the savings banks saw their liabilities diminish (and therefore their ability to lend money was curtailed). As a consequence they had to turn from long-term to short-term business in order to survive. Nonetheless, the government's decision in 1921 to lift most of the restrictions that prevented savings banks from operating as universal banks meant that after stabilization in 1924 the savings banks experienced an impressive recovery as popular saving recovered. The move to more universal banking activities also meant that savings banks reduced their mortgages as assets and increased current account advances.

It was therefore the inflation of the interwar years that truly consolidated the savings banks' place in the local economy. As inflation worsened, the federal states found themselves forced to liberalize restrictions on the activities of the savings banks to provide local markets with liquidity and ensure that basic local needs, such as food, clothing, and housing, were met.[26] However this was not just an emergency response but it was also motivated by the belief held by many federal governments that the commercial banks were not providing the *Mittelstand* with sufficient funds. In fact, in regions where the big Berlin banks had taken over provincial banks they generally provided less credit to the *Mittelstand* than the provincial bank had done.[27] The behaviour of the commercial banks during hyperinflation had alienated many of the smaller depositors who now flocked to the savings banks.[28]

Theo Balderston has discussed the relationship between the credit banks and firms in the interwar period by looking at net short-term indebtedness to the banks. This measure shows that the large firms' relationship with the banks was a much more independent one that is normally portrayed in the literature, and that these firms were getting cheaper loans from foreign banks. Furthermore, during the period of inflation, the *Reichsbank* tried to enforce a credit squeeze by reducing the number of rediscounted bills brought in by the commercial banks. This led businesses to complain of credit shortages and the formation of large concerns has been seen as a reaction to the problems caused by these shortages.[29] As was happening in Britain, the creation of cartels and combines was attributed by one contemporary observer to the difficulty of medium-sized firms of getting long-term capital from the banks, as these preferred to lend to older and larger organizations.[30] By creating their own house banks, or setting up trusts to allow capital movements between large concerns, enterprises were trying to free themselves from the control and tutelage of the banks.[31] As a consequence of the rising independence of big businesses from the banks during the period of inflation, the banks lost the ability to influence the direction of industrial policy and the process of industrial concentration. As Gerald Feldman states: 'To a considerable extent the great bankers were being reduced to intermediaries in the industrial concentration process.'[32] Nevertheless, by the late 1920s the development of German industry was constrained by the availability of external credit and internal resources. Harold James has estimated that between 1925 and 1928 some investment was still paid out of undistributed profits. However, after 1929 the volume of investment financed through internal capital fell drastically. Even during the mid-Weimar period, corporate profits were reduced by high levels of taxation. Firms turned to the banks and from 1925 to 1929 bank loans accounted for the major part of industrial investment.[33] Yet most bankers preferred to concentrate their loans on a few big borrowers and their favourite sectors for investment were textiles and food production, especially breweries, showing a remarkable lack of entrepreneurial spirit. From 1927 to 1929 a subcommittee of the Inquiry into German Conditions of Production and Sale analysed the state of German banking and showed that the great banks concentrated their loans on big borrowers and that small firms had to use alternative sources, namely the cooperative and savings banks.[34] Industries that consisted predominantly of small firms obtained a smaller proportion of their credit from the commercial banks than other branches of industry and small firms complained about the reluctance of the credit banks to make small advances.[35]

However, any state-sponsored solution to the credit problems of small and medium firms and the long-term problem of how to promote investments in industry during the period of inflation was strenuously opposed by the big banks, who feared any form of competition and state intervention. In fact some of these banks saw the crisis as the opportunity for the German economy to eliminate small enterprises, seen as elements of backwardness. Hence these banks' opposition to any change in the law to allow savings banks' reserves to be tapped for capital investment in small and medium-sized firms, despite the fact that most of the savings banks' funds came from the *Mittelstand*.[36] Nevertheless, by lifting the restriction on the proportion of current account lending to savings account deposits in 1924, the government extended the savings banks' ability to make commercial advances. By doing this the government showed that the opposition of the big banks to competition did not stop it from enacting legislation to protect the savings banks. Most of the policies pursued by the Weimar Republic were aimed at facilitating the growth of large combines, in the belief that rationalization would lead to recovery and the restoration of workers' real wages to pre-war levels.[37] However, the functions provided at a local level by the savings banks played an important part in reducing the population's hardship and political conflict, both important aims for the Weimar governments.

Government action was instrumental also in preserving the cooperative banks from the effects of hyperinflation as this had wiped out much of their equity and many cooperatives had closed. Through the *Preussenkasse* (the cooperative banks' central bank) the state provided the remaining cooperative banks with much needed capital. In addition, the *Preussenkasse* aided cooperative banks by pursuing a countercyclical interest rate policy, maintaining low and constant interest rates on cooperative bank deposits and loans. Even though the number of urban cooperative banks declined from 1,549 in 1913 to 1,349 in 1925, after that the remaining banks steadily increased their balance sheets. By 1930 approximately one quarter of all urban *Mittelstand* firms and 50 per cent of all farmers were cooperative members.[38] During the interwar period, banking cooperatives helped the *Mittelstand* from dying out by supporting small firms and craftsmen.[39]

The consolidation of these two banking groups and the rising strength of the big commercial banks led to increasing levels of competition and conflict. The cooperative and commercial banks objected to the incursion of the savings banks into short-term lending and argued that this sort of business was a taxable commercial activity and therefore did not belong in the tax-free savings banks sector. To defend their growing engagement in commercial banking activities, the savings banks had to develop a new self-definition of their social and economic role. They declared that their role was to fill the gaps left between the large commercial banks and the small cooperative banks (which lent mostly to the craft sector), such as in the area of public infrastructure and *Mittelstand* lending. The savings banks characterized their role as providing an essential counterweight to the growing centralization and concentration of the economy.[40] The conflict was resolved in 1928 when the Prussian government came down strongly in favour of the savings banks by issuing new tax regulations, keeping current account and *Mittelstand* lending tax-free to savings banks. At this point the three banking groups decided to establish a private (albeit sanctioned by the State) competition accord in which the commercial banks agreed to drop their opposition to the savings banks' commercial activities if they agreed in turn to refrain from engaging in large industrial loans. The market was thus segmented, with the cooperative banks lending to the craft and farming sector, the savings banks to the middle classes and to small and medium-sized firms, and the big banks to big business.

The 1931 banking crisis induced a reorganization of German banking. The effect of the crisis was to reduce greatly the number of big banks and their assets, leaving only three big Berlin banks placed under state supervision.[41] The savings banks' assets were also reduced as the federal governments had borrowed heavily from them and when the crisis hit they could not repay their loans. To protect the savings banks from further abuse by local public authorities, the national government transformed the savings banks into legally independent banks while providing them with emergency capital. The cooperative banks survived the 1931 banking crisis relatively well, which suggests that the craft sector was not particularly injured by the crisis.

The commercial banks used the banking crisis to attack the activities of the savings banks. The head of the *Reichsbank*, Hjalmer Schacht, however, defended the savings banks, and the Imperial Bank Sector Law (*Reichskreditwesengesetz*, or KWG), passed in 1934, reconfirmed the right of the savings banks to exercise commercial banking activities. The banking commission that had prepared the KWG cited the overextension of credit on easy terms to large firms by commercial banks, to the detriment of small and medium-sized firms, as one of the causes of the 1931 crisis. The aim of the KWG, therefore, was to preserve the liquidity of the system by ensuring that the *Mittelstand*'s need for capital was satisfied.[42] On the other hand it has been argued that the instability experienced by the whole banking system, but in particular by the credit banks, was due to the increased competition for deposits and loans during the interwar period from foreign banks, and savings banks. Fierce competition led the banks to follow quite aggressive policies that accepted low liquidity and low profitability, thus weakening them.[43] While in Britain the creation of a banking oligopoly made the system more stable, in Germany competition between different groups of banks worsened the already fragile state of the credit banks.[44] Nevertheless, the existence of a banking system made of three groups of banks, serving different segments of the market ensured the provision of finance to small provincial firms avoiding, to a certain extent, a credit gap. This segmentation of the system (both in terms of supply and demand) was not just the result of market forces, but also of political intervention. The nature of the interaction between the economy and the state becomes clear by looking more closely at the structure of German industry at this time.

THE STATE AND GERMANY'S INDUSTRIALIZATION

The story of Germany's industrialization is one well known to most economic and business historians and has been dominated by the rise of big firms. As Alfred Chandler has stated: 'The German experience [up to the 1940s] . . . is closer to that of the United States than to that of Britain.'[45] He based this statement on the observation of the histories of Germany's 200 largest manufacturing enterprises. These showed him that German entrepreneurs were much more able than their British counterparts to invest in the plant and workforce necessary to enjoy economies of scale and scope, and to develop marketing facilities and managerial hierarchies. Two-thirds of Germany's largest companies were clustered in metals, chemicals, and machinery, while in Britain the top 200 largest firms were to be found mostly in those sectors producing consumer goods.[46] The most distinctive feature of German capitalism, according to Chandler, has been the development and support given by the state to cartels and inter-firm cooperation, developing what Jürgen Kocka has defined as 'organised capitalism'. The years between 1870 and the First World War have been identified by Kocka as those which saw the rise of the modern firms. These were also the years when Germany overcame its relative economic back- wardness, overtaking in terms of growth of output per capita the other continental states, and in some areas even Britain. Germany's relatively late industrialization is the reason given by Kocka to explain the earlier development of large integrated firms in Germany, compared with Britain. Germany's old set of commercial and artisan structures were unsuited to industrialization and proof of this is that the most important industries in the German industrial revolution—railroads, manufacture of machinery, and chemicals—had very few predecessors. Therefore, when German entrepreneurs, impressed by Britain's example, decided to imi- tate her, they had to fund factories almost from scratch.[47]

Large firms developed in those German regions which had at the beginning of the nineteenth century very little protoindustrial activity because skilled small property holders were missing, and which had large numbers of landless peasants. These new industries became verti- cally integrated because there was very little local industry and handicraft skills to draw on. These regions were the Ruhr Valley, northern and eastern Westphalia, the Prussian province of Saxony, Berlin, Silesia, and many of the old medieval cities such as Hanover, Kassel, Nuremberg, Augsburg, and Munich. Even where protoindustrial landscapes emerged, such as the linen industry in Silesia or textiles and handicrafts in Bavaria, these collapsed in the face of mechanized competition at the beginning of the nineteenth century, based as they were on an impoverished rural propertyless class of labourers rather than rural property holders.[48]

Expansion, diversification, and integration, the hallmarks of German firms before (and after) 1914, were all the consequence of the absence of areas with a well-developed industrial tradition. As Kocka states: 'Small, highly specialised, single function personal enterprises were more clearly dominant in the first phase of industrialisation [in Britain] than they were in Germany.'[49] This view of Germany's industrialization, however, ignores the existence of dynamic centres of craft-type industrial development in Rhineland and Saxon regions as early as the eighteenth century, export-oriented and specializing in textiles and ironwares. The existence of these centres and their need for transport links would explain, for example, the development of the railways and the source of the initial investment in them. Richard Tilly connects the existence of skilled craftsmen and innovative entrepreneurs characteristic of 'protoindustrialization' to the factory-type industrial growth of the nineteenth century. Tilly also considers how increasing productivity in the late eighteenth century in some agricultural areas could have contributed significantly to economic growth and the development of domestically produced non-agricultural goods in the early part of the nineteenth century.[50] Even after 1870, when Germany's industrialization seems to be taken over by large, integrated, capital goods producing firms, these centres of early industrialization, specializing mostly in finished and semi-finished goods, did not disappear.

The story of Germany's industrialization can also be told from the point of view of small firms by focusing on the development of what Gary Herrigel has defined 'the decentralised industrial order'. This story starts in the seventeenth century and shows the growth of regions specialized in specific industrial sectors with production based around merchants, outworkers, and the role of regional governments. The growth of mechanized production in Britain was the external shock that refined the specific nature of German industrialization. Germany specialized in the goods that the British did not produce or in sections of the market that British goods did not enter. Though over a century and a half mechanized factory production took over the domestic industry of the regions, factory production and decentralized, production-fragmented, subcontracting networks coexisted to form regional economies. Over time, agglomerations of decentralized, interconnected outworkers evolved into agglomerations of decentralized, interconnected small and medium-sized firms, with no wholesale movement of workers into large units. The four main regions were Württemberg, the Rhineland, Thuringia, and Saxony, specializing mainly in textiles and metal goods. The strategy pursued by firms in these regions was not to compete with the cheaper British goods but to use cheap inputs from Britain and process them into high quality and high value added goods. In these regions, alongside the development of a decentralized production system based on a myriad of small and medium-sized firms, new institutions emerged to help decentralized producers acquire the capital, labour, and technical knowledge they needed to carry out their flexibly specialized market and production strategies. These institutions were technical training institutes and cooperative regional banks.[51]

Regional prosperity in the early nineteenth century was important to regional governments also in the context of the spectre of German unification. German regions had to remain competitive so as not to be gobbled up by other European states or by the German nation. However, industrialization had to be of a certain kind, not based on large factories because this created the possibility that political autonomy might be challenged by private concentrations of power. Governments wanted to promote industrialization in the interest of welfare and prosperity. This strengthened their political power, but they also wanted to ensure that the small and medium-sized character of production was preserved, as this type of industrial structure was easier to control and presented less of a political threat. In these regions the existence of local private banks and later of savings and cooperative banks, which could lend to craftsmen and small and medium-sized firms, meant the preservation of this type of decentralized industrial structure.[52]

The interwar period presented these regions with some substantial challenges as the competitive environment began to change and traditional markets in Germany and Europe became more difficult to retain and enter. As the markets became uncertain various governance strategies were devised to control this uncertainty and to maintain the decentralized system of production rather than concentrate. Some industries like chemicals found this too difficult and the decentralized form of production was abandoned. Price cartels, term-fixing cartels, and specialization cartels were established and cooperation between small and medium-sized producers was achieved thanks to the activity of trade associations. The difficulties of the interwar period also changed the structure of the country's big business organizations as cartelization and the expansion of the combine system[53] increased the pace of industrial concentration, especially in iron, steel, and coal.[54]

Many German economists and managers during the late 1920s, and after, wrote about the 'rationalization boom' of the period. The substitution of capital for labour, investment in technology, and plant rationalization to achieve assembly-line production were seen as representing the 1920s. These were the same objectives of the British rationalization literature, with Germany (and the USA) as the prime examples of successful application. German contemporaries, however, saw these as also being the cause of the depression because of the massive misdirection of resources and an irrational pursuit of bigness. Inflationary reconstruction had sparked off a process that Feldman has defined as 'hectic concentration, unprecedented speculation and the building of huge economic empires'.[55] Elsewhere, James has defined the Depression as 'the price for technical hubris'.[56] A contemporary observer also noted in 1931 that Germany's rationalization was not the result of planned re-organization of the whole industry, despite the rhetoric that surrounded it, but instead financial amalgamations, central selling, and output regulation were carried out at different times between 1924 and 1928 as responses to different contingencies.[57] Instead of technical advances and improvements there was a sectoral maldistribution of investment that created overcapacity in some basic heavy industries and textiles.[58] Even in steel there was very little technical modernization and the most important technical improvements were in the saving of energy. This was made possible by the concentration of ownership, which led to the creation of the giant group *Vereinigte Stahlwerke*, concentrated and vertically integrated. It is probably the achievements of the steel industry that were foremost in British minds concerned with German power. The large scale of the German plants and the level of integration of the processes contrasted with the sad state of British steel in the interwar period, where new projects were not built in the right place, or were not big enough for scale economies to be achieved. Nevertheless, despite a certain amount of 'negative rationalization' through the closure of smaller firms, speciality steel continued to be produced by small firms. Another example was the car industry. Here Ford and Opel were still building modern, labour-saving plants, but these American-style plants were not typical for Germany. As a mass product the German car was not really competitive. In the 1920s, German roads were still poor and the most common form of transport was the train. Cars were luxury products and customers required customized vehicles rather than a mass product. In 1929 there were still seventeen major producers of cars, mostly small firms which did not try to develop a mass market.[59]

The rise of Germany's steel and coal industries was what most worried British observers. However, they were probably less aware that by 1913 Germany had become the second largest producer of machine tools in the world and the biggest exporter. This industry in Germany was made of small and medium-sized firms, with strong links to each other and the regions in which they were placed.[60] Rationalization through concentration was attempted but without much success, mostly because of the great variety of manufactured products, the tendency to cater to highly specialized markets, and the 'spirit of independence among many of the smaller and older firms'.[61] The industry remained fragmented, with an average size of plant of 45.5 persons in 1925 and 39.5 in 1930. An American commentator, Robert Brady, shows the awareness of contemporaries of the importance of the machine tool industry: 'the fortunes of the machine industry have a peculiar importance for any economic system ... the more highly mechanised an industrial system becomes, the greater the pivotal role of the machine producing industry'.[62]

Small firms in the regions of decentralized production and the large firms in the 'autarkic regions'[63] came to clash in the political sphere after Germany's defeat in 1918. The collapse of the Imperial regime after 1918 generated a strong movement for the creation of a unitary state and for political centralization that would ultimately control strong, centralized producer associations. The focus was on the large, autarkic firms in the economy and on the creation of corporatistic forms of state control like those developed during the war economy. In the same way as was happening in Britain, the ideal of rational, centralized planning united radical socialists, corporatists, and technocrats.[64] Centralization, however, was strongly opposed by all of the regional governments that had traditionally been engaged in the process of decentralized production, and by autarkic Bavaria, who wanted a federalist state to protect its Catholic culture from Protestant, north German political forces. The voice of the regional governments proved strong enough to scupper the plans of the centralizers and to achieve a federal government, though the lack of political unity between the states meant that they were unable to achieve fiscal autonomy. The removal of financial autonomy at a local and regional level reduced the regions' ability to isolate themselves from the social and economic priorities that emanated from the centre. The changes that took place in the constitutional structure of German politics with the formation of the Weimar Republic dealt a serious blow to the existence of decentralized systems. To deal with the burden of reparations, the federal government was given the right to issue direct taxes, while municipal and regional governments had this power taken away from them. As a result much of the funding that had been invested in industry, in such areas as technology transfer and development, dried up. In addition, in order to fund their activities firms began borrowing heavily from the local municipally owned savings banks, and as unemployment and inflation increased, savings decreased and the banks had less and less money to lend to businesses. This is when the ability of the savings and cooperative banks to use their voice to gain the state's support proved to be important, as shown earlier in the chapter. Their ability to lend to local economies allowed the decentralized system of production to survive.

By the end of the 1920s, the conflict between those who wanted to strengthen decentralized government and those who instead aimed for further centralization became so acute that a constitutional reform conference was called. The position of large firms towards the Weimar Republic had been mostly neutral as long as political structures did not interfere with production. Nevertheless there was strong opposition to central planning, nationalization, and the establishment of factory councils, proposed by successive Weimar governments, as these threatened firms' tradition of self-government. The increase in taxation, to pay for the state's extensive programme of social welfare, was also viewed with little sympathy. Despite ideological neutrality, it soon became clear that the social aims of the new republic were at odds with the economic imperatives of big business. Moreover, autarkic producers, despite their propensity for interfirm cooperation and the creation of combines, resented every attempt by the state to create corporatist arrangements because of a profound mistrust of state interference. When in 1927 increasing levels of regional and local governments' expenditure threatened the country's creditworthiness and therefore foreign capital investments, large businesses joined forces in calling for constitutional reform. The aim was to rationalize the structure of public administration by eliminating regional and municipal bureaucracies as this inflated the cost of government and led to higher taxes, high levels of spending, and indebtness. The creation of a unitary state was seen as the best way to rationalize decision-making and expenditure. This position on constitutional reform placed the autarkic producers in direct conflict with the decentralized industrial order, whose regional governments were threatened. Big business was in direct conflict with local industrial interests and this conflict constituted one of the central obstacles to an institutional accommodation of either form of industrial order within the Weimar Republic.[65] The political and economic history of the Weimar period could thus be characterized by a constant conflict between local governments allied with decentralized producers against the interference of the national state whose aims were centralizing (both politically and industrially).

CONCLUSION

Table 3.3 highlights sharply the size of the small firm sector in the interwar period. The large increase shown in 1931 was a consequence of the depression when many unemployed industrial workers set up their own activities. The chapter has shown how these firms had their own banks, the savings and cooperative banks, and how these prospered alongside the growth of those areas characterized by decentralized production. In Britain the state played a marginal role in the regulation of the banking system, while in Germany it was active in mediating between the different types of banks. The decision to mediate the conflict and regulate competition was an active choice, dictated by the political decision to protect small firms and their local economies. The term used in much of the literature on small firms in Germany is *Mittelstand*, middle estate, and it includes artisans,

Table 3.3. Germany: size of firms (manufacturing and craft), by number of employees, 1925 and 1933 (%)

| | 1–5 | | 6–50 | | 50+ | | Total | |
	Firms	People	Firms	People	Firms	People	Firms	People
1925	87	22	11	23	1.8	55	1,852,737	12,704,135
1933	91	34	8	22	1	44	1,903,420	8,998,753

Source: For 1925, *Statistisches Jahrbuch für das Deutsche Reich* (Berlin, 1931), 82–3; for 1933, *Statistisches Jahrbuch für das Deutsche Reich* (Berlin, 1935), 118–19.

shopkeepers, and small business owners. However, *Mittelstand* is much more than just a definition of size such as *Kleingewerbe* (small business); it implies the existence of a social class, whose collective history is pre-modern, and whose ideological roots are to be found in pre-industrial individualism very different from middle-class, white-collar workers and professionals.[66] The *Mittelstand* in Germany was a powerful conservative body, as it was in France and Italy, but not in Britain, mostly because small-scale entrepreneurs in that country were not able to organize themselves. This socio-economic group showed 'a disposition towards moral indignation at different value organisations, an inclination towards collective panic, a readiness to demonise all forces which threaten the traditional social order—these seem to be characteristics of the mentality of the lower middle classes', as Winkler has written.[67]

Whether or not the Weimar governments recognized small firms as positive agents of growth, they still had to reckon with their political weight, at a time of deep unrest and conflict between social and economic groups. Unlike what happened in Britain, small firms in Germany were able to achieve an identity as a group, to make their voices heard, by associating at a national, regional, and sectoral level. By 1895 the need to gain influence at national and state level led the industrial *Mittelstand* to create the BDI (*Bund der Industriellen*),[68] to address the problem of the growth of cartels that were making raw materials such as iron, steel, and coal expensive for small and medium-sized firms.[69] After 1918, regional groupings such as the Association of Saxon Industrialists and sectoral ones such as the *Verein Deutscher Maschinenbau-Anstalten*, the trade association of the engineering industry, contributed to the political weight of the decentralized industrial order. Conflict between regions, between different industrial systems, and between banks representing different social and economic groups resulted in the failure of the centralizing design of the state. There is no doubt that this generated further instability, both political and economic, but it did ensure the survival of strong local economies. The comparison with France, in Chapter 4, shows that such conflict cannot be assumed to be the natural outcome of the difficulties of building a nation state.

NOTES

1 Donaubauer, *Die Konzentration im Deutschen Bankgewerbe 1848–1980*.
2 Tilly, 'Policy, Capital and Industrial Finance in Germany'. A comprehensive summary of the literature concerning the growth of big banks and their connection with industry is provided by Wellhöner and Wixforth, 'Finance and Industry'.
3 Kocka, 'The Rise of Modern Industrial Enterprise in Germany', 92.

4 Thomes, 'German Savings Banks', 156.
5 Deeg, *Finance Capitalism*, 240.
6 Thomes, 'German Savings Banks', 144.
7 Fischer, 'Das Deutsche Handwerk im Strukturwandel des 20. Jahrhunderts', 346.
8 Thomes, 'German Savings Banks', 147.
9 Ibid., 148–50.
10 Ibid., 151.
11 Balderston, 'German Banking', 566. For the earlier stages of industrialization in a specific region and the positive role played by the savings banks in mobilizing small savings see Tilly, *Financial Institutions and Industrialization*, 126–9.
12 Herrigel, *Industrial Constructions*, 55.
13 Thomes, 'German Savings Banks', 153–6.
14 Ibid., 157.
15 Deeg, *Finance Capitalism*, 34.
16 Hardach, 'Banking in Germany', 272.
17 Deeg, *Finance Capitalism*, 241.
18 Herrigel, *Industrial Constructions*, 53; Deeg, *Finance Capitalism*, 35.
19 For banking in Württemberg see Loewenstein, *Geschichte des Württembergischen Kreditbankwesens*; for the Rhineland see Tilly, *Financial Institutions and Industrialisation in the Rhineland, 1815–1870*.
20 Hardach, 'Banking in Germany', 273.
21 Eschwege, 'Hochfinanz und Mittelstand', in *Die Bank*, May 1908, quoted in Hardach, 'Banking in Germany', 273.
22 Tilly, 'German Banking 1850–1914'.
23 Ziegler, 'The Origins of the Macmillan Gap'.
24 Ibid., 199.
25 Hardach, 'Banking in Germany', 273.
26 Thomes, 'German Savings Banks', 155.
27 Between 1914 and 1921 the eight Berlin banks had absorbed eighty-three provincial banks, thus providing themselves with a truly national network of branches used to gather deposits from the provinces and channel them towards large business. Deeg, *Finance Capitalism*, 40.
28 Hardach, 'Banking in Germany', 275–80.
29 Balderston, 'German Banking', 568.
30 Warriner, *Combines and Rationalisation in Germany*, 10–11.
31 Kocka, 'Entrepreneurs and Managers in German Industrialisation', 570.
32 Feldman, *The Great Disorder*, 276–7.
33 James, *The German Slump*, 132.
34 Ibid., 139–43.
35 Balderston, 'German Banking', 594. The *Verein Deitscher Maschinenbau-Anstalten*, the trade association of the engineering industry, made mostly of small and medium-sized firms, complained that big firms were given preferential access to credit by the great banks. James, *The German Slump*, 140.
36 Feldman, *The Great Disorder*, 269.
37 Ibid., 656–6.

38 Deeg, *Finance Capitalism*, 241.
39 Kluge, *Geschichte der Deutschen Bankgenossenschaffen*, 107–11.
40 See also Balderston, 'German Banking', 575.
41 The central government, through the central bank, held more then 90 per cent of the equity of the Dresdner bank; 70 per cent of the Commerzbank and 35 per cent of the Deutsche bank. Deeg, *Finance Capitalism*, 242.
42 Deeg, *Finance Capitalism*, 43–4; and Hardach, 'Banking in Germany', 285.
43 Balderston, 'German banking between the wars', 554–605.
44 Cottrell, *Industrial Finance*, 243–4.
45 Chandler, *Scale and Scope*, 393.
46 Ibid., 22–3.
47 Kocka, 'The Rise of the Modern Industrial Enterprise in Germany', 78.
48 Hardach, 'Banking in Germany', 72.
49 Kocka, 'The Rise of the Modern Industrial Enterprise in Germany', 108.
50 Tilly, 'Germany', 176–81.
51 Hardach, 'Banking in Germany', 43–51.
52 Hardach, 'Banking in Germany', 55.
53 Cartels were amalgamations of legally and economically independent companies, usually in the same production line, for the purpose of fixing prices and sales and production quotas, while combines brought together independent enterprises under one management to achieve economies of scale and scope.
54 For details of this see: Feldenkirschen, 'Big Business in Interwar Germany'; Feldenkirschen, 'Concentration in German Industry 1870–1939'.
55 Feldman, *The Great Disorder*, 272.
56 James, *The German Slump*, 147.
57 Warrimer, *Combine*, 31.
58 James, *The German Slump*, 149.
59 Ibid.,150–3.
60 Herrigel, 'Industry as a Form of Order'.
61 Brady, *The Rationalisation Movement*, 142, 148.
62 Ibid.,139.
63 Herrigel, *Industrial Constructions*, 72.
64 Ibid., 125.
65 Ibid., 132–9.
66 Wengenroth, 'Small-scale business in Germany', 118. In the 1960s the *Institut für Mittelstandsforschung*, Institute for Middle-estate Research, still argued the *Mittelstand* was a qualitatively separate form of personal enterprise with a distinct mental attitude of the entrepreneur. These arguments consciously rejected Anglo–Saxon notions of 'small firms' as being merely quantitative; Wengenroth, 'Small Scale Business in Germany', 134.
67 Winkler, 'From Social Protectionism to National Socialism: The German Small Business Movement in Comparative Perspective', 16–17.
68 Not to be confused with the post-1945 *Bund der Deutsche Industrie*, also known as BDI.
69 Herrigel, *Industrial Constructions*, 122.

4

Small Firms and the *Synthèse Républicaine*

While the existence in Germany of systems of decentralized production made of small firms could be explained as the resistance of previously independent states towards centralization, this explanation is not valid for France. France's eighteenth-and nineteenth-century industrialization occurred in the political context of a unified nation state, with a strong central government. As a result, the persistence of small firms into the twentieth century had different roots.

From the end of the First World War until 1930, France achieved one of the world's fastest rates of growth. Between 1922 and 1929 GDP grew by 4.4 per cent annually, thanks to the expansion of new sectors, such as electricity, chemical, mechanical engineering, and rubber.[1] This period was also characterized by an increase in the size of establishments, especially in these new industries,[2] and these years can be seen as those when France's large firms established themselves.[3] Until recently the historiography of this period has consigned small firms to a marginal role in this process, when not seeing them as elements of retardation.[4] In contrast, Michel Lescure's in-depth analysis of small and medium-sized firms in France during the 1920s shows that, far from occupying a marginal place, small and medium-sized firms played a central role in the process of growth. While large firms developed standard goods for a growing mass market, the smaller firms rapidly expanded specialty production. However, one of the factors identified by Lescure as holding back small and medium-sized firms and preventing them from fulfilling their full potential during these years was the availability of credit, as commercial banks increasingly rationed finance to their smaller customers.[5] Compared with Britain, however, this gap was narrower thanks to the existence of a segmented banking system. Furthermore, the institutional environment was much different from Britain's, one where the state was active in filling this gap. The reason for this difference is the place occupied by small- and medium-sized firms in the social and political identity of the French Republic.

SMALL FIRMS: THE HEART OF THE REPUBLIC

The establishment in 1892 of the Meline tariff signalled France's final and wholesale embracing of protectionism. Jules Meline, the minister who devised this last round of tariffs, meant to protect an economy of small, independent workshops and farmers. In his mind France was not suited to follow the path of mass production as Britain and Germany had done. Industrialization would only drain the countryside and create cyclical depression and unemployment. Accordingly, he encouraged marketing cooperatives, easier farm credit through the establishment of the *Crédit Agricole*, rural industries, and lower taxes for artisans.[6]

The figures from the 1906 Census shown in Table 4.1 suggest an industrial structure that was very fragmented. But the degree of fragmentation varied depending on the industry, with iron and steel being more concentrated than food production. The predominance of small firms was due to sectors that were the traditional domain of small-scale industry, like food production, the wood industry, and laundry. Others where 'collective manufacturing' survived, such as the clothing industry, were still very much based around the small family firm. The survival of these firms was due to the fact that they produced goods either of very high or very low quality and that wages were kept at a very low level.[7] The small scale of these firms allowed them to adapt quickly to changes in demand, especially for high quality, specialty products. Despite the preponderance of small firms in traditional sectors, the small establishments in 1906 did not look doomed to disappear but were in fact 'heralds of the future' as François Caron has defined them. Caron applies this definition to the crowd of subcontractors who worked for large establishments and to the growing number of repair and maintenance one-man firms that were taking over from traditional artisans, such as electrical workshops and garages. Before the First World War, for example, there were 150 different firms engaged in the automobile industry and this industry epitomized the true nature of French industry, an industry oriented towards the production of a great variety of quality goods. The low degree of concentration in the car industry meant that innovative design and a gamut of choices could be offered, rather than cheaper cars

Table 4.1. France: distribution of the workforce according to industrial plant size, 1906–36 (%)

	1906	1926	1931	1936
0–4	53	35	28	33
5–10	5	6	6	6
11–20	5	5.9	6.6	6.1
21–100	11.8	15.9	17.8	16.5
101–500	13	17.7	19.8	18.3
500+	12.2	19.5	21.8	20.1

Source: Lescure, 1999 p. 146.

produced using mass production methods. Caron maintains that this is why throughout the 1920s many industrialists thought that rationalization of production could have only limited development in France.[8]

From the beginning of the twentieth century, France developed holding companies instead of the corporate form. The limitations of the French financial market made the creation of financial holdings a sensible alternative to large integrated firms, as holdings could circulate capital within the group according to the various sections' investment needs. At the same time industrialists were associating themselves both in lobbying groups and cartels to fight off the rising threats of socialism, trade unionism, and foreign competition. The most powerful national federation of the period was the *Union des Industries Métallurgiques et Minières* created in 1901. Other pre-war cartels were the *Comité Français de la Filature de Coton* that grouped the cotton spinners of Lille, Rouen, and the Voges. These producers seized control of the domestic market, expanded their plant, and specialized in different branches of production under the protection of a cartel that fixed prices and production quotas. Similarly, coal companies in the Nord and Pas-de-Calais, under threat from Belgian and Ruhr coal cartels associated to fix prices and production quotas. The law in theory prohibited cartels but these were rarely prosecuted and never convicted. The *Comité des Forges*, the umbrella organization for iron and steel companies, modelled itself on its German counterpart to demand protective tariffs and favourable purchasing policies from the government.[9]

Big establishments were to be found in textiles, iron and steel, processing of metals, and mines, though here again the size of the establishment depended on the type of production: for example, carding was more concentrated than spinning, and this was more concentrated than weaving. Especially in sectors characterized by fluctuating demand, the existence of small-scale specialist firms also allowed larger firms to use subcontractors, rather then employ their own capital. The census of 1906 showed the importance (at least numerically) of small firms and confirmed the view of politicians across the political spectrum that small retailers, artisans, and entrepreneurs occupied a place of considerable importance both in social and economic terms. In the decades just before the First World War the aim of public policy was to maintain the country's 'balanced economy'. This meant a mix of agriculture and industry where the rural sector played a very important part in maintaining France's self-sufficiency and also protected traditional values and institutions, while small firms were placed at the heart of the republican synthesis (*au cœur de la synthèse républicaine*). The interests of small firms were not only represented by the centre-left Radical party[10] but also by the parties of the right, both liberal and conservative, for whom small-scale capitalism was the bulwark against socialism.[11] The programme of the Radical party was one of maintaining an equilibrium among industry, commerce, and agriculture to isolate France from the turmoil that reigned in other nations such as the USA, where industrialization was progressing much faster. Discriminatory taxes were introduced to defend independent shop-keepers from chain retailers and department stores and to help small farmers and small firms survive.[12]

The end of the war in 1918, however, showed all the weaknesses of the French economy, and for modernizers like Etienne Clémentel (Minister of Commerce and Industry) and Louis Loucheur (Minister for Industrial Reconstruction and Clemenceau's main adviser on industrial questions) this weakness was caused by the insufficient level of concentration and by the excessive individualism of small businessmen. Both believed that France was threatened by German cartels and that France could excel by copying the German example. In 1917, Loucher said: 'I am convinced that we can create in every corner of France the same great factories as those in Germany; I know that we can do better [than Germany] in economic performance.'[13] In the 1920s the 'modernizing' movement *Redressement Français*, led by businessman Ernest Mercier (who had been on Lou-cheur's staff during the war), wanted the French economy to adopt the methods that, in their eyes, made the American one so successful.[14] At the same time, however, the 'modernizers' wanted to preserve artisan firms, seen as particularly suited to the aptitudes and tendencies of the French people. To reconcile these two aspirations the modernizers of the *Redress-ment* saw large and small firms not in competition with each other but as complementary.[15]

Several different groups saw rationalization as the solution to France's perceived backwardness. Rationalization in France, as in Britain, meant industrial concentration, the assembly line, product standardization, mass marketing, scientific management, cartels, and technology. Trade union groups and the left championed it because, in a world where production could be rationalized, abundance would reign, labour would receive its fair share, more leisure and higher possibilities for consumption, and workers as producers would eventually replace the capitalists. Clearly the easiest way to attain all this was through national-ization. However, within the Radical Party, whose constituency was mostly in rural and provincial France, there was a strong feeling that rationalization would have decimated its electoral base.[16] Etienne Clém-entel, for example, who believed in the power of consortia to modernize France, was also instrumental in the creation in 1917 of the law that reorganized the Popular banks as vehicles of credit for small entrepre-neurs.[17] It is clear that there existed a tension within the state generated by these conflicting aspirations, to make the French economy 'modern' while protecting not just small firms but also a way of life, the republican synthesis. To this effect, during the 1920s a large number of fiscal and legal devices were instituted to assist small firms.[18]

The 1920s saw fast changes in the structure of industry in terms of size and products. During this period it was the engineering industries which were most dynamic while textiles and leather declined in import- ance in terms of their share of output.[19] This growth was attained thanks to large-scale technical changes and by a reorganization of production methods that became more and more openly capitalistic. It was based on the emergence of a mass consumer market and on equipment invest- ment. An analysis of exports, however, shows that this period was char- acterized by the survival, and in some case the prosperity, of certain sectors of traditional French production, such as silk and woollen goods, and by the growth of 'new' products, such as machinery, tools, and chemicals.[20]

Table 4.1 shows a clear shift away from very small units (those employ- ing fewer than ten people) towards larger establishments, consistent with the view that investment in machinery and energy led to larger produc- tion units. Though the industrial structure remained fragmented, many of the firms in France came under the more or less direct control of large enterprises, thanks to the creation of cartels and holding companies.[21] The high number of small-medium establishments hid the presence of large enterprises, such as Peugeot, Renault, Kuhlmann, Saint-Gobain, Citröen, which did develop vertical integration.[22] During the interwar period, concentration developed in the form of loosely articulated holding com- panies that achieved financial integration without effectively controlling production. The state also intervened with the creation of public and semi-public companies, such as the *Mines de Potasse d'Alsace*, the *Office National Industriel de l'Azote*, and the *Compagnie Française des Pétroles*. Holding companies proved to be very effective in raising capital while still leaving space to individual producers. Saint-Gobain with its 150 sub- sidiaries was representative of the way French industry merged in the 1920s. Other holdings were common in sectors that required substantial capital investments such as chemicals, electricity, metals, and heavy industry.[23] Though all firms suffered during the Depression, few bank- ruptcies occurred and this fact suggests that the financial holdings created in the 1920s acted as a shelter for firms as they could receive assistance from other firms in the group.[24] The Depression induced the creation of more holdings to regulate production and prices and the economy came to be dominated by 'extended oligopolies'. These, however, were typical of the capital and semi-finished goods while consumer goods kept a much more scattered production structure.[25] As in Britain, cartelization was seen as a response to the turbulence of the market, and as a way of regularizing it. The government moved to encourage cartels though in some cases, such as shoe manufacturing, where large enterprises threatened to take over an artisanal industry, the state imposed arrange- ments between firms aimed at freezing the status quo.[26]

The absence in France of large industrial groups such as ICI or IG Farben is seen by Maurice Lévy-Leboyer not as a sign that the economy 'failed' to modernize but as a consequence of the smallness of the markets, the lower level of urbanization, the absence of national channels of distribution (which accidentally favoured small firms as they could retain their local markets), foreign competition from within, and the slow growth of consumer demand. Under these circumstances it is not surprising that with a narrow and dispersed home market and a specialized workforce the size of firms remained small. The small scale of these firms allowed the continued production of luxury products such as silk in Lyon, but also of goods as diverse as steel cables, fire extinguishers, machine tools, cardboard, and electrical material.[27] The specific constraints the French economy was under meant that businessmen and managers could not have replicated the American model before 1945. Therefore the holding company was not the expression of some supposed 'failure' of the economy but an alternative model. Furthermore, at the beginning of the twentieth century France was comparable to Britain in terms of the weight of the top 100 firms in the economy. The difference resided in the organizational structure which favoured combines and holdings rather than corporations. French medium-sized firms (those employing between 100 and 500 people) also accounted for a larger share of output than British ones, especially in sectors like food preparation, leather, wood, and specialized metallurgy.[28] The difference between the two countries became more marked in the interwar period. The share of output of large firms decreased while medium-sized firms became stronger in sectors such as building, mechanical engineering, chemicals, and textiles.[29]

In any case, the performance of French economic growth demonstrates that over the long period this compared favourably with that of Britain. It has been defined as a failure by historians such as Landes because of the lack of accurate quantitative data and because of a single-track vision of industrialization, based on the British example. French industrialization was slower, and more gradual, with each region taking advantages of its own endowment of natural and human resources. Substantial industrialization was combined with the continued expansion of the handicraft sector and small-scale production. Since the 1960s, any characterization of France as a 'failure' has been revised to show the quantitative and qualitative merits of this alternative model of industrialization.[30]

SMALL FIRMS AND THE INSTITUTIONAL CONTEXT

The continued growth of small and medium-sized firms and their contribution to the economy in the interwar period needs to be placed in its institutional context. This allows us to highlight further the differences between France and Britain and the reasons behind these. Between 1891 and 1913 the number of banks increased from 42 to 132 and so did the total size of their balance sheets, though this grew faster indicating the existence of a relative process of concentration. However, the share of the combined balance sheets of the four big banks, *Crédit Lyonnais, Société Générale, Comptoir d'Escompte de Paris,* and *Crédit Industriel et Commercial,* became smaller over the same period, showing the growing importance of medium-sized, regional banks during this phase of growth of the economy. This period saw a process of concentration taking place at a regional level, as many local banks were taken over by the larger, regional banks.[31]

As part of the French government's preoccupation with small firms, in 1911 an extra-parliamentary commission on banking was set up. The commission identified the closing down of local banks as a problem for the supply of capital to small firms. The commission considered that the closure of local banks meant that long-term personal credit, issued by local bankers with knowledge of local conditions, could hardly be replaced by short-term credit issued by branches acting on rules dictated by head offices in Paris. The setting up of the commission was the state's response to the concerns that small firms had been voicing since the late nineteenth century as the banking landscape of the country changed. An active response was followed by practical measures: in 1917 the reorganization of the *Crédit Populaire* created another supplier of credit to the smaller units in the economy and in 1919 the *Crédit National* was created to supply to small and medium-sized firms with medium-and long-term loans.[32]

In order to understand its significance, the state's intervention and the re-organization of lending to small and medium-sized firms must be seen as part of the overall development of French banking. The role of France's big banks in promoting industrialization has been assessed positively by Maurice Lévy-Leboyer.[33] However, a reassessment of the activities of the whole spectrum of banks has shown that in the period before 1914 local banks played a more important part in the overall process of growth than did the national banks. In 1870 there were between 2,000 and 3,000 unit banks.[34] Most of these were small, local, private banks, launched by merchants and manufacturers to respond to local needs, as in the British case. These banks provided their clients with both short- and long-term credit and their funds were considerable as large firms resorted to them by either taking loans or selling parcels of shares to the banks. Chatillon-Commentry, the fourth largest metallurgic firm in France in 1880, financed the building of several of its plants by using credit from a group of local bankers. In the north of the country, banks such as *L. Dupont* or the *Caisse Commerciale du Nord* provided the sugar and textile industries with long-term capital. The local bankers of Lyon, like *Aynard, Guérin,* and *Veuve Morin-Pons* were all present in the regional industries (mining, metallurgy, textiles), either as managers or shareholders. In Lorraine the iron and steel industry developed thanks to the active role played by the local banks such as *Weill Lévy et Compagnie, Banque Lenglet,* and *Banque Thomas.* Lévy-Leboier and Lescure consider that a banking system made of local units was more suitable for an economy where small and medium-sized firms were the most prominent. This made the role of the large joint-stock banks, such as the *Crédit Mobilier* analysed by Gerschenkron, less crucial than he originally hypothesized.[35]

The national banks began extending their branch network in the early 1880s and, from the mass of local banks, some regional joint-stock banks emerged as the scale of industrial firms also increased with the growth of the economy. Banks such as *Crédit du Nord, Société Lyonnaise de Dépôts,* or *Société Marseillaise de Crédit* became the agents behind regional industrialization by rolling-over short-term advances and in the case of new industries by placing securities issues with the public.[36] In the case of regions where the speculative nature of the local economy meant that savers preferred to invest their money in things such as houses or public securities, banks such as the *Société Marseillaise de Crédit* would hold shares and bonds of regional companies, becoming a substitute for the lack of dynamism of local savings. In contrast with the active role played by the eastern and southern banks, most regional banks in Lille or Lyon did not become involved when new industries were launched. Overcommitment to the older industries (75 per cent of the board of the *Crédit du Nord* came from textiles by 1890), coupled with their role as short-term credit suppliers, made their attitude towards new industries more conservative. Banks in more established industrial regions played a limited role in the supply of long-term capital, as these regions were the ones with the smaller industries or with industries such as textiles, which needed cash for running costs rather than large sums for capital investments.[37]

By 1914 banks' customers were still mostly urban upper and middle class or large and medium-sized enterprises, when in fact 58 per cent of industry consisted of firms employing fewer than ten people and 55.8 per cent of the population were living in rural areas. The decline of private banks was matched by the increase in the number of joint-stock banks and by an increase in specialization as large banks gave up their role as universal banks to become deposit banks (as in the case of the *Crédit Lyonnais*). At a regional level, however, the country banks continued to operate as universal banks, by rolling-over short-term industrial credits so that overdrafts, often without any security, became long-term credits.[38]

In the 1920s local and regional banks were still the main source of finance for firms employing fewer than 100 people mainly as medium-term loans disguised as short-term advances. Though some large firms were heavily in debt with regional banks, these types of firms tended to use the larger, national banks. The main difference between these two types of banks was that regional banks were able to reduce the cost of lending to small firms by using proximity to reduce transaction costs, while the banking practices of the national banks were guided by rule books issued by the central administration. The effect of reducing risk by better information was the high level on non-secured advances, especially in the period before the First World War. In 1909, for example, in the *Société Nancéienne de Crédit*, non-secured advances amounted to 52 per cent of the total. However, the relationship between small firms and local and regional banks progressively weakened during the 1920s. The first reason for this was the gradual disappearance of local banks from the turn of the century onwards. These had been facing competition from savings, regional, and national banks and from the Bank of France and had been reduced to engaging in risky shareholdings in local industrial companies. As a result many collapsed at the turn of the century. The second factor was the growth of regional banks between 1900 and 1930. In order to compete with the national banks, the regional banks extended their branch network by taking over local banks, and from 1900 to 1923 the number of branches available to the eight main regional banks in the north increased from 24 to 364. The greater geographical spread weakened the benefits of proximity, and hence the propensity to lend to small firms, and increased the banks' desire for liquidity.[39]

Despite the increase in concentration, local and regional banks were still the main source of finance for small firms. In 1926 loans from regional banks represented 65.4 per cent of total bank debt for firms employing fewer than 100 people.[40] The link between small firms and regional banks was the strongest in those areas where these dominated, the north and north-east and in Alsace.[41] In 1926 regional banks in these regions provided 74 per cent of bank loans to local firms, far higher than in any other region. Such high levels of local lending were a function of the connection between local economic health and that of the banks. However, what determined the banks' preference for industrial lending was the size of the bank. The larger the bank the lower the degree of engagement with industrial customers. Hence the larger commercial banks made a smaller contribution to industrial lending than did the regional banks. The reason for this was the centralized nature of these banks. This influenced their ability to assess the risk of firms in the periphery and, as the banks' main concern was to invest their funds in the safest way, this led them to divert their funds elsewhere, while lower transaction costs meant that local and regional banks could engage with local businesses.[42]

TRANSACTION COSTS: A CASE STUDY

Lescure's study of the relationship between banks and local firms in the Choletais (Maine-et-Loraine) from 1900 to 1950 brings some interesting insights into this relationship. The productive system of the Choletais was distinguished by the existence of two industries. One, of pre-industrial origins, was textiles, located within Cholet and relatively concentrated, employing in 1930 about 10,000 people. The second, relatively more recent industry, created in the 1870s and 1880s, was shoemaking, which absorbed the workforce made redundant by the mechanization of the textile sector. Shoemaking was made of very small firms, located in the countryside, and also employing about 10,000 people, mostly within their homes. The local supply of credit was structured around two poles, the first one consisting of banks embedded in the local economy with a decentralized structure, and the second one consisting of branches of the national banks. The first pole was represented by a local bank, the *Banque Delhumeau*, which since 1890 had been the only local bank of Cholet and by the *Banque Populaire du Maine-et Loire d'Angers*, established in 1924. The second pole was represented by the branches of the *Crédit Lyonnais*, in Cholet since 1891, and the *Banque National de Crédit*, which had opened a branch in Cholet after 1918.

Up to 1914 the local bank had almost the total control of local credit, both within Cholet and in the surrounding countryside, while the branch of the *Crédit Lyonnais* tagged behind. In 1913, to increase its resources and keep up with the growth of local industry, *Banque Delhumeau* merged with another local bank in nearby Anger. In 1918 another local bank, this time in Saint-Nazaire, was taken over and a new name was given to what had become a regional bank, the *Crédit de l'Ouest*. Despite the increase in its resources the bank lost its control over local credit. The larger textile firms became more attached to the *Crédit Lyonnais* and to the *Banque National de Crédit*, while the smaller textile firms and the rural, smaller shoemaking firms remained clients of the *Crédit de l'Ouest*. This segmentation of the market was furthered in 1924 by the establishment of the *Banque Populaire du Maine-et Loire d'Angers*, whose clients were firms smaller than those that borrowed from the *Crédit de l'Ouest*. Older and more embedded in Cholet than the younger popular bank, the *Crédit de l'Ouest* was better able to secure bigger urban clients while the popular bank became the banker of the smaller establishments in the countryside, mostly shoemakers.

As competition between the banks increased during the interwar period, the local banks lost clients to the national banks as these had more to offer to the larger, urban firms. However, the local banks were able to defend their activity by expanding their operations to smaller, more rural, firms. These firms were in theory more risky, as the nature of the industry and their dispersed localization increased transaction costs for those banks, like the national ones, that did not have a detailed knowledge of the entrepreneurs and their activities. Proximity allowed the local banks to reduce these costs. The long-term relationships that the local banks established with the smaller, local firms allowed them to

continue reducing assessment and monitoring costs and hence to maintain a different client base to that of the national banks. After 1924 the
Crédit de l'Ouest came under the control of the *Crédit Industriel et Commercial*. Despite having become part of a national bank, during the 1920s, it
did not reduce its links with the firms of the Choletais. During the 1930s,
however, increasing levels of centralization of decision-making reduced
the advantages of relationship banking accrued by the *Crédit de l'Ouest* in
the previous years, as the procedures for the collection of information and
analysis of risk became increasingly centralized. The gap in the provision
of finance for smaller firms was filled by the *Banque Populaire*, while the
larger firms continued as clients of the *Crédit Lyonnais* and of the *Banque
National de Crédit*.[43]

THE TROUBLED 1920S AND THE CREDIT GAP

One of the consequences of the turbulence of the interwar period was the
search for liquidity by the banks and this is shown by the shift in the
composition of advances. The commercial portfolio of the banks grew
faster in nominal value than loans and overdrafts, and within the commercial portfolio it was Treasury bills, rather than bills of exchange that
took the largest share. This development produced a loosening of the
links between the banks and the economy, in particular with small and
medium-sized firms, as current account loans were the most suitable kind
of credit for them. As in Germany, the deficiencies of the banking system
led the larger firms to set up their own banks (e.g. the *Electro-Crédit* by the
Compagnie Générale d'Electicité), further loosening the relationship between banks and firms. After 1927 the recovery of the economy increased
the availability of deposits and as a consequence the willingness of banks
to lend. To regain their industrial customers, most of the large banks
launched financial subsidiaries specially designed to provide medium-
term loans to enterprises.[44]

The commercial banks' disengagement from the economy, in terms of
their willingness and ability to lend, can be estimated by looking at bank
credit as a proportion of national income. These credits dropped from 32 per
cent in 1913 to less than 20 per cent in the 1920s, down to 18 per cent in 1935.
The decrease in intervention by the banks was a consequence of the increasing demands made on them by the state. The First World War and after that
the birth of welfare increased state debts and the banks had to increase
public bonds as a share of their portfolios. At the same time public institutions were increasing their weight as sources of funds for French business:
after 1919 the *Crédit National* and the popular banks were required to
support small and medium-sized businesses and the *Crédit Agricole* was
restructured as a national state institution to support farmers.[45]

After the relative concentration experienced by the banking system before 1913, the interwar period was favourable to de-concentration, as more banks were created in the wake of the positive economic climate. However, the delay in leaving the gold standard brought a wave of banking crises, the first one in 1930–1 and the second one in 1935. Between 1929 and 1937, 670 banks went bankrupt, but of these only 276 were joint-stock banks. The highest number of casualties was among the regional, universal banks because of their closer links with industrial firms. The only large bank to fail was the *Banque National de Crédit*, replaced after liquidation by a new bank, the *Banque National pour le Commerce et l'Industrie*. The response of the banks to the crisis was once again to reduce lending and increase their liquidity. This was also a consequence of a contraction in deposits, due also to the competition from the savings banks who saw their deposits multiply by 3.8 between 1926 and 1936, while those of the commercial banks increased only 1.3 times.[46]

The debate in France as to whether the banks have supported sufficiently the economy has been raging since the mid-nineteenth century. At various stages in the history of the French economy, banks have been accused of being too conservative, too devoted to liquidity and short-term lending, and of not acting in a more entrepreneurial fashion. The period between the end of the First World War and the Second World War was a difficult one for the French commercial banks and the banks themselves were acutely aware of their inferiority, especially compared to the English big five. In 1911 the deposits of the *Crédit Lyonnais* were 89 per cent of those of the Midland bank, while in 1936 they had fallen to 19 per cent. The Midland bank alone had more resources than the five largest French banks. The French banks blamed the smallness of their deposits on the unfair competition of the state's sponsored banks. However, this was justified, in the public eye, by the perceived lack of support given by the private banks to the economy. The banks' survival of the turbulence of the interwar period confirms that their conservative strategy of favouring liquidity and short-term lending was a successful one. In this respect the more dynamic regional and local banks paid dearly for their support of industrial firms, as many failed, or were taken over after the crisis of 1929.[47] The Depression was 'the hecatomb of the local bank'[48] and this undoubtedly reduced the provision of finance to small firms. However, there were other public and semi-public institutions that helped fill the gap: the savings banks and the popular banks.

The French savings banks had been created by private enterprises in the first part of the nineteenth century and then placed under state supervision after the economic difficulties of the 1880s. In 1881 the state created a parallel institution in the form of postal savings banks. The post office network allowed the savings banks to absorb the savings of those large parts of rural France where there were no bank branches and in many cities the savings banks served small businesses. One of the reasons why savings banks were a more attractive option than commercial banks was that they paid higher rates on their deposit accounts. In 1913 the banks were paying 1.5 per cent on deposit accounts and the savings banks 2.75 per cent. The state's guarantee of the deposits also inspired customers' confidence. By 1913 there were 15.1 million savings banks passbook holders in France. This averaged more than one passbook per household. In 1935 the number of passbooks had increased to such an extent that on average every other Frenchman owned a savings bank passbook.[49] In 1931 the banks' interest rate on deposits had dropped to 1 per cent while the savings banks' was 3.5 per cent, and the ceiling on passbooks was raised to 20,000 francs from the 7,500 it had been before. Furthermore, the savings banks tended increasingly to receive the trading capital of small and medium-sized industrial and commercial firms. By 1937 the deposits collected by the savings banks almost equalled those of the commercial banks, but the deposits collected by all the public financial institutions (*Banque de France*, savings banks, *Caisse des Dépôts*, *Crédit Agricole*, and popular banks) amounted to more than double those of the commercial banks.[50]

While the savings banks occupied a strong place in rural France, the popular banks were a more urban phenomenon. Created around the middle of the nineteenth century, and following the German model of self-help cooperatives, they were slow to develop because of the competition from local banks.[51] They were rescued from a slow decline thanks to the state's decision in 1911 to establish a commission to investigate the problems concerned with the provision of credit to small and medium-sized firms. Concerns about the existence of a possible gap had been growing since the end of the nineteenth century. The demand for credit from family concerns was growing but their traditional suppliers, the local banks, were finding it difficult to resist the competition of larger institutions. As the local banks amalgamated with other banks to become regional institutions they left a gap, and small borrowers in particular found themselves at a disadvantage. The commission set up in 1911 to investigate these problems came to a number of conclusions and the legislation that followed (in 1917) identified the popular banks as the best type of institution to provide short-term loans to small firms. The urban, mutual nature of these banks made them, in the eyes of the legislators, ideal vehicles to provide small, local entrepreneurs with capital.[52] Until 1936 the Treasury supplemented the banks' capital by providing them with interest-free advances. These were repaid by levies of between 10 to 20 per cent on their profits.[53] In 1921 the banks associated to create a central organization, the *Caisse Centrale*, to centralize deposits and the purchase of government securities and provide clearing facilities. This was followed in 1929 by the establishment of a supervisory body, the

Chambre Syndicale, for the purpose of exercising supervision of the banks' activities. Each popular bank was required to subscribe to a common fund held by the *Chambre*, to which the state also channelled the advances to the movement.

Before the Second World War, the state exercised its influence on the activities of the popular banks through direct advances, regulation, and direction of policy. The popular banks were also used as channels to lend money to specific categories of firms. For example, in 1923 the *crédit artisanal* was established. Special loans were made to cooperative unions of artisans and to their members in the form of short-term and medium-terms loans, repayable in ten years, at special rates. The funds employed derived from allocations made by the state and the popular banks were, in this instance, acting as agents of the Treasury, being reimbursed for the cost of managing these loans.[54]

The development and expansion of public and semi-public credit institutions with state backing was, after 1913, the most crucial change in the structure of French banking. It showed the state's willingness to develop an interventionist approach towards the economy and in so doing pursue social and political goals by protecting the class of small entrepreneurs and artisans.[55] In some cases the state intervened on its own, and in others together with the big private banks (as in the case of the *Crédit National*), but in all cases only when the commercial banks had left a gap. The role of the state was not to compete with the commercial banks but to complement them. The case of the popular banks is the clearest. The 1911 enquiry highlighted the fracture between the *couches moyennes*, the middle classes, rural and urban, and the big banks. The big banks had, since 1870, been trying to get these classes to deposit their savings with them but in return these clients felt that they were being slighted, especially with regard to the financing of innovation and of equipment. The excuse the banks gave was that they could not lend to small and medium-sized entrepreneurs when the only guarantee they could offer was their personal capabilities. Social aspirations and economic needs were, therefore, behind the proliferation of the popular banks.[56]

CONCLUSION

During the interwar period, despite the establishment of the popular banks and of the *Crédit National*, the gap in the provision of finance to small firms did not close. Contemporaries accused the boards of these two institutions of being in collusion with big business and of diverting savings and state funds to them. An assessment of the lending activities of the popular banks and of the *Crédit National* shows that it was only a small proportion of the lending of the banking system as a whole, reaching 3 per cent in 1930. While their lack of resources limited their impact, this does not explain why they did not lend much to small firms.

The assessment method used by the *Crédit National* to reduce risk was extremely complex but was not able to eliminate completely information asymmetry and this meant that advances had to be protected by a high-level mortgage. For this reason it was mostly medium-sized firms that made up the clientele of the *Crédit National* and firms employing more than 100 people were more likely to be granted a loan than the smaller firms. This selective top slicing is explained by the level of security demanded by the institution granting the loan, as insufficient guarantees accounted for 72.7 per cent of refusal of requests for credit. The best placed firms were those that could offer other securities apart from the current value of their industrial assets. Small firms were at a disadvantage as most of them could offer no securities other than their industrial assets and the most heavily penalized were new firms in which all available finance had been used to set up the concern. The rate of credit acceptances dropped from 68 per cent in the case of the longest-established firms (those that had been operating for more than fifty years) to 37.5 per cent in the case of those firms which had been established for less than five years. The popular banks were also more likely to lend to medium-sized firms, because of the higher level of security offered.[57] However, as these banks, unlike the *Crédit National*, were local institutions, their behaviour varied depending on the degree of competition from other banks in the locality.[58] The problem faced in the 1920s by these institutions alternative to the commercial banks was not that they were unwilling to lend to small firms, but how to guarantee loans to firms that did not possess sufficient collateral.[59]

Lescure's in-depth analysis of the financial needs of small firms during the interwar period and of the limits of the banking system suggests that France also suffered from a 'Macmillan gap'. In a comparative perspective, however, France's banking system was marked by a much higher level of competition and segmentation than Britain's. The example of Cholet, given earlier, shows that the presence of different types of banks meant that smaller firms were not left out, despite the expansion of the local banks. In fact it was competition that ensured that smaller, rural firms could still find a lender.

Before and after the First World War, the expansion of the national banks into the provinces to increase their deposit base did put a strain on the local banks, which reacted by amalgamating with other local banks, creating strong regional banks. One of the reasons why the local banks did not succumb to the national credit institutions was that the latter were not really interested in the type of lending the local banks did, but rather in increasing their deposit base. The willingness of the local and regional bank to lend locally, in the form of long-term advances on current account, meant that the national and local banks could share the same geographical space but serve different markets.[60] Higher levels of lending to industrial and commercial customers did reduce the liquidity of local and regional banks. The high number of bankruptcies among these banks during the Depression does show the inherent instability of the system. Nevertheless, the presence of semi-public lending institutions, the popular and savings banks provided small firms with alternative sources of finance.

NOTES

1   Measures of French economic growth can be found in Carré, Dubois, and Malinvaud, *French Economic Growth.*
2   Cahen, 'La concentration des établissements en France de 1896 à 1936'.
3   Lévy-Leboyer, 'The Large Corporation in Modern France'; for a specific case study see Friedenson, *Histoire des usines Renault.*
4   Landes, *Unbound Prometheus*, chapter on France; Lévy-Leboyer, 'Le patronat français, malthusien?'.
5   Lescure, *PME et croissance économique.*
6   Kuisel, *Capitalism and the State*, 18–19.
7   For small firms' contribution to the early stages of industrialization see: Piore and Sabel, *The Second Industrial Divide*; Bergeron, *Les capitalistes en france (1780–1914)*; Nye, 'Firm Size and Economic Backwardness'.
8   Caron, *An Economic History of Modern France*, 174–5.
9   Kuisel, *Capitalism and the State*, 21–6.
10 This party came to power for the first time in 1902, and was in and out of power until 1940.
11 Lescure, *PME et croissance économique*, 244–7.
12 Kuisel, *Capitalism and the State*, 16.
13 Louis Loucheur, writing in the *Bulletin des Usines de Guerre*, 27 August 1917. Quoted in Kuisel, *Capitalism and the State*, 50.
14 For more details on the *Redressement Français* and the modernizers see Kuisel, *Ernest Mercier, French Technocrat.*
15 Lescure, *PME et croissance économique*, 245–7.
16 Kuisel, *Capitalism and the State*, 78–90.
17 Albert, *Les banques populaires*, 49.
18 Lescure, *PME et croissance économique*, 248–50.
19 The share in industrial value added in constant prices of the engineering industries rose from 18 per cent in 1913 to 25 per cent in 1929. Over the same period the share of textiles, clothing, and leather fell from 40 per cent to 28 per cent. Caron, *An Economic History of Modern France*, 231.
20 Ibid., 231–7, 256–7.
21 Caron and Bouvier, *Histoire économique et sociale*, 781–9.
22 Lévy-Leboyer, *Histoire de la France industrielle*, 277.
23 Ibid., 244–64.
24 Lévy-Leboyer, 'The Large Corporation in Modern France', 149.
25 Caron, *An Economic History of Modern France*, 365.
26 Kuisel, *Capitalism and the State*, 95.

27   Lescure, *PME et croissance économique*, 289–313.
28   Daviet, 'Some Features of Concentration', 68–78.
29   Caron and Bouvier, *Histoire économique et sociale de la France*, 773–4.
30   This revisionist literature has been summarized effectively by Cameron and Freedman, 'French Economic Growth'. For the nineteenth century and a comparison with Britain see Crouzet, 'French Economic Growth in the 19th century Reconsidered'; for an extensive comparison with Britain see O'Brien and Keyder, *Economic Growth in Britain and France, 1780–1914*; for the twentieth century see Carré, Dubois and Malinvaud, *French Economic Growth*.
31   Bouvier, *Un siècle de banque française*, 122–3.
32   Lescure, *PME et croissance économique*, 252–64.
33   Lévy-Leboyer, *Les banques européennes* and Lévy-Leboyer, 'Capital Investment and Economic Growth in France, 1820–1930'.
34   Plessis, 'Le "retard français": la faute á la banque?'.
35   Lévy-Leboyer and Lescure, 'France',167.
36   Lescure, 'Banking in France in the inter-war period'.
37   Lévy-Leboyer and Lescure, 'France', 170.
38   Lescure, 'Banking in France', 315–17.
39   Lescure, 'Banks and Small Enterprises', 318–19.
40   Lescure, *PME et croissance économique*, 178–80.
41   In Alsace the Crédit Mutuel acted like a regional bank, see Gueslin, *Le Crédit Mutuel*.
42   Lescure, *PME et croissance économique*, 182–7.
43   Lescure, 'Entre ville et campagne'.
44   Lescure, 'Banking in France', 329.
45   Gueslin, 'Banks and State in France from the 1880s to the 1930s.', 85.
46   Lescure, 'Banking in France', 133.
47   Plessis, 'Les banques, le crédit et l'économie'.
48   Caron, *An Economic History of Modern France*, 125.
49   Gueslin, 'Banks and State in France from the 1880s to the 1930s', 76–9.
50   Ibid., 78, tab 4.7.
51   For the early years of the banks see Albert, *Les banques populaires*, 10–30.
52   Ibid., 36–7.
53   Wilson, *French Banking*, 239–40.
54   Ibid., 239.
55   Apart from the reorganization and funding of the popular banks and the creation of the *Crédit National*, other public institutions created in the interwar period were in 1920 the *Caisse Nationale de Crédit Agricole* and the *Banque Française du Commerce Extérieur*; in 1923 the *Caisse Centrale du Crédit Hôtelier*; in 1936 the *Caisse Nationale des Marchés de l'État* and in 1938 *Caisse Centrale de Crédit Coopératif*.
56   Bouvier, *Un siecle de banque française*, 145–52.
57   Lescure, 'Banks and Small Firms in France', 322–5.
58   Albert, *Les banques populaires*, 82–138.
59   Lescure, *PME et croissance économique*, 325.
60   Willis and Beckhart, *Foreign Banking Systems*, 597–603.

5

Italy's Alternative Model of Industrialization

Italy's industrialization began later than that of its neighbours. In the nineteenth century, even the most advanced (in terms of capital accumulation) of the Italian states, Piemonte and Lombardia, had not reached the levels of industrialization of German states such as Saxony.[1] Nevertheless, in the twenty years before Unification, certain sectors of preindustrial origins, such as textiles, especially cotton and silk, and mechanical engineering saw a rapid development as wealthy landowners sought to diversify their investments.

Italy's industrial history before Unification was one of regions with very different levels of wealth, agricultural development, and industrial specialization that had been determined by their separate political histories, and by their factor endowments. The leading regions were Piemonte, Lombardia, and Liguria, while the southern states lagged far behind. In 1911, 55 per cent of the industrial value added was produced in the 'industrial triangle', 29 per cent in the north-east and centre and only 16 per cent in the south.[2] The industrial structure of these regions was different, with technologically advanced industries in the north that had stronger elements of vertical and horizontal integration, while in the north-east and the centre there were industrial districts with low technological levels. The link between industrial activity and agriculture remained very strong in most regions well into the post-1945 period, with the greater part of firms being small and presenting a mixture of craft skills and outwork.[3]

SMALL FIRMS AND THE 'DUAL MODEL' OF ECONOMIC DEVELOPMENT

In 1911 the sectors where small firms were preponderant, such as clothing, shoes, furniture-making, small mechanical production, and food, contributed to two-thirds of industrial production. As consumption increased these sectors grew. In 1914, 12 per cent of those employed in manufacturing worked in food production and the other 'light' sectors employed one-third of the rest in firms that on average employed five to six people. These firms had low capital intensity and value added but were commercially very dynamic, adapting production to rapidly changing fashions, and exporting specialty goods. These sectors developed outside the industrial triangle, in the north-east and part of the centre, and had the great advantage of bringing the per capita income of these regions closer to the richer ones in the north, unlike those regions such as Umbria and Campania where state intervention had placed large industrial settlements. In 1911 the value added per worker in the industrial triangle was L1,400, in Emilia, Toscana, and Marche it was close to L1,000 while in Umbia and Campania it did not reach L500. By raising income levels small firms also influenced the levels of consumption in these regions allowing these regional economies to develop.[4]

In the more 'modern' sectors the few firms that succeeded were born large because of the constraints imposed by technology. The examples that dominate the literature are iron and steel production (Terni), shipbuilding, cannons, and locomotives (Ansaldo), mechanical engineering (Breda, OM), cars (Fiat), fertilizers (Unione Concimi), chemicals (Montecatini), and electricity (Edison).[5] All these sectors were highly concentrated and dominated by few firms. The high capital intensity of these sectors and the smallness of their markets meant that to develop vertical and horizontal integration firms had to rely heavily on state orders and on the mixed banks for funds.

Despite Italian historians' interest in the country's large firms, Table 5.1 shows that in the interwar period the industrial structure was still polarized between a very few large firms and a multitude of small ones. These were the firms that helped to stabilize the economy during the 1920s, by absorbing the excess labour force, first the demobilized soldiers and later on during the economic crisis.[6] In the 1920s small firms were quick to associate at a local level with the *Comitati delle Piccole Industrie*. These bodies were used to lobbying the government, for example for a revision of the industrial census, as an accurate measurement of the weight of small firms in the economy would give these a stronger hand in negotiating for State support.[7] However, already in 1919 a Central Consultative

Table 5.1.   Italy: employment in manufacturing by size of firm, 1927–51 (%)

Firm size	1927	1937–9	1951
1–9	37.8	36.4	32.1
10–99	21.7	20.7	22.1
1–99	59.5	57.1	54.2
100–499	21.2	20.9	20.4
500+	19.2	22.3	25.4

Source: Colli, 2002, 80.

Committee for small enterprise had been created by the government, as it could not ignore the position held by small firms from an electoral point of view and in terms of their contribution to the export bill.[8] Nevertheless, apart from some general expressions of interest and support, the Fascist regime which came into power in 1922 displayed little more than benign neglect of small firms. In fact, many of the economic measures taken by the regime damaged them. The artificial overvaluation of the lira in 1926 when Italy rejoined the gold standard, for example, harmed small firms' export capabilities. By inducing a strong deflation of internal demand it also hurt those firms that produced consumer goods, such as shoemaking in the Marche and in Vigevano, silk in Como, straw hats in Carpi, wool in Prato, marble in Carrara, and gloves in Napoli.[9] Small firms' ability to make themselves heard by the government was also hurt by the regime's decision to limit the membership of the *Confindustria* (the industrialists' association) to firms employing more than five people.[10]

Much of the literature on Italy's economic performance before 1945 has stressed the failure of the economy to modernize. This failure was represented by the persistence of a dualistic structure made of a majority of small-scale firms, labour intensive and specialized in consumer goods and of a very small number of oligopolistic firms, large-scale, capital intensive, and dependent on protectionism and the government's demand for its output.[11] However, Stefano Fenoaltea's work on the contribution of manufacturing to the economy shows that as late as 1911 the 'modern' sectors (metal working, engineering, chemicals, coal and oil processing, rubber, and photographic materials) accounted for less than a third of manufacturing value added. Despite the growth of these industries during the 1930s, in 1938 they still accounted for only 45 per cent of the value added, much less than in Britain or in Germany.[12] Jon Cohen and Giovanni Federico have suggested that although these figures might seem to confirm the view that Italy failed to modernize, they could in fact indicate an alternative path to development, one based on dynamic consumer industries, whose strength was based on a wise use of the country's natural endowments.[13]

The view that Italy's 'modern' sectors were uncompetitive because they were highly concentrated and dominated by oligopolies has also been revised. Giannetti, Federico, and Toninelli have show that before 1914 manufacturing was marked by low levels of concentration not just in the traditional and light sectors but also in the heavy sectors like chemicals and iron and steel. The sectors with the highest levels of concentration (but still low compared to Britain, France, and Germany) were mining, oil refining, car-making, rubber and synthetic fibres.[14] In the interwar period there was a small reduction in the overall concentration and the only sectors to increase their level of concentration were electrical generation and chemicals. These results show that the economy was more competitive than the 'dualistic' model of Italian industrialization, few large firms in capital intensive sectors and many small firms in the labour intensive ones, would suggest.[15] In fact Italy's model of industrialization emerges as one characterized by small firms whose strategies of product diversification, occupying niche markets, adapting imported technology, and using simple production structures can be seen as propulsive growth factors, rather than negative ones.[16] Furthermore, the case of Fiat with its more than 500 subcontractors working for it in Torino before the Second World War suggests firstly that, as in France and Germany, small and medium-sized firms provided large firms with flexibility.[17] Secondly, to paint Italy's model of industrialization as a divide between small (and by implication backward) firms and large 'modern' ones, is too rigid an interpretation.

The notion that Italy's industrialization was an alternative to the model based on large-scale integrated firms has to be placed in the context of the slowdown in the growth rates of its GDP and GDP per capita, compared with the Giolittian period (and with the period after 1945). Rather than being found in the industrial structure of the country, the reasons for this slowdown were a result of Italy's reliance on the international economy for imports and capital. The slowdown of trade and trade flows in the 1920s and their collapse after the Depression were particularly damaging for a small, open economy like Italy's.[18] The policies enacted by the Fascist regime to attempt to isolate the economy worsened the situation and growth during the Fascist period fell sharply below trend.[19]

SMALL BANKS FOR SMALL FIRMS

More than in any of the other three countries studied in this book the structure of Italian banking resembled closely that of the rest of the economy. There were very few large banks and a multitude of small and medium-sized ones with a mostly local clientele. As in the case of the other three countries, this structure was not the result of accident, but of design.

Banking in Italy goes back as far as the fourteenth century. One of the largest banks at the end of the twentieth century, the *Monte dei Paschi di Siena*, was established in 1472, and many other large banks date back to the sixteenth century. By the beginning of the nineteenth century, however, most of these ancient banks had disappeared but two new types of banks had emerged: the savings banks and the banks of issue. The latter were linked to the various Italian states, such as *Banca Nazionale degli Stati Sardi* in Torino, the *Banca Nazionale Toscana* in Firenze, and the *Banca dello Stato Pontificio* (subsequently *Banca Romana*) in Roma. In 1861, when Italy achieved political unification, there were already more than 130 savings banks[20] and shortly after unification two commercial banks were created, the *Societá di Credito Mobiliare* and the *Banca di Sconto e Sete*. Between the end of the nineteenth century and the beginning of the twentieth, as the country industrialized and foreign capital came in, more commercial banks were set up, such as the *Credito Italiano*, the *Banco di Roma*, the *Banca Commerciale Italiana*, and the *Banca Nazionale del Lavoro*. In 1874 there were more than 120 commercial banks. Apart from the savings banks there were other semi-public institutions, the *banche popolari*. These popular banks were credit cooperatives, developed by Luigi Luzzatti along the lines of the German model devised by Schulze Delitsch. The first popular bank opened in Lodi in 1864 and by 1890 there were 738, mostly in the northern and central regions of the peninsula. In addition in 1875 postal savings banks were set up and in 1883 urban commercial banks, such as *Banco Ambrosiano di Milano* and the *Banca Cattolica Vicentina*, were allowed to establish rural cooperative banks.

Table 5.2 shows the substantial share of assets held by the savings banks before the First World War and the increasing importance of the popular banks, such as the *Banca Popolare di Milano* and the *Banca Popolare di Novara*. The popular banks were fast becoming the main source of funds for local economies made of small and medium-sized commercial and manufacturing activities, while the commercial banks were instead starting to become involved with larger concerns acting more and more like universal banks. These banks' lending to a still very fragile industrial system led to the first bank crisis and to the Bank Law of 1893 which created the central bank, the *Banca d'Italia*, through the merger of the main banks of issue. In many regions the banking crisis of 1893 had the effect of making local banks more active and increasing competition between savings, popular, and regional commercial banks.[21] Moreover, the collapse of some of the largest banks in the country left a gap that was quickly filled by foreign bankers, at first German then Austrian, Swiss, and French. Their intervention led to the creation of two of the most important investment banks of the time, the *Banca Commerciale Italiana*

Table 5.2. Structure of Italian banking, share of total assets, 1874 and 1914

	Banks of issue	Savings banks	Popular banks	Rural banks[a]	Commercial banks	Postal savings banks	Rural mortgage banks
1874	40.9	18.5	5.6		29.5		5.5
1914	26.4	20.1	9.3	2.6	19.3	16	6.3

[a] This included the few surviving pledge banks.

Source: Zamagni, 1990, 183.

(Comit) and the *Credito Italiano*.[22] These, and two other, the *Banco di Roma* and the *Banca Italiana di Sconto* developed along the model of the German universal banks, lending short-, medium-, and long-term loans to private and industrial customers, helping in the placement of shares, keeping a certain amount of these and directly financing the activity of firms through constantly rolled-over overdrafts. The rise of these four banks was spectacular and by 1914 they had a combined share of 14.7 per cent of the total assets of the banking system.[23] These banks became involved with Italy's rising capital goods firms producing railway stock (Breda), iron and steel (Terni, Falk), ships (Odero-Orlando), rubber (Pirelli), and electricity (Edison) and whose strength was based on the state's promotion. The positive role of these banks in propelling forward Italy's industrialization was analysed in 1962 by Alexander Gerschenkron but has since then been revised.[24] These banks' asset structure might have been similar to that of a universal bank, but in fact they concerned themselves more with normal banking activity than with industrial strategy. Prior to the First World War they also avoided permanent ownership of industrial concerns. It was only in the early post-war period that the economic crisis made it impossible for firms to repay their debts and the banks became their main stakeholders.[25]

The development of the Italian banking system along its regional lines was the result of the country's fragmentation before 1860, the strong separation of the countryside and town, and the early advantage smaller commercial, popular, and savings banks had gained in local economies. Most of the local commercial banks had been set up according to principles based around Catholic solidarity and some, such as the *Banca Cattolica Vicentina*, had grown substantially. Before the First World War most of these banks had associated in a national federation to create a central clearing institution, the *Credito Nazionale*. The regional segmentation of the system (and its political origins) proved to be one of the barriers to the development of Italy's national banks in the years before the Bank Law of 1936, and one of the reasons why these banks remained embedded within their local economies and did not grow in the same way as their European counterparts.[26]

During the nineteenth century, of the various types of banks, the savings banks were those most able to expand their deposit base, especially in the provinces. Savings banks in the 1870s held half the deposits of the whole banking system, and by 1935 they still had the largest share of the market.[27] In the early stages of their development savings banks' funds were used mostly to purchase public bonds, often issued by local bodies to finance public works. Over time, however, the savings banks, created by the local middle classes to encourage savings among the working classes, established a bond with the emerging entrepreneurial middle class. The popular banks instead gained an early strong foothold in local economies by supporting first local merchants and, later on in the century, small businesses by discounting bills (although their share of the market for deposits was much smaller).[28] This linking together of local political authorities, businesses, and banks has been defined by Giovanni Ferri as 'municipal capitalism'.[29]

The organization of the savings banks, based on boards made up entirely of local representatives, made these banks the institutional nexus of mediation between the economic and political interests of the various components of the local society. This meant that these banks also became the places where local financial resources were transformed in industrial capital. Because of this, these banks did not act as if profit was their ultimate goal but instead as supporters of local entrepreneurship and local economic development.[30] A good example of this can be found in the activity of the *Cassa di Risparmio di Milano*, Milan's savings bank, and one of Lombardia's biggest banks (in terms of deposits). Between 1870 and 1931 the bank changed the composition of its lending, increasing discounting and advances for working capital parallel to the increase in the industrial activity of small and medium-sized firms within the city.[31] The savings bank, however, had to compete for this type of clientele with the city's popular bank, the *Banca Popolare di Milano*, created by Luzzatti in the early 1870s for the purpose of supporting crafts and small firms and offering more competitive interest rates than the savings bank did.[32]

Before the First World War savings and popular banks held the larger share of the market for loans (mainly as discounted bills) thanks to their advantage in the assessment of risk over the commercial banks. Their connection with the local economy meant that they could select their clients more efficiently than the commercial banks could. As assessment and monitoring costs were higher for those banks not so closely connected to the territory, like the commercial banks, these preferred to invest their funds in industrial shares and government bonds. It was this early tradition of support of local economies that allowed many smaller banks to survive the opening up of the market and the national banks' competition after the First World War, and the crises of the 1920s and 1930s.[33]

The development of the banking system before the First World War can be measured by the increase in the number of branches. Between 1906 and 1913 these increased by approximately 25 per cent, from 2,072 to 2,567. The sector to expand the most was that of the popular banks in the north of the country, the bank that most represented the savings of the provincial middle classes, showing the growing strength of this socio-economic group. After the war the expansion of branches became even faster, and by 1923 the total number of branches in the system had increased to 7,800 (without including at least 2,000 rural cooperative banks). While there had been a decrease in the total number of banks between 1913 and 1923, after this year the number increased again, reaching its peak in 1927 with a total of 1,683 banks.[34] This process of expansion was connected with the growth of regional economies and ran counter to the concentration that was occurring in France, Germany, and Britain. In the meantime the Italian banking system had also become more regulated.

In 1922, after the collapse of the *Banca Italiana di Sconto*, the savings banks were the fastest to grow. Savers' confidence in the stability of the system had been dented by the collapse of the *Banca Italiana di Sconto* and the savings banks looked safer as these, together with the pledge banks, were the only banking institutions whose activity was regulated by the central bank. In 1920 the savings banks' share of deposits had increased to 27 per cent and to 44 per cent in 1936.[35] Between 1922 and 1925, deposits overall increased by 11 per cent annually and loans by 9 per cent, while the profits of the banks also rose very fast.[36] The rapid growth of the economy between 1922 and 1925, based on easy exports due to an under-valued currency and low labour costs,[37] induced many commercial but also savings and popular banks to overextend their lending to the private sector and take in shares as a form of guarantee. The end of the boom came in the spring of 1925 with a sharp fall in the stock market. This was followed by strong deflationary measures imposed by the government in preparation for rejoining the gold standard. The slowdown of the economy weakened all the banks. The chaotic expansion of banks and branches and the absence of effective regulation to protect savers' deposits concerned the central bank and in 1926 legislation was passed that gave it the power to authorize the opening of new branches, the creation of new banks, and mergers.[38] In particular the law sought to strengthen the savings banks by imposing the takeover of the smaller ones by the largest provincial savings bank. The central bank also had the authority to close down pledge and savings banks in the same town, if too many banks meant too much competition.[39] The law of 1926 also freed up completely the lending activities of the savings banks, allowing them to become even more involved in the local economy in which they operated. The legislators thought this to be important to avoid a credit gap, due to the growing instability of local commercial banks.[40] Clearly, the aim of the law and of the *Banca d'Italia* was to intervene in the structuring of the market by promoting limited concentration, while reducing competition, and ensuring a stable provision of funds to regional economies. Furthermore the *Banca d'Italia* was given the power to collect the accounts of all the banks and inspect their activities on a regular basis. The fragmented nature of Italian banking meant that this activity of control could only be pursued effectively by a decentralized structure and the *Banca d'Italia* set up offices in the largest provincial cities.

The central bank aimed to be able to control the expansion of the banks in order to avoid both an excessive fragmentation and dispersion of resources, while preserving the existence of a system where different types of borrowers and savers could be served by the most appropriate type of bank. The existence of a segmented banking system with a strong element of localism was the priority of the central bank together with the defence of savings. Thanks to the powers given by the government to the central bank to close those banks whose activities were thought to endanger their clients' savings, by 1929, 435 banks had been closed. At the same time the expansion of the largest credit institutions had been checked by limiting the number of branches they could open and preventing mergers, to avoid the repetition of the collapse of the *Banca Italiana di Sconto*.[41]

Much of the historiography on Italian banking has attributed its instability to the banks' excessive involvement with industrial finance. This on one hand prevented the emergence of a financial market and on the other exposed the system to the fluctuations of the international economic cycle. More recent work, however, has indicated that the instability of the Italian banking system before 1936 was due to more complex reasons than the relationship between banks and industry, namely the existence of two almost separate banking worlds. The large national banks, which were the main lenders to big business, suffered from limited levels of liquidity as most of the deposits were held in the periphery by local banks and invested locally in smaller concerns. The central bank was not able to act as a conduit and balance this mismatch in liquidity. After the crisis of 1907, the *Banca d'Italia* attempted to establish systems of cooperation between the different types of banks but with little success. At the same time, however, the central bank pursued an active policy of encouragement of the diffusion of the smaller banks as a way of reducing risk. This seems to have been the only option open to the central bank to stabilize an inherently unstable system as cooperation and regulation failed.[42]

The turbulence of the interwar period revealed the structural weakness of the banking system, and in particular that of the large mixed banks. Their liquidity depended on the conditions of the stock market and every fall reduced the banks' margin of safety. The smallness of the market and the presence of many unscrupulous speculators (more often than not connected to the banks themselves) made the system more fragile, with the banks often in a captive position in relation to their industrial customers, leading them to ask for progressively fewer guarantees.[43] As a consequence, the national banks attempted to increase their share of deposits by opening branches in the provinces where competition became ferocious leading to the closure or amalgamation of a number of small, local banks. By 1921 the commercial banks had managed to overtake the popular banks in terms of their share of the deposits market. However, the collapse of one of the largest commercial banks, the *Banca Italiana di Sconto*, in 1921 and the serious crisis of the *Banco di Roma* in 1923 led savers to move their deposits back to the popular and savings banks.[44] In fact, both popular and savings banks benefited from 'first movers' advantages in terms of deposits, having acquired the larger share of the market before the First World War. After 1925 the economic crisis and increasing levels of competition led to a process of concentration. Thanks to the promotion of the mergers between savings banks by the *Banca d'Italia*, their number fell from 416 in 1926 to 246 in 1936. During the same period the number of popular banks was reduced from 660 to 447, while the number of commercial banks went from 416 to 246.[45]

The crisis of 1930, which followed in the wake of the world economic slump, demonstrated the flaws of the country's banking structures. In 1934 the three major banks, the *Banca Commerciale Italiana*, the *Banco di Roma*, and the *Credito Italiano*, which held the shares of most of the failing Italian firms (especially in the state-promoted iron and steel sectors), were taken over by the government, and their shares transferred to the newly created and state owned *Istituto per la Ricostruzione Industriale* (IRI). State control was meant to be a temporary solution, waiting for an upturn in the economic cycle that would allow private investors to come forward. In the following years few buyers appeared to purchase the companies held by IRI and, in 1937, state ownership was made permanent. IRI, by taking over the control of the three banks and of the shares they owned in the bankrupt firms, became the largest state-controlled holding company of the western economies.[46]

The big banks were not the only ones to be hit by the crisis. Since 1925 a number of local commercial banks had gone bankrupt and, despite the intervention of the national federation, closures continued during the following years. These banks were salvaged by the *Banca d'Italia* after 1931 by forcing the takeover of smaller banks to create regional institutions, such as the *Banca Cattolica del Veneto* and the *Banca Provinciale Lombarda*. The funds for these rescues were provided by the Treasury and other national banks, such as the *Banca Nazionale del Lavoro*, generating a complex interlocking of interests and ownerships.[47]

The creation of IRI and the rescue of the banks led in 1936 to the basic banking legislation that was to regulate the system until the mid-1970s. The new law made the collection of savings and the granting of credit functions of 'public interest', therefore justifying and requiring control by the government. This definition of banking allowed the state to take the lead in promoting the accumulation and distribution of capital. Besides exercising supervision, the central supervisory authorities were given the power to control credit both for the development of the national economy and for the creation of savings. Most importantly, a clear line was drawn separating medium-term credit to industry from short-term credit. The intention was to separate short-term finance (for working capital) from medium- and long-term finance and especially from industrial credit.

Nevertheless, the separation of the two functions was never quite absolute, as the provision of medium- to long-term credit to industry was to be performed by sections within the banks and by special institutions controlled by the government and owned by the banks.

The Italian banking institutions were divided into six groups. In 1938 there were six public law banks (*Istituti di Diritto Pubblico*), three banks of national interest (*Banche di Interesse Nazionale*), 170 ordinary commercial banks (*Banche di Credito Ordinario*), 294 popular banks (*Banche Popolari*), 97 savings banks (*Casse di Risparmio*), and 1151 rural and artisan banks (*Casse Rurali e Artigiane*).[48]

The crisis of 1930 and the salvaging of the banks gave the chance to economists, like Alberto Beneduce, to promote through IRI the concept of the state that Francesco Saverio Nitti had advocated in the second decade of the century. Nitti, Giolitti's successor as prime minister, saw the state as a force that could stimulate economic development by direct intervention in specific industrial sectors and through long-term planning. This intervention was to be conducted by autonomous bodies, that would behave like enterprises, such as IRI.[49] The industrial activity of IRI was flanked by the financial activity of the *Istituto per la Mobilizzazione Industriale* (IMI). IMI provided large industrial concerns with medium- and long-term finance by placing bonds representing various industrial sectors on the market. These bonds were purchased by the public through the banks, by the banks themselves, by other institutional investors like the insurance companies, and by foreign investors.

The rigid regulation of the banking system by the Bank Law of 1936 left the market little scope and had its origins in the economic thought behind the creation of the state controlled IRI and IMI. The Bank Law was drawn up by the economists Menichella, Saraceno, De Gregorio, and Beneduce in 1933 at IRI. In that year a report was sent by them to Mussolini, with a plan to redefine the structure of the banking system.[50] The report stated that ten large national banks were too many and that other large regional banks, like the *Istituto San Paolo*, or a savings bank like the *Cassa di Risparmio delle Provincie Lombarde*, were dealing with the same markets. Too many banks were competing in the same areas, offering similar kinds of services. The fierce competition among these banks for deposits and loans meant that losses were incurred which had eventually to be borne by the state. The structure had to be made more rational, and the sphere of activity of each bank, in terms of geographical territory and sector of the economy served, had to be defined and controlled.[51]

Donato Menichella, head of IRI in 1933 and later head of the *Banca d'Italia*, commented that he hoped for a backing off of the large banks, whose role in his opinion should be that of discounters for the smaller, regional banks. In his view this would lead to a strengthening of local credit institutions which were the only ones that could serve local economies adequately.[52] The marked preference of the leaders of IRI and the *Banca d'Italia* for smaller banks led in the banking law of 1936 to the establishment of clear boundaries to the activity of the commercial banks, such as the restriction to short-term lending only, while no such restrictions were placed on the savings banks.[53]

One of the results of the financial crisis of 1931 was the reduction in the overall number of banking institutions. Though the largest number of closures were among the smaller commercial banks, the reduction in the number of banks did not really mean an increase in concentration as the variety in the type of banks and their territorial presence was preserved. The crisis gave the central bank the opportunity to force the banks to trim their branch network and, after 1936, enforce territorial competence by linking it with the size of the banks' capital. The regions most affected by the decline in the number of banks and branches were those in the south, where many medium-sized banks were replaced by two expanding national banks, the *Banco di Napoli* and the *Banca Nazionale del Lavoro*, while in the north local banks filled the space left by the closure of larger banks.[54]

CONCLUSION

In Italy after unification, as in France and in Germany at the same time, those who debated the desirability of an industrial system which included small firms argued about issues that went beyond those of industrial efficiency. Small firms were seen as essential preservers of social stability, both in the countryside, where they provided an alternative source of income,[55] and in cities, where they reduced the destabilizing impact of unionization and workers' unrest.[56] Small firms, often rural and domestic in nature, were seen as the element that would allow the country to industrialize without generating excessive social tensions.[57] Small-scale production was also recognized as more suited to a country poorly endowed with natural resources and with badly connected markets.

The industrial ideology that developed during this period was heavily marked by catholic paternalistic solidarity, which led many entrepreneurs, in Veneto, Lombardia, and Toscana to develop a decentralized system of production that kept production units small and reduced the opportunity for labour conflict. Instead, the development of large businesses was connected with a strong technocratic tradition whose proponents were men such as Leopoldo Pirelli, who was trained at Milan's Technical University. In Piemonte and Lombardia this technocratic tradition led entrepreneurs to associate very early and in 1906 Gino Olivetti created the first industrial association, whose membership quickly spread to the rest of the industrial triangle and in 1912 had 1,893 member firms. The third ideological element that characterized Italy's early industrialization was the nationalistic-military one, whose origins were to be found among the Genoese firms involved in shipbuilding and mechanical production. This ideology spread rapidly to other industrial regions, linked as it was to the aim of making the country economically independent and militarily powerful.[58]

In the early years after unification, the tension between the anti-industrialist camp, who wanted to preserve Italy's agricultural character (seen as a competitive advantage), and those who wanted to make it a 'modern' economy meant that the state had to cast itself in the role of economic mediator. The resolution of the conflict meant more than just finding a way of reconciling two different social groups (the landed aristocracy on one side and the urban, industrial middle class on the other) as it implied the state's direct intervention in the economy. The first example of this was the establishment of a tariff on manufactured goods in 1878.

The events that led to the creation of Terni in 1884 and that gave the country its first large-scale iron and steel company show the commitment to industrial scale of the newborn Italian state. Terni was created to allow the production of steel for warships. Amatori and Colli describe the events that linked Vincenzo Breda, owner of a large enterprise and an expert on state contracts, and Benedetto Brin, minister for the navy, who strongly believed that Italy needed a navy of large destroyers instead of a fleet of fast and small fighting units. The events that led to the creation of Terni, its subsequent history of costly mistakes,[59] and the personalities involved, including bankers, shows the power of the ideology that connected industrial size, military strength, and a country's international position.[60] However, the dangers inherent in the link between state, army, and heavy industry were identified in the 1880s by illustrious economists such as Wilfrid Pareto. At the same time industrialists, academics, and journalists were highlighting the merits of a system based on small and medium-sized firms as this held together industry and agriculture, a system that was developing a seamless transition into industrialization, without social and environmental fractures.[61]

The persistence of small firms can also be explained by examining the reaction of some of Italy's most prominent businessmen to American labour organization theories. In Italy after the First World War, as in the other three countries studied here, the USA defined the road to industrial development. Taylor's writings and the American system of manufacture showed Italian entrepreneurs how production could be organized and costs controlled. More than that, mass production seemed to promise widespread prosperity and consumption and this gave it an appeal to a wider public, not just to businessmen and technicians. Nevertheless, just as it was happening in other countries, the Italian way to industrial development was the result of a hybrid of the original American model. One of the most authoritative observers of Italy's economic history, Duccio Bigazzi, attributed this not to a conservative resistance but to a process of selective adaptation. At least until the post-war 'economic miracle', Taylorism and Fordism were not copied blindly, even within the most 'modern' of the country's firms. One reason was the limits imposed by the smallness of the consumer market, but there was also a resistance on the part of the workforce and middle management to the impersonality of the Taylorist shopfloor.[62] Nor were all the entrepreneurs who visited the USA, such as Pirelli, Rossi, and Olivetti, convinced that large scale was the best way to organize society and business. This belief, together with a realistic view of the limits of vertical integration given the structure of the market, meant that even the larger firms relied on networks of small firms to provide them with components (and absorb workforce during times of contraction).[63]

In the context of this book, Italy's case presents the most extreme example of state intervention in shaping the banking system. It would be easy to dismiss the rigid segmentation of the market, to match the size and type of bank to the size and type of customer, as a piece of Fascist corporativism. However, the bank laws of 1926 and 1936 were, *inter alia*, explicitly aimed at protecting local economies. These laws allowed the nationalistic-military state, with its commitment to large-scale capital goods industries, to coexist with the catholic-paternalistic state, with its preference for small firms. The structuring of the banking system was the outcome of the dialectical process between different groups that had taken place since the early days of Unification.

NOTES

1 In comparative terms, in 1860 there were about 500,000 cotton spindles in the whole of the country, against the 30 million in Britain and 2 million in Germany. Zamagni, *Dalla periferia al centro*, 41.
2 Ibid., 111–12.
3 In 1936, 52 per cent of the population were still employed in agriculture and only 25.6 per cent in manufacturing. Zamagni, *Dalla periferia al centro*, 49.
4 Amatori and Colli, *Impresa e industria in Italia*, 113.
5 More details on Italy's largest firms can be found in Zamagni, *Dalla periferia al centro*, 491–545; Amatori and Colli, *Impresa e industria in Italia*, 59–79 and 145–69 provide extensive details and a bibliography on the histories of Italy's large firms.
6 Colli, *I volti di proteo*, 50 and 211.
7 The first census had taken place in 1911 and had excluded units employing less than five people.
8 Colli, *I volti di proteo*, 51.

9   Amatori e Colli, *Impresa e industria in Italia*, 179.
10 Colli, *I volti di proteo*, 53.
11 See for example, Castronovo, *L'industria Italiana dall'ottocento a oggi*; Amatori, 'Italy'.
12 Fenoaltea, *Il valore aggiunto dell'industria*.
13 Cohen and Federico, *The Growth of the Italian Economy*, 48.
14 Giannetti, Federico, and Toninelli, 'Size and Strategy of Italian Enterprises', 495–8.
15 For a full explanation and presentation of the historiography on the dualistic nature of Italian industrialization see Federico, *The Economic Development of Italy since 1870*.
16 Battilossi, 'Mercati e concentrazione', 290.
17 Castronovo, *Fiat*, 598–9.
18 Cohen, Federico, *The Growth of the Italian Economy*, 24.
19 Rossi and Toniolo, 'Catching Up or Falling Behind?'.
20 Of these 15 were in Lombardia, 22 in Piemonte, 9 in Veneto, 5 in Emilia Romagna, 27 in Toscana, 51 between Lazio, Marche, and Basilicata and only one in the southern regions. Zamagni, *Dalla periferia al centro*, 179.
21 Conti and La Francesca, *Banche e reti di banche*, 387.
22 For more details on these 'German' banks see Hertner, *Il capitale tedesco in Italia*.
23 Zamagni, *Dalla periferia al centro*, 193.
24 Gerschenkron, 'Notes on the Rate of Industrial Growth in Italy 1881–1913'.
25 Cohen and Federico, *The Growth of the Italian Economy, 1820–1960*, 60.
26 On the other hand it is unlikely that, given the limited amount of savings held by the population, Italian banks could have grown to the size of their European counterparts.
27 Conti, 'Processi di integrazione e reti locali', 339.
28 Ibid., 399–401.
29 Cesarini, Ferri, and Giardino, *Credito e sviluppo*, 17–55.
30 Barcellona, *Casse di Risparmio*, 12.
31 The growth of manufacturing within Milan, from workshops to larger concerns is well described in Colli, *I volti di proteo*, 142–9; the history of the Cassa di Risparmio di Milano is told by Bachi, *La Cassa di Risparmio delle provincie Lombarde* and by Cova and Galli, *Finanza e sviluppo locale*.
32 Piluso, 'Il mercato del credito a milano dopo l'unita', 543.
33 Conti, 'Processi di integrazione e reti locali', 388, 431–2.
34 Polsi, 'L'articolazione territoriale del sistema bancario Italiano', 223–4.
35 Cohen and Federico, *The Growth of the Italian Economy*, 58.
36 Toniolo, in 'Il profilo economico', 40, does not give more details on the banks' profits, apart from revising downwards his earlier estimates in Ciocca and Toniolo, 'Industry and Finance in Italy, 1918–1940', 121.
37 Rossi and Toniolo, 'Catching Up or Falling Behind?'.
38 For a detailed analysis of the events that led to the banking law of 1926 see Guarino and Toniolo, *La Banca d'Italia*, 46–56.
39 Lamandin, *Le concentrazioni bancarie*, 30.
40 Conti, Ferri, and Polsi, 'Banche cooperative e fascismo', 13.

41 Polsi, 'L'articolazione territoriale del sistema bancario', 227–45.
42 Conti, 'Le banche e il finanziamento industriale', 447–54. The existence of a fragmented banking system is also shown by the fact that between 1878 and 1907 there was no convergence in terms of the interests rates charged in different regions.
43 Ibid., 468, 475.
44 Polsi, 'L'articolazione territoriale del sistema bancario', 226.
45 Conti, Ferri, and Polsi, 'Banche cooperative e fascismo', 16.
46 Ciocca and Toniolo, 'Industry and Finance in Italy 1918–1940'.
47 The events surrounding the crisis and subsequent rescue of the catholic local banks has been analysed by Toniolo, 'Il profilo economico', 58–66.
48 Banca d'Italia, *Bollettino statistico*, 1938. The figure for rural and artisan banks also includes foreign banks.
49 Bonelli, 'Alberto Beneduce, il credito industriale e l'origine dell'IRI', 72.
50 Cassese, *Come e' nata la legge bancaria*.
51 The text of the report is contained in Menichella, *Scritti e discorsi. 1933–1966*.
52 Cotula, Gelsomino, and Gigliobianco, *Donato menichella*, 103.
53 Conti, 'Le banche e il finanziamento industriale', 487.
54 Polsi, 'L'articolazione territoriale del sistema bancario', 258 and the table on 260.
55 For a good example of this see Cento Bull, *From Peasant to Entrepreneur*.
56 Urbanization and the development of the factory with its connected social problems are discussed in Della Peruta, *Milano: lavoro e fabbrica 1815–1914*.
57 The views of Italy's industrial bourgeoisie, including those of Alessandro Rossi, are analysed in Baglioni, *L'ideologia della borghesia industriale nell'Italia liberale*.
58 Zamagni, *dalla periferia al centro*, 141–5.
59 A detailed history of Terni can be found in Bonelli, *Lo sviluppo di una grande impresa in Italia*.
60 Amatori and Colli, *impresa e industria in italia*, 45–6, 49.
61 On the anti-industrialist option at the end of the nineteenth century see Segreto, 'Storia d'Italia e storia dell'industria', 7–12.
62 Bigazzi, 'Modelli e pratiche organizzative', 899.
63 Ibid., 913–15.

PART II

SMALL FIRMS AND BANKS AFTER 1945

6

The Demise of Small Firms in Britain

As a consequence of the Depression and the war, between 1930 and 1950 industrial concentration in Britain did not increase in terms of the share of the market controlled by the top 100 firms. Output, though, did become concentrated in fewer firms as they reaped the benefits of the building of larger plants after the merger wave of the 1920s. Concentration increased again in the 1950s and 1960s, both in terms of the share of the market of the top 100 manufacturing firms and of their share of net output, which increased from 26 per cent in 1953 to 40 per cent in 1970. At the same time the number of firms employing 200 people or less declined from 136,000 in 1935 to 60,000 in 1963, while their share of output fell from 35 to 16 per cent.[1] Table 6.1 shows the persistent decline in the share of employment provided by small and very small firms, starting from the 1930s. As in the 1920s, mergers were the main cause of this increase in concentration and of the reduction in the number of small and medium-sized firms.[2]

During the 1950s and 1960s, as industrial concentration increased, the British economy experienced its fastest rates of growth. However, these were lower than those of its competitors. These higher productivity levels in continental European economies have been attributed to a number of factors, but in particular to the spread of American technology and

Table 6.1. Britain: employment and employment share, by size of firm 1930–73

	All establishments ('000)	Establishments employing less than 200 people (%)	Establishments employing less than 50 people (%)
1930	5,179	43	19
1935	5,409	44	19
1948	6,871	37	16
1951	7,382	35	—
1954	7,537	33	14
1958	7,781	32	14
1964	7,960	31	12
1968	7,870	29	12
1970	8,033	—	—
1973	7,616	27	11

Source: Hughes, 1993, 28

systems of work organization, while Britain's falling behind has been seen as a result of a 'failure' to adopt these methods.[3] The following chapters qualify the extent of the 'Americanization' of Germany, France, and Italy, whereas what is suggested here is an alternative view of looking at the issue of whether British industry underwent 'Americanization'.

THE BRITISH ECONOMY AND 'AMERICANIZATION'

The resistance of British businessmen to the adoption of cost-saving devices, such as standardization, materials handling, and quality control, is a theme that pervades historical accounts of the post-war period. In recent studies of post-war Britain the resistance to industrial Americanization has been taken as a sign of backwardness, one of the elements which contributed to the decline of British manufacturing.[4] Jim Tomlinson and Nick Tiratsoo have attributed the failure of British industry to adapt to a 'highly specific set of historical circumstances which predisposed management to both a limited willingness and limited capacity to follow the American example'.[5] Jonathan Zeitlin instead attributes this resistance to an attachment to more 'flexible' ways of production, more suited to the British market.[6] Interpreted in this way, resistance becomes a much more positive force, an attachment to an alternative way of production and an adaptation of methods that could work within this alternative model.

In fact, rather than resist, many engineering firms, for example, adopted and adapted American methods of production, but this adaptation was the result of positive and negative tensions. On the one hand British manufacturers realized that design diversification, for example, could be a competitive advantage. They saw that Britain's markets (at home and abroad) were smaller and more diversified than American ones and that excessive standardization would cause production rigidities.[7] On the other hand, even if they had embraced Americanization British firms faced a number of obstacles imposed first by the Labour and later by Conservative governments in order to achieve macroeconomic objectives. Shortages of fuel, power, labour, raw materials (such as steel), and later of capital made expansion and investment plans difficult. In fact Tomlinson and Tiratsoo suggest that the Conservative government of 1951–64 did not wholeheartedly embrace Americanzation,[8] as this implied support for decartelization and deconcentration policies.[9] Moreover, despite traditional tensions between government and state institutions, they were both in line when it came to industrial policy. In particular the Bank of England and the Treasury's uninterest in industrial policy sorely restricted the Conservative's and later Labour's ability to intervene in the economy.[10] The Bank and the Treasury were more concerned with Britain's international position and the strength of sterling than with industry. Their control over monetary matters and public expenditure meant the existence of a very powerful force *within* the state whose interests clashed with those who wanted to promote industrial policy.[11] Given the lack of government support it is hardly surprising, therefore, that manufacturers took those elements of Americanization that could be adapted to existing conditions rather than opt for a massive rehaul of plant and equipment.

The case of the engineering industry shows that 'Americanization' was not necessarily a prerequisite for competitiveness. British engineering firms abandoned their indigenous methods of productive organization only between the mid-1950s to the mid-1970s, under pressure from the government, and, as a result of mergers and takeovers, imported more clearly 'American' methods of production, such as multidivisionalization. As Zeitling has pointed out, this strategy did not make the sector more competitive and it lost market share at home and abroad. By the 1980s the competitive difficulties experienced by British engineering firms were being attributed by contemporaries to their inability to match the standards of product innovation and flexibility set by the Germans and the Japanese in meeting the demands of increasing diverse and volatile international markets.[12]

According to much of the literature on this subject, Britain's loss of competitiveness in the post-war period was the result of a failure to adopt more 'modern', 'American' methods of production. At the same time, however, Britain had the industrial structure that most resembled that of the USA, in terms of concentration of output and size distribution. Rather than a failure of adaptation, Britain's competitiveness suffered because of the limited scope for the development of flexible methods of production, as a consequence of the decline of small firms. Moreover, this decline affected the innovative capability of the economy. As Edith Penrose has argued so convincingly, a growing economy possesses 'interstices' left open by the expansion of larger firms, as their growth opens up new opportunities for investment. It is the struggle between small firms to occupy these spaces that tends to induce innovation in the process of production and in the variety of products.[13]

At the end of the 1960s the Parliamentary Committee of Inquiry on Small Firms (the Bolton Committee) ascertained that the British economy suffered from a long-term decline in the number of small firms. The committee's report revealed that while this decline was being experienced by all the developed countries the process had gone further in Britain than elsewhere. The implications of these findings in terms of Britain's industrial competitiveness were spelled out in a study of small firms and technological innovation commissioned by the Committee and carried out by the University of Sussex. The study found that small firms accounted for approximately 10 per cent of the important innovations selected for the investigation over the period 1945–70. Their share of innovation was half of their share of employment and output but more than twice their share of research and development expenditure, suggesting that the innovative *efficiency* of small firms was greater than that of large firms.[14] While in no way suggesting that all small firms were sources of technological change, the committee argued that, because of the impossibility of selecting 'winners', the decline in the total number of small firms had important implications for the stock of potential innovations and therefore on economic performance. The innovative potential of small firms justifies establishing whether the environment in which they found themselves in the post-war years allowed them to develop this potential.[15]

THE POLITICS OF INDUSTRIAL CONCENTRATION

In the 1950s and 1960s the decline of small firms was the result not just of an economic trend but of barriers to growth. The political context in which we must place this decline was one dominated by the rhetoric of economic concentration. The longest standing adverse comparison of British and American industry was the scale of its units of production. The whole 'rationalization' movement of the interwar period was spawned from the argument that Britain suffered from too many small units and that the model to follow was that of mass production of standardized goods. This argument persisted in the post-war period, following the observation that since 1930 there had been a slowdown in industrial concentration. As a consequence, in 1946 a Parliamentary working party investigation was set up into the production practices of consumer goods industries. This found that size was not unanimously thought to be important. One of the members of the working party, the economist John Jewkes, pointed out that mass production would generate inflexibility and that standardization and bulk selling would not benefit industries that instead relied on quality products, fashioned to suit the demands of consumers.[16] Nevertheless, the majority view remained that British firms were not large enough in scale. For this reason Sir Stafford Cripps agreed to the establishment in August 1948 of the Anglo-American Productivity Council, under the auspices of the Marshall Plan, so that trade unionists and businessmen could go to America and study their methods. On their return these teams all stressed the need for British industry to emulate American methods of production to increase productivity.[17]

The events that followed, however, had as much to do with politics as they did with the economy. Despite the slowdown in concentration, in 1951 the Conservatives inherited a still very cartelized economy and some very limited pro-competition legislation in the shape of the 1948 Monopolies Act.[18] As most Conservative ministers were not in favour of a pro-competitive environment the Monopolies Commission was never given independent power. The Conservative government's attitude towards monopolies is shown by the establishment of the Restrictive Trade Practices Act in May 1956. The Act was supposed to introduce the effective abolition of the British cartel system by declaring collective practices unlawful. In fact, what it did was favour the development of large, transnational firms. The Act made the registration of all agreements between two or more persons on prices and discounts, quotas, or methods of manufacturing obligatory. What the Act omitted were the activities of large firms in monopolistic positions. Certain types of agreements, such as 'sole agency' agreements used by large transnational firms were also left out of the legislation. Helen Mercers reports how, for example, two American firms operated 'sole agency' agreements in agricultural machinery which aimed

to cut off the smaller British manufacturers from the best dealer outlets, and they [could] do this because they manufactured a complete range of products whereas the smaller British firms concentrate on one or two machines and could only offer a complete range if several of them worked together.[19]

The Act came at the same time as the role of the Monopolies Commission was downgraded, although Chancellor Peter Thorneycoft wanted its complete abolition, to take the issue of monopolies completely out of the public domain. The Monopolies Commission was retained (albeit with reduced powers) only because its elimination would have meant opening the government to the criticism that it was concentrating its efforts on the restrictive practices of small and medium-sized firms while leaving monopolies alone. In any case Thorneycroft was convinced that the Monopolies Commission should be run by top-ranking industrialists.

The Act banned the collective enforcement of RPM (resale price maintenance) while at the same time strengthening the power of the individual manufacturer to enforce his resale price by allowing him to take legal action against a price cutter. This was another example of the support given to large manufacturers. The Act also gave firms the incentive to substitute their cartel agreements with concentration, expanding in scale. It also threatened the activities of trade associations because of their price-fixing activities. The trade associations, however, provided also some very important services to their members, mostly small and medium-sized firms, such as arranging exhibitions, joint advertising, and sharing technical knowledge. Over time, and especially during the war, trade associations had developed a continuous relationship with government departments and had become accepted by the government as part of its system of intermediaries. The curtailment of their activities further damaged small firms, despite rhetoric which claimed the Conservatives to be the party of small enterprise.[20] In fact for many Conservatives the future of industry was in the hands of large concerns and the Monopolies Commission's purpose was purely to assuage the public's fears that concentration would not harm their interests.[21]

Unlike their laissez-faire attitude towards concentration during the interwar years, after the Second World War the attitude of governments in Britain was to become more directly active in the promotion of mergers. This applied even more so to Labour between 1964 and 1970, as the feeling within the Party was that larger units would be, in the long run, better for employment. To promote these in 1966 the Labour government created the Industrial Reorganisation Corporation (IRC) to assist mergers. The IRC was set up because, in the words of its first report', there was a need for more concentration and rationalisation to promote the greater efficiency and international competitiveness of British industry. The changes which had so far taken place in this direction ... did not yet match the economy's requirements.'[22] The eleven-man board of the IRC was staffed mainly by representatives of Britain's top corporations and had the authority to draw up to £150 million of public funds[23]. The IRC's unusual status, created by the state but run by businessmen, gave it an aura of independence and allayed businesses, fear of government intervention and interference. The IRC, however, did not publish any detailed explanation for its beliefs in the virtues of size nor any calculations of the prospective benefits deriving from the gigantic mergers it organized. The merger of English Electric and General Electric, for example, was backed by the belief that 'it must be in the national interest to create the strongest possible companies, in terms of managerial, financial, technical and other resources, to compete in international markets'.[24] It is not surprising that the representatives of big business thought that creating giant corporations was the best way of developing the economy and that this was akin to an act of faith. After all these were men who said: 'We don't feel the need for economists ... and we don't believe in volumes of analysis. It is not a question of analysing the problem ... what is needed is action.'[25] The Labour government was also behind the establishment of the Shipbuilding Industry Board which tried to enlarge shipbuilding firms by promoting mergers among them. In 1967 the British Steel Corporation was created to bring together the fourteen largest steel makers under public ownership, and create large integrated steelworks. During the 1970s, nationalization was extended to shipbuilding and aerospace, resulting in further concentration. Although businessmen tended to oppose nationalization, many welcomed government promotion of mergers as these came with financial packages to help their ailing firms. The enhancement of profits also made mergers desirable as they meant the restriction of competition and, in some cases, the achievement of economies of scale.[26]

Some of the mergers of the 1960s and early 1970s resulted in successes, as in the case of General Electric Co. and Glaxo, but others did not stand the test of time, as in the case of British Leyland and Courtaulds. In fact, it has been suggested that much of the 1960s merger activity had not improved efficiency, but had only reduced competitive pressures on managers and increased their salaries.[27] The poor financial performance of many of the 1960s mergers and the slowdown of the stock market after the oil shock of 1973 halted the growth of mergers and demergers started to take place.[28]

Ultimately, Labour's attitude towards small firms was a fundamentally hostile one, a reaction to the observation that many of them subjected their workers to poor pay and working conditions. The difficulty of unionizing workers in small units also made small firms distasteful to the party. This attitude was at odds with Labour's stance on industrial democracy, as smallness could be seen as an important element in creating effective democratic structures.[29]

MONETARY POLICY AND ITS IMPACT ON SMALL FIRMS

The hostility, or at best indifference, of governments to small firms during these years resulted in their inability to perceive the damage that their economic policies inflicted on them. The 1950s and 1960s were years of unprecedented prosperity as unemployment virtually disappeared and earnings rose faster than prices. Much less perceivable at the time, however, were the recurring balance of payments crises and the spectre of inflation, both of which threatened the stability of the pound and consequently Britain's international position. After the war, successive governments strove to achieve the goal of 'maintaining a high and stable level of employment' that had to be achieved together with price stability, and budgetary stimuli were used in the belief that these would control aggregate demand.[30] As a consequence the economy of these years was characterized by cycles of expansion followed by deflation in which policies dictated by the government were used to counteract balance of payments crises or changes in the level of unemployment.

Between 1951 and 1962, monetary policy was one of the main tools used by successive Conservative chancellors to manage consumer demand, in the attempt to maintain full employment while controlling the balance of payments and defending the value of the pound in the 'run-up' to the achievement of full convertibility. Government policy to manage the growth of aggregate demand included raising the bank rate, the imposition of controls on hire purchase and on the Capital Issues Committee, and exercising pressure on the banks to restrain their lending.[31]

All firms, regardless of size, saw their activities curtailed by monetary policy, but small firms bore the brunt of the credit restrictions as, unlike large companies, they had no other source of finance beyond their banks.

In 1956 a survey conducted by the Oxford Institute of Statistics tried to determine how important bank lending was to small firms in the manufacturing sector.[32] The most important source of funds for the small firms in the survey was savings derived from past profits. Clearly the availability of this source of finance depended partly on the profitability of the firm, partly on the amount of tax, and partly on the firm's policy with regard to the distribution of profits.[33] The analysis of the finance of expenditure showed that the small firms in the sample were likely to retain profits in order to finance expenditure on operating assets. While this finding helps support the idea that small firms in the first half of the 1950s relied a great deal on internally generated sources of funds for the provision of their long-term capital, it is necessary to consider whether self-financing might have been, in fact, evidence of financial constraint. Small firms could have been forced to rely heavily on their savings because of a scarcity of external finance, therefore trimming their investments to suit these savings. On the strength of this consideration the survey concluded that the growth of small firms was probably inhibited by the lack of sources of long-term external funds. This conclusion was reinforced by the discovery that the most rapidly expanding firms in the survey were those that relied less on internally generated funds and more on external sources, while the slow growing firms were self-financed.[34]

The survey also established that the main source of external finance available to small firms was bank overdrafts. While bank credit was understood to be short-term in nature, its availability allowed firms to free savings for long-term investments. While in the 1950s only 35 per cent of public companies had overdrafts, 47 per cent of the small firms in the survey had overdrafts and on average these overdrafts represented almost 20 per cent of net assets, twice the average for quoted companies.[35] Small firms also tended to have overdrafts for longer periods than quoted companies. Most interestingly the survey revealed how the younger firms in the sample (those founded after 1940) made extensive use of bank loans, compared with firms funded before the Second World War, showing how small, young, and rapidly growing firms were more dependent on borrowing from the banks.[36] For small and medium-sized firms the adoption of new machinery was conditional on their ability to raise money from their banks since overdraft facilities, though nominally not used for capital purposes, could release resources for the purchase of machinery or the expansion of premises.[37] Since innovation in small firms takes the shape of a cumulative process and is determined crucially by the firm's liquidity at the moment of the decision to change either process or product, liquidity will determine the extension and the articulation of the first steps towards change. Moreover, any uncertainty regarding the future availability of funds will condition the firm's willingness to risk change.[38] Hence the crucial role that banks play in the 'life cycle' of small firms. In its infancy, a small firm's growth potential (and hence its potential for innovation) could therefore be seriously damaged by any curtailment in bank lending.

Under the Labour government of 1945–51 bank lending increased relatively rapidly. By mid-1951 advances to all categories of customers had doubled since the end of the war. Simultaneously the rise of advances was further affected by inflation and by the build-up of stocks caused by the outbreak of the Korean War. In April of that year Hugh Gaitskell, then chancellor, felt compelled to ask the banks 'to maintain a restraint in their credit policy',[39] thus showing his fundamental misunderstanding of the direction of causality in a pegged rate system and of the policy framework in which he was operating. The Chancellor left it to the banks to decide the day-by-day selection and discrimination of lending but he let it be known that the banks were to favour projects concerning exports, agricultural development, transport, and the production of raw materials, and not to approve lending for speculation or overcapitalization. In November 1951 the banks, after numerous meetings with the Governor of the Bank of England, agreed to be firmer about advances to 'less essential industries' but in return requested an increase in the bank rate.[40] By the end of 1952 bank lending had fallen by 14 per cent in real terms.[41] Although the officials at the Bank of England considered monetary policy to be working and regarded the fall in advances as 'encouraging', in the main the boards of the London clearing banks were sceptical of Treasury policies.[42] For instance, the Midland bank knew that the brunt of the restrictions was being felt by the smaller and more vulnerable borrowers, namely those in the 'Personal and Professional' category.

This restrictive phase was followed by a more expansionary orientation of policy within the 1953 budget, easing the pressure on banks, and reducing bank rate. By 1955 the economy was booming, requiring an increasing amount of imports and pushing the balance of payments back into deficit, while prices and wages kept rising. In July, the Treasury had to ask the banks to achieve a 'positive and significant reduction' in lending, but how the banks were to achieve this was left up to them.[43] The Committee of London Clearing Banks decided to reduce advances by limiting the number of new applications accepted, decreasing existing limits and restricting the availability of finance to hire purchase companies and to customers in the 'Personal and Professional' category (their smaller customers). The aim was to reduce advances by a total of 10 per cent by December and memoranda were sent to branch managers with detailed instructions on how to deter customers.[44] By August advances had declined in the 'Food', 'Retail', 'Other Financial', 'Personal and Professional', 'Other textiles', and 'Nationalized Industries' categories[45] as customers kept away from the banks fearing that 'it [was] no use asking'.[46]

Despite a further rise in the bank rate in February 1956 to 5.5 per cent, the Treasury repeated its requests to the banks to maintain their restrictions on advances. The bank rate was lowered a year later to 5 per cent, only to be increased to a 'crisis rate' of 7 per cent in September, following the foreign exchange crisis.[47] Calls for reduction in advances continued over these years, with the Chancellor (Harold Macmillan first and Peter Thorneycroft after him) taking the unprecedented step of regularly summoning the representatives of the commercial banks instead of dealing with them through the Bank of England, to remind them of the seriousness of the government's policy.[48] Between 1955 and 1958 advances fell by a further 13 per cent in real terms until a rise in unemployment prompted the government to relax all controls in September 1958 and let the economy expand again.

As bank lending was not classified on the basis of the size of the borrower's business it is not possible to determine exactly the fluctuations in lending to small firms. It is possible, however, to proxy this by using the figures for advances to the 'Personal and Professional' category of borrower as this group included advances to cover 'the provision of working capital for professional purposes, such as the purchase of machinery for a small manufacturer'.[49] In real terms between 1951 and 1958, advances to this group of borrowers fell by 40 per cent while advances as a whole fell by 18 per cent.[50] Reducing advances to smaller customers was much easier than denying credit to larger, corporate businesses, as the chairman of Lloyds, Sir Oliver Franks, candidly admitted.[51] The banks had to bear in mind that the Treasury gave preference to sectors involved in exports and at the time as much as the forty largest companies produced 30 per cent of exports, while small firms only contributed directly to a quarter.

The continuation of the credit squeeze led to recurring questions regarding the impact of this measure on small firms. The representatives of the banks, in their meetings with the Governor of the Bank of England, reported the occurrence of a number of failures amongst the smaller concerns, though this did not trouble them unduly, as the level of bad debt was still very low.[52] Memoranda were circulated internally to the Bank, showing the increasing figures for bankruptcies, and by the end of 1956 the Bank was well aware that the credit squeeze was having an adverse effect on small firms.[53] Nevertheless, there is no mention in the Bank of England's files of possible measures that could be taken to avoid the credit restrictions from forcing small firms into liquidation.[54]

The absence of concern about the impact of this policy on the real economy is well documented by the following episode. In July 1955 the MP for Wednesbury (a Black Country constituency) lamented the effect the credit restrictions were having on small firms in his constituency. He defined the Black Country as the 'stronghold of family business'; within ten miles of Wednesbury Town Hall there were no fewer than 10,000 small manufacturing concerns each employing fewer than fifty people. Most of these firms worked as subcontractors to the car industry and the MP feared that since these firms were not *directly* involved in exports they would suffer badly from the restrictions.[55] In his view, a reduction in credit would affect the small manufacturers very seriously since 'the people running these small family concerns have always been taught to look to the banks for money with which to modernise and expand their business. They know nothing of the money market.' Addressing Parliament, the MP asked the government to impose on the banks some sort of regulation which would prevent them from reducing advances at the expense of smaller customers. He was answered by the Economic Secretary to the Treasury, Sir Edward Boyle, in terms that left little doubt that the fate of small firms was not one of the major concerns of the Treasury in formulating policies to curtail demand and maintain low inflation. One of the Treasury's aims was 'to encourage firms to postpone their marginal investment plans and, whenever possible, to postpone replacing their fixed assets'. Credit restrictions were to accomplish this and, in the words of Sir Edward, the Government '[were] right to attempt to reduce internal pressure by asking the banks themselves to take what steps they regard[ed] as necessary to reduce the volume of credit'. The smaller businesses were not to be protected from the 'full rigours' of the government's policy.[56]

The Oxford Survey of 1956 aimed also at establishing the impact of the credit restrictions on a sample of small and medium-sized manufacturing firms, none of which were quoted on the stock exchange. Between 1950 and 1956, of the firms in the sample, 35 per cent had had to order less capital equipment than originally planned and/or reduce stocks of materials and parts. The two main reasons given for this reduction were the difficulty of rising finance (43 per cent) and the fear that the credit restrictions would reduce demand and therefore sales (46 per cent). For most (72 per cent) of those firms who had had to reduce investment plans and/or stock because of the difficulty of rising finance, the main problem was not the higher cost due to increased interest rates but the availability of finance. In other words, of the 876 firms who replied to questions concerning the impact of the credit restrictions, more than 10 per cent had had to reduce their expansion because of the difficulty of raising money. Interestingly, the survey shows how, within the sample, the smaller firms (employing fewer than seventy-five people) were more affected by financial difficulties induced by the credit restrictions, while the bigger firms were more concerned with the possible drop in sales. This demonstrated the biased nature of the restrictions, a bias that has not been highlighted in the literature on this subject.[57] By focusing on bank lending, the credit restrictions inevitably affected small firms more than large ones as these had recourse to other sources of finance, such as the capital market.

In 1959, in their evidence to the Committee on the Working of the Monetary System (the Radcliffe Committee) the representatives of the Association of British Chambers of Commerce (ABCC) stated that from the onset the effect of the credit restrictions had been more serious for 'small firms and particularly [for] progressive and expanding companies'. Growth-oriented small firms had been particularly affected because 'restriction of bank advances [had] an appreciable effect on plans for capital extension or replacements. Doubts as to the availability of bank credit [led] to the abandonment of schemes for capital expansion.' Small firms were singled out by government policy as their borrowing was confined to bank loans and though these were not normally used for medium to long-term projects the ABCC confirmed that this had become the norm by the second part of the 1950s.[58]

To back up the reports collected from its membership, the ABCC carried out a survey to ascertain the extent of the impact of the credit restrictions on their membership since 1957. In March 1958 questionnaires were sent out to individual member companies through seventy-two affiliated chambers of commerce, and by mid-April 3,404 answers had been returned.[59] The findings of the survey allowed the ABCC to support

Table 6.2. Survey by the Association of British Chambers of Commerce, March 1958. To the general question: 'Have you since September 1957 experienced . . . ?' (percentage of replies saying 'yes')

Size of firms (by employment)	Under 100	100–250	250–1,000	Over 1,000
Turnover reduced	58	51	50	39
Stocks or work in progress reduced	43	37	31	21
Fixed investment projects reduced	24	25	25	23
Fixed investment projects postponed	31	35	34	30
Asked to reduce overdraft[a]	16	13	8	8
Had overdraft reduced[a]	14	11	8	7
Taken steps to reduce overdraft[a]	31	30	29	28
Other short-term finance obtained	7	8	6	3
Machinery purchased on instalment terms	6	9	4	5
Credit squeeze affected ability to carry out export business	10	8	6	3
Forecast contraction for 1958	46	44	42	33

[a] This per cent is an underestimate as the Association calculated that at least 25 per cent of firms did not have an overdraft.

Source: Committee on the Working of the Monetary System, 1959, 89.

Table 6.3. Summary of main findings from Birmingham Chamber of Commerce questionnaire

Size of firm by capital	Under £10,000	Under £100,000	Under £250,000	Over £250,000	Total
Turnover reduced (%)	42	49	33	28	42
Overdrafts seriously restricted (%)	13	10	7	9	10
Used alternative sources of finance (%)	6.5	4	4	5	5
Postponed or cancelled plans since 1955 (%)	38.5	29	23	24	30
Total number of questionnaires returned	184	252	94	80	610

Source: Committee on the Working of the Monetary System, 1959, 88.

the more impressionistic evidence that the Association had collected for the 1951–6 period: small companies were more adversely affected by the credit squeeze than large ones, as detailed by Table 6.2.

Table 6.2 shows how on all counts the firms employing fewer than 250 people were those that experienced the most difficulties, while the firms employing fewer than 100 people were those most affected by the banks' reduction in lending. The smaller firms also tended to resort more to sources of short-term finance other than banks and to purchase machinery using hire purchase.

The results of the ABCC survey mirrored those from an earlier survey carried out in October 1957 by the Birmingham Chamber of Commerce. Table 6.3 was tabulated using answers from 610 manufacturing firms, and shows that 42 per cent had experienced a reduction in turnover since 1955, and that the reduction was more marked in the case of firms with capital of less than £100,000. The main reasons given for this reduction were increased competition, tightness of money among customers, hire purchase restrictions, and shortage of capital. The restrictions on borrowing affected firms differently depending on their size. Of the smaller firms (those with less than £100,000 capital) 23 per cent had their overdrafts seriously restricted while the larger firms suffered to a lesser extent. More small firms had to postpone or cancel plans for expansion than large firms. Of these postponed plans almost half were intended to promote exports either directly or indirectly, showing how, in this case at least, the credit restrictions were achieving quite the opposite to the government's aim of improving the balance of payments.[60]

The FBI gave evidence on the impact of the restrictions to the Radcliffe Committee on the strength of 1,595 replies to its questionnaire.[61] The questionnaire sought to establish members' reactions to the government's monetary and fiscal policies, including the credit squeeze during the period 1955–7.[62] The questionnaire was extensive but Table 6.3 focuses on the relationship between firms and banks.

The evidence from the FBI is useful because it confirms how the impact of the credit squeeze on overdrafts was inversely proportional to the size of the firms. Of the firms that were required to reduce their existing overdraft limit, 47 per cent employed fewer than 200 people and of those who were asked to reduce their overdrafts, 60 per cent were small firms, while 64 per cent were refused an increase. Conversely, only 28 per cent of the firms whose requirements had been met in full were small firms. The results of these three surveys indicate that monetary policy, in the form of credit restrictions, did not affect all firms in the same way. In fact, the paper submitted to the Committee by the FBI stated that 'the impact of the credit squeeze on overdrafts appears to decrease as the size of the firm increases. The requirements of the larger firms have been very fully met.'[63]

Two of the industrial associations which gave evidence to the Radcliffe Committee were bodies that represented mainly small firms. One of these was the National Union of Manufacturers (NUM). In 1958 the NUM had a membership of more than 5,000 firms, mainly small and medium-sized, and its recognized function was to represent the views and interests of such firms. The evidence presented to the Radcliffe Committee was collected primarily from the smaller firms (mainly employing fewer than fifty people). In the memoranda submitted to the Committee, the NUM recounted how,

when a small firm needed finance, it always turned to its Bank, relying on the local Manager's knowledge of local affairs to assure him that the risk was a good one and confident that his agreement was all that was needed to secure an overdraft. Few old established firms have not in their early years been saved by the help of a long-sighted bank manager.[64]

According to the NUM the credit restrictions had

seriously curtailed this traditional, flexible and convenient method of finance; and it had operated much more to the detriment of the smaller firm than to that of the bigger. The restrictions had seriously impaired a traditional, and certainly valuable, part of the local business system. That the Banks have reduced their overdraft facilities, and that this has affected mainly the smaller firm, there is no doubt; and it is further true that many firms, in circumstances in which they would have normally have approached their bank, have not done so for fear of a rebuff.[65]

The NUM, though strongly deploring the impact of the restrictions on the relationship between local bank managers and local businesses, revealed how the curtailment of borrowing had made little difference to the smaller firms' willingness and ability to borrow as they were able to negotiate loans from finance houses, but at considerably higher rates of interest (up to 20 per cent per annum). Thus the main effect of the credit squeeze had been to force borrowers to pay higher rates of interest than would otherwise be necessary. The small firms did not regard a higher rate of interest as an adequate reason for not borrowing, but just as one among many increased costs to be passed on, as far as possible, in higher prices,[66] thus defeating the government's aim (in imposing the credit restrictions) of reducing inflation. Furthermore, the existence of alternative sources of finance blunted the effectiveness of restricting bank advances as a policy instrument, showing what a narrow view of the operation of the monetary system the authorities had.[67]

The point that small firms' ability to invest had suffered from the restrictions was made at length in the evidence presented by the Engineering Industries Association (EIA). The EIA had a membership of 3,500 firms of all sizes, representative of most sections of the engineering industry in Britain. The Association told the Committee how the credit restrictions had led many small and medium-sized businesses to postpone or cancel plans for a new plant. Successive 'squeezes' had made it clear that it was not safe to rely on bank overdrafts as a means for financial expansion. Though the banks' business was not to supply permanent capital, small engineering firms would nonetheless use overdraft facilities for capital purposes, particularly for the acquisition of plant and machinery.[68] In times of prosperity a small engineering firm would use 'five or ten thousand pounds' of its overdraft to finance projects such as factory extensions in the knowledge that the project would be amortized out of the profits made following expansion and the banks would accept the firm's point of view.[69] Prior to the credit squeeze the banks were prepared to 'roll-over' the loans they made for periods of longer than five years.[70] A 'tremendous number of small and medium-sized engineers relied on bank overdrafts' and furthermore, in most cases, the companies with overdrafts were the ones that wanted to expand.[71] Therefore, the curtailment of overdraft extensions had discouraged many small and medium-sized firms from even considering expansion and they had been forced to 'make do' with machinery which ought to have been replaced to the extent that these firms felt that 'they were being prevented from increasing their efficiency'. Not surprisingly small firms blamed the credit restrictions for hindering them 'from offering genuine competition in markets which [were] monopolised by larger producers who, because of their age, [had] financial resources which [were] not available to the smaller and younger firms'.[72] Though the small firms might have been prone to exaggerate the effect of the squeeze on their competitiveness, the Association was worried that Britain was damaging its productive efficiency by continuing credit restrictions for too long. This adversely affected fixed capital accumulation as output was being maintained without the requisite modernization of plant taking place.[73]

THE CREDIT RESTRICTIONS AND THE 'MACMILLAN GAP'

By reducing the supply of funds available in the economy the credit restrictions were a contingent factor that inadvertedly worsened an existing problem: the gap in the market for the provision of finance to small firms for capital investment. Following the Macmillan Committee recommendation, the government and commercial banks had joined forces in 1945 to create the Industrial and Commercial Finance Corporation (ICFC), to provide venture capital to small firms. ABCC, however, revealed to the Radcliffe Committee how there was demand for medium to long-term capital that was not being satisfied by ICFC. One of the reasons why demand was not being satisfied was not because firms failed to offer worthwhile projects, but because the resources of ICFC were limited. This was confirmed by the statement of the Chairman of ICFC, Lord Piercy, in presenting the accounts of the Corporation for the year ending March 1957. In Piercy's words, 'the volume of investment was maintained at a high level, but the Corporation was short of funds to deal with all the applications which might justifiably [have been] accepted'.[74] The number of customers on the Corporation's books on 31 March 1958 was only 629 and a total of £56 million had been invested. Piercy himself felt that this was not enough, but also that it was as much as the ICFC could do within the statutory constraints put on its resources. And when asked by the Radcliffe Committee whether he thought the 'Macmillan gap' still existed he answered in the affirmative.[75] Admittedly, it was in Piercy's interest to paint a negative picture, in order to convince the government to allow ICFC to raise part of its funds in the market, thus reducing the banks' control over it. Nevertheless, his views were echoed by the ABCC. These felt that the provision of finance for small firms, especially new and expanding ones, was not adequate to the volume of demand and that if some more comprehensive and adequate form of finance could be established worthwhile projects would be carried out.

This point was also made by the EIA which pointed out that while the 'Macmillan gap' might have become smaller due to the introduction of institutions such as ICFC, they required a body which could provide relatively small sums (up to £10,000) for start-up businesses on a three to seven year loan. The spokesman for the EIA suggested that this need could be met by industrial banks 'on the continental model' or by local finance companies with officers familiar with local conditions, to replace the loss of the wealthy local (pre-war) investor.[76] The development of a more comprehensive form of finance would have been of great assistance to the many private companies which '[played] such a vital role in the country's economy and [were] hampered in their development through the lack of adequate finance'.[77] This difficulty was particularly felt by small firms as these had no other outside source of finance except for the banks and if these could not accommodate such companies, either because of the limitation on advances or the perceived risky nature of the business, then small firms would remain bereft of capital. The ABCC claimed that

[i]t is becoming more and more difficult to find the necessary financial backing to start up a new venture which cannot offer much security, but which may hold out great promise for long-term development, i.e. the form of risk capital which was provided by private individuals in the past and which was without doubt the foundation of many of the large and prosperous businesses of today.[78]

Furthermore, ICFC was not known by many firms, and

[a]lthough they may have been sent documents, it is much more natural for them to go to their bank manager with whom they have done business for years, whom they know and trust. They are timid. A lot of small businesses shrink away from coming to a finance house in London, if they can borrow from their own bank.[79]

Despite the fact that ICFC had regional offices at the time, this was not sufficient to make it known to small firms.[80]

The findings of the Oxford survey provide further evidence that during the 1950s there were many small firms that could not or would not deal with ICFC. Respondents to the Survey were asked whether over the period 1950–6 they had ever 'tried to get funds from any other institutions specialising in the finance of small and medium sized businesses' [such as ICFC]. Of the 1,021 firms which answered this question 95 per cent had not tried, 1 per cent had tried and succeeded, 3.6 per cent had tried and been rejected. Of the firms who had not tried, 50 per cent had not heard of such institutions and the other 50 per cent did not want any interference.[81] Moreover, one of the problems the ICFC encountered in making itself known to potential customers was the reluctance of the banks to advertise the Corporation's activities, either because of the fear of losing potential customers or, in the case of some branches, ignorance.[82]

Clearly these firms thought the credit restrictions were hindering their investment plans, and therefore their competitiveness. Or at least this is what firms *said*. The view could be taken that it was in businesses' interest to make themselves heard and therefore what they said did not necessarily reflect reality. In terms of general welfare the government's use of monetary policy for macroeconomic purposes had a negative impact, as it generated uncertainty.[83] In these conditions, therefore, it might have been entirely rational for firms not to engage in costly investments. However, the British economy in the 1950s was growing at an unprecedented rate and despite uncertainty over the availability of bank loans some small firms chose not to wait, but instead exercised their option to invest by taking out loans with finance houses and buying machinery on hire purchase agreements.[84]

The finance houses, however, did not escape the Treasury's notice and restrictions were imposed on the terms of hire purchase in 1952, when the minimum deposit on consumer goods, including motor vehicles, was increased to 33 per cent and the hire period reduced to 18 months. The controls were kept in place with varying degrees of harshness until October of 1958.[85] This had a double effect that in the view of EIA was worse than the bank credit restrictions. First, the frequent alterations of policy caused violent fluctuations in the demand for finished goods and this interfered with the flow of production of subcontractors and manufacturers of components. Second, the restrictions on hire purchase, relating to capital equipment, caused many firms to refrain from embarking upon modernization and expansion of their plant since 'owing to the shortage of capital facilities engineering firms [had] resorted to hire purchase for the acquisition of machinery'.[86]

Nevertheless, in the second half of the 1950s the need for funds was such that, despite its cost[87] and the government's restrictions, hire purchase on industrial equipment increased rapidly. In 1955 well over 50 per cent of hire purchase for this category of goods was being used by small firms and in the three years between December 1955 and December 1958 the use of hire purchase by small firms doubled. Following the end of the credit squeeze the steep rise in the use of hire purchase between October 1958 and December 1959 reveals the extent of pent-up demand for finance.[88]

Treasury officials and ministers believed that direct lending controls would have an effect on monetary conditions. In fact these controls led to increasing levels of disintermediation as institutions such as the finance houses, not affected by credit ceilings, were given an artificial advantage over the commercial banks. This lack of understanding on the part of policymakers not only led to a substantial section of British industry being forced into borrowing capital in an inefficient way, but also to the commercial banks being turned into a declining public utility whose only role was to say 'no'.[89] However, a collection of reports on the structure of British industry, published in 1958, shows that the provision of finance to the larger firms was more than adequate thanks to the many sources available, including banks. It was the smaller firms, such as those in the new industries, which encountered substantial difficulties and they remained reliant on internally generated funds.[90]

In its concluding report, the Radcliffe Committee commented on the situation in the following terms: 'there is a danger, which it is socially and economically desirable to avoid, that the growth of small firms may be impeded because they lack some of the facilities open to large companies for obtaining capital'.[91] The Committee concluded that the 'Macmillan gap' had not been bridged as, in the main, small firms and new entrepreneurs could only use their banks as a source of finance. During the 1950s the problem was compounded by the government's policy of restricting credit since small firms—that category of firms that had no other source of external funds except for banks—suffered a decrease in the availability of bank loans.

By 1960 the Treasury had become aware that the credit squeeze did not reduce overall borrowing and that although bank lending was reduced borrowers were using other sources. The banks themselves were purchasing finance houses to find another outlet for their lending. In fact, the only effect of the credit squeeze was 'to restrain the development of capital projects to industry'.[92] During the 1960s there were three main periods of credit restraint: from July 1961 to October 1962, from November 1964 to April 1967, and from November 1967 to the end of 1969. In each of these period the authorities used selective criteria that were applied to bank lending through qualitative controls (indicating who to lend to, such as to export companies, and who not to lend too, including personal customers and hire purchase) and quantitative controls, such as ratio requirements, special deposits, and interest rate agreements. The effectiveness of these measures is difficult to evaluate and it is probable that their main impact was, as noted by the Radcliffe Committee ten years earlier, to drive frustrated borrowers to other sources of credit. Although during the 1960s the government did try to include financial intermediaries other than the banks, these other institutions were not subject to cash and liquidity ratio requirements or to special deposits. As during the 1950s the state found it easier to attempt monetary policy by putting pressure on a small number of institutions.[93] The 1960s credit restrictions were identified by the Bolton Committee (just as Radcliffe had done ten years earlier) as one of the factors which hampered small firms' ability to invest, while at the same time recognizing that these firms were those most affected by government restrictions on bank lending.[94]

CONCLUSION

Small firms in Britain carried on their work in an atmosphere of political hostility, or at best indifference. Neither the Conservative nor the Labour party felt that this group had enough political or economic weight to make it worth protecting. Small firms had to wait until the late 1970s for some positive discrimination from the government. There is little evidence to disprove the assumption made by the Bolton Committee in 1971 that small businessmen were conservative in politics (and therefore more likely to support Conservative governments), and that they had a tendency to mistrust initiatives of the Labour governments. This can explain the insignificance of the small firm lobby as a political factor: one party took its loyalty for granted, while the other dismissed it.[95] The absence of a party professing strong attachment to the interests of small businesses meant that there was no space for these in the machinery of policy. The credit restrictions are just one example of the consequence of this indifference.[96] Banks were asked to reduce their lending and they did so by following the easier route, by lending less, or not at all, to their smaller customers, whose reliance on bank loans for investments was the greatest. While it is not possible to quantify the impact of the credit restrictions, there is some evidence to suggest that during these years small firms were not only declining in number but also in productivity compared with their main competitors abroad, as capital investments were postponed or cancelled because of lack of funds[97].

Moreover, the comparison with the other continental European countries shows that during these years British small firms remained small, as we do not observe the expansion of the medium-sized sector that occurred in these other countries. During the 1950s and 1960s, the British firms who used overdrafts and hire purchase were more likely to be young and dynamic and the link between external finance and growth was confirmed by a later study funded by the Social Science Research Council on a sample of small firms. This study found that there was a strong relationship between financial postures and the performance and aims of a company. Those firms that did not complain of financial problems were also more likely to be liquid, satisfied with their performance and size, and to have rather restricted goals. Instead those firms whose chief executives described their financial problems as an obstacle to progress were in the top third in terms of growth performance. These firms were also thinking of expanding their business over the following five years and were already borrowing from other sources.[98] *Ceteribus paribus* the transition from small to medium size seems to rest on the availability of external finance, and the relatively low level of output from Britain's medium-sized firms suggests that they, in turn, were prevented from making the transition to a larger scale.[99] Chapter 7 shows that small firms' difficulties were not only due to government indifference but were strongly linked to the very nature of British banking.

NOTES

1 PP 1971, Committee of Enquiry on Small Firms, *Report*, 59–60 (hereafter Bolton).
2 Bolton, *Report*, 10–11.
3 Examples of this view can be found in: Glyn, et al., 'The Rise and Fall of the Golden Age'; Crafts and Toniolo, 'Postwar Growth: An Overview'.
4 Broadberry and Crafts, 'British Economic Policy and Industrial Performance in the Early Post-War Period'; Crafts, ' "You've Never Had It So Good"?'.

5   Tomlinson and Tiratsoo, 'Americanisation beyond the Mass Production Paradigm',129.
6   Zeitlin, 'Americanizing British Engineering?'.
7   Ibid., 134.
8   Tomlinson and Tiratsoo, *Thirteen Wasted Years*.
9   On the detail of the commitment of US officials to these policies see Killick, *The United States and European Reconstruction, 1945–1960*.
10 Tomlinson, 'Conservative Modernisation, 1960–1964: Too Little, Too Late?', 31–3.
11 Hall, 'The State and Economic Decline', 282–7.
12 Zeitlin, 'Americanizing British Engineering?', 152.
13 Penrose, *The Theory of the Growth of the Firm*, 222–8.
14 Bolton, *Research Report No 6*.
15 The findings of the Bolton Committee were confirmed by other, later studies: Geroski, *Market Structure*.
16 *Working Party Reports: Cotton*, note by Professor Jewkes, 242–9. Jewkes had a particular interest in small firms, and in Chapter 4 of his *Sources of Invention* he showed their contribution to innovation.
17 Hannah, *The Rise of the Corporate Economy*, 140–2.
18 Despite the Labour party's manifesto commitment to an anti-monopoly policy, this was not pursued with any urgency. Despite the establishment of the Monopolies Act in 1948, the government did not challenge the prerogatives of the private sector, focused as it was on nationalization. See Tomlinson, *Public Policy and the Economy since 1900*, 225.
19 Letter from the Director of Fredk. Burgess Ltd to the President of the Board of Trade, 23/4/1956, quoted in Mercer, *Constructing a Competitive Order*, 128.
20 Harris, *Competition and the Corporate Society*.
21 Mercer, *Constructing a Competitive Order*, 125–48.
22 IRC, *First Report and Accounts*, 5.
23 In 1969, the eleven-man board of the IRC included the chairmen and managing directors of four corporations in the top 100, including the chairman of no 2. See Bannock, *The Juggernauts*, 136.
24 IRC, *Report and Accounts for the Year Ended 31st March 1969*, 13.
25 Roger Brooke, second in command at IRC, quoted in Bannock, *The Juggernauts*, 137. Until its abolition in 1970, after the Conservatives came back to power, the IRC was involved in the mergers of firms in the computer, electrical engineering, motor-cars, ball bearing, and scientific instruments industries.
26 Hannah, *The Rise of the Corporate Economy*, 151.
27 Particularly critical of the 1960s and early 1970s mergers have been: Meeks, *Disappointing Marriage*; Cowling and Stoneman, *Mergers and Economic Performance*.
28 An overall assessment of mergers and demergers during the 1970s can be found in Gourvish, 'Beyond the Merger Mania'.
29 Tomlinson, 'Socialist Politics and the "Small Business" '.
30 HMSO, *Employment Policy White Paper*, 1944, 1.

31 British policymakers at the time did not understand that under a pegged exchange rate system where Britain was not the reserve centre, direct controls could not affect aggregate monetary conditions. In fact it was the country's external position, vis-à-vis its Bretton Woods peg, that determined whether monetary policy had to be tightened or could be relaxed. See Bordo and Eichengreen, *A Retrospective on the Bretton Woods System*.

32 For a full analysis of the sample and methodology used in the small businesses survey see Bates, *The Financing of Small Businesses*, Appendix A.

33 Ibid., 36.

34 Ibid., 56–7.

35 Tew and Henderson, *Studies in Company Finance*, 90–1.

36 Bates, *The Financing of Small Businesses*, 90–3.

37 For a contemporary assessment of the banks' contribution to small firms financing in the 1950s see Piercy, 'The MacMillan Gap and the Shortage of Risk Capital', 4.

38 Amendola and Gaffard, *The Innovative Choice*, 40–3.

39 Hansard, *House of Commons Debates*, 10 April 1951, cols 841–2.

40 Bank of England Archive (hereafter BEA), Chief Cashier Private Files, 7/11/1951, C40/687. The first rise in the Bank rate since 1939 occurred in November 1951 when it was increased by half a per cent to 2.5. After that first rise, changes to the rate were always included with the other elements of monetary policy. Between November 1951 and November 1958 bank rate rose, or fell, thirteen times, reaching its highest rate at 7 per cent in September 1957. See Dow, *The Management of the British Economy 1945–60*, 253.

41 Quarterly figures (in current terms) from Bank of England, *Statistical Abstract*.

42 BEA, Chief Cashier Private Files, 2/11/1952, C40/687.

43 BEA, Statement sent by the Chancellor to the Bank, C40/689.

44 BEA, Minutes of meeting of Committee of London Clearing Banks, 26/7/1955, and Report on advances, 31/10/1955, C 40/689.

45 BEA, Report on advances, quarterly figures, 16/8/1955, C40/689.

46 BEA, Governor's note on interviews with bankers, 3/10/1955, C40/689.

47 Worswick and Ady, *The British Economy in the 1950s*, 305.

48 Dow, *The Management of the British Economy 1945–60*, 255.

49 BEA, Advances and the control of inflation files, 12/7/1949, C40/686.

50 Long-term series of figures for advances (in current terms) can be found in Bank of England, *Statistical Abstract*, (1970), vol 1, 68–70.

51 Lloyds Bank Archive, Sir Oliver Franks, 'Bank advances as an object of policy', Winton File, 1950, 5–6.

52 BEA, Confidential reports from the banks, 16/3/1956, C40/691.

53 BEA, Memo on the number of bankruptcies, 12/9/1956, C40/692.

54 With the proviso that bankruptcy figures are difficult to interpret due to the obvious problem of establishing a correct lag period, it should be noted that their number for the manufacturing sector (businesses and individuals) had increased steadily from 1945 and between 1955 and 1956 had risen by 14 per cent. However between 1956 and 1959 the number of bankruptcies fell slightly, by about 5 per cent, only to rise steadily again until 1963. The number

of bankruptcies in 1960 was 17 per cent higher than it had been ten years earlier. Nevertheless, the absolute number of bankruptcies in the manufacturing sector remained small (177 in 1950, 207 in 1960), compared with the total number of firms in the economy. However, the number of firms being forced into liquidation by the credit restrictions might have been higher. Indeed the secondary literature on small firms and finance does make this connection. The absence of data on the liquidation of unincorporated firms (most small firms) in this period makes it impossible to test this hypothesis. The bankruptcy figures are taken from Board Of Trade, *Bankruptcy. General Annual Reports*.

55 Only those firms who figured as exporters were supposed to receive advances from their banks.

56 Parliamentary Debates, *Hansard*, vol. 554, 1413–25, 28 July 1955.

57 The sample used in the survey was considered to be representative of all British manufacturing firms within the size limit of 11–499 employees. For a description of the sample and a more extensive analysis of the survey's findings see Lydall, 'The Impact of the Credit Squeeze on Small and Medium-sized Firms'.

58 PP 1959, Committee on the working of the monetary system (hereafter Radcliffe), *Memoranda of Evidence*, Cmd 827, vol. 2, 85.

59 Distribution of answers by employment size: 1,679 firms employed fewer than 100 people; 725 employed between 100 and 250 people; 685 employed between 250 and 1000 people; while 315 employed over 1,000 people; this distribution of firms is not surprising as the membership of the chambers of commerce reflected more closely the distribution of firms in the economy than FBI did, since the majority of its members were large firms. The survey was taken at the end of what the Association termed 'a classic period in [the] recent monetary history', the six months from September 1957 to March 1958 when the Bank Rate stood at 7 per cent. See Radcliffe, *Memoranda*, vol. 2, 88.

60 Ibid., 88.

61 Distribution of answers by employment size of the firms: 593 employed fewer than 200 people, 447 employed between 200 and 700, while 555 employed more than 700 people. Unsurprisingly the majority of firms that returned the questionnaire were medium–large, public companies; this was not representative of the structure of British industry but rather of the membership of the FBI. In all three surveys, conducted by ABCC, Birmingham Chamber of Commerce, and FBI, the answers represented 20–25 per cent of the total number of questionnaires sent.

62 The following figures are different from the ones published in the memoranda of evidence because these calculated percentages on the total number of questionnaires returned. The estimates presented here are based on the total who in fact answered the questions.

63 Radcliffe, *Memoranda*, vol. 2, 118.

64 Ibid., vol. 2, 137–8.

65 Ibid., vol. 2, 137.

66 Idem.

67 Ross, 'British Monetary Policy and the Banking System in the 1950s', 205.

68   Radcliffe, *Memoranda*, vol. 2, 108.
69   Radcliffe, *Minutes*, qn 6330.
70   Ibid., qn 6333.
71   Ibid., qn 6335.
72   Radcliffe, *Memoranda*, vol. 2, 108.
73   Radliffe, *Minutes*, qn 6352.
74   Radcliffe, *Memoranda*, vol. 2, 86.
75   Radcliffe, *Memoranda*, vol. 3, 198.
76   Radcliffe, *Memoranda*, vol. 2, 110 and *Minutes*, qn 6404.
77   Radcliffe, *Memoranda*, vol. 2, 86.
78   Idem.
79   Radcliffe, *Minutes*, qn 11,123.
80   Ibid., qn 1.1,124.
81   Bates, *The Financing of Small Businesses*, 79.
82   Radcliffe, *Minutes*, qn 11,123.
83   Dixit and Pindyck, *Investment under Uncertainty*.
84   Carnevali, 'Did They Have it so Good?'.
85   In the summer of 1954 all controls were lifted only to be reinstated in February
     1955 but in 'softer' terms. The minimum deposit was reduced to 15 per cent
     and the hire period extended to twenty-four months. A year later the controls
     were tightened, the minimum deposit increased to 50 per cent of the value of
     the purchased good and for the first time the controls were extended to
     finance on industrial plant and machinery. See Radcliffe, *Memoranda*, 29.
86   Radcliffe, *Memoranda*, 109 and *Minutes*, qn 6,365.
87   15–20 per cent on a reducing balance, compared to 5–7 per cent charged by
     the banks.
88   Carnevali, 'Did They Have it so Good?', 28.
89   Capie, Goodhart, and Fisher, *The Future of Central Banking*, 26.
90   Burn, *The Structure of British Industry*, 182.
91   Radcliffe, *Final Report of the Committee*, para 932.
92   PRO, T230/815 'Credit Control of the FH—Economic Aspects of Policy
     1960–7, Appendix I, May 1960.
93   Croone and Johnson, *Money in Britain 1959–1969*, especially ch 3.
94   Bolton, *Report*, 155–63.
95   Ibid., 93.
96   The Bolton report contains more examples of the negative impact of policies
     that were seemingly neutral. Bolton, *Report*, 95–6.
97   Bannock, *The Smaller Business in Britain and Germany*, 56–7.
98   Boswell, *The Rise and Decline of Small Firms*, 219–22.
99   Driver and Dunne, *Structural Change in the UK Economy*, 100–14.

7

Credit Rationing in Britain after 1945

In 1959 the representatives of the London clearing banks told the Committee on the working of the monetary system (Radcliffe Committee) that 'they could comfortably lend more on overdraft if only they could find more credit-worthy customers'. The Committee responded that the banks were underlent because their criteria of creditworthiness were extremely narrow.[1] Furthermore, bankers recognized that they often refused loans to customers who were creditworthy at the interest rate charged.[2] The banks were strongly opposed to any official suggestion that they should ration their loans on the basis of price rather than by quantity and borrowers willing to pay higher rates were turned down. On one hand, this behaviour was perfectly rational as lending is beset with problems of unequal information and moral hazard.[3] Higher interest rates would have sent good customers to rival banks, and might have attracted riskier projects. On the other hand, however, at a time when the economy was booming banks specialized in only the highest quality loans to a degree that implies profit-satisficing risk aversion.[4] Hire purchase companies charged their business customers much higher interest rates without experiencing major insolvency problems and the evidence presented in Chapter 6 suggests that there were many small firms who were perfectly creditworthy customers yet whose demand for funds was left unsatisfied by banks.

Further proof of the existence of a strategy of low-cost loans to low-risk borrowers is the very low level of bad debt experienced by the clearing banks. Between 1945 and 1962, for example, average bad debt written off was less than 0.1 per cent of Barclay's outstanding advances. The bank was *explicitly* taking few risks, as shown by the very low level of bad debt reserves; while 2.5 per cent of advances had been set aside as bad debt and doubtful debt reserves in 1945, by 1959 the reserves had fallen to 0.4 per cent of advances.[5] Between 1942 and 1959, at the Midland Bank net new provisions for bad debt were necessary only in three years. During the 1960s, net provisions were lower than 0.5 per cent of total advances,[6] nothing like the figures of 3 per cent annually as seen in some years in the 1930s and 1990s. These figures show that the banks were taking virtually no risks, possibly not the best strategy in terms of bank profitability or more broadly for the British economy.[7]

The existence of 'an unsatisfied fringe of borrowers' has been attributed to a market mechanism that excluded potential customers who were either too risky or whose risk was too expensive to assess. Nevertheless, it has also been suggested that the banks' perception of risk might have been too conservative.[8] The banks' bias against small firms was most probably the result of their profit-satisficing behaviour but also the direct consequence of the centralized and concentrated nature of the banking system, as this skewed their perception of risk, as shown in the following pages.

FURTHER CONCENTRATION IN BANKING

By 1957 there were eleven members of the Committee of London Clearing Banks. Barclays, Lloyds, Midland, National Provincial, and Westminster had a national network of branches while District and Martins were much smaller and concentrated in northern England. Williams Deacons and Glyn Mills were owned by the Scottish Royal bank while Coutts was owned by the National Provincial. The National Bank, predominantly an Irish bank with few branches in London and other areas of England, was the last one of the London clearers.[9] Scottish banking also underwent a process of amalgamation and by the end of the 1950s the number of banks had been reduced from eight to five. Increasing the size of the banks was seen as important to fight off the threat that large Scottish firms might look to London for their financial requirements.[10] The English banks had started their encroachment of the Scottish market in the interwar years. In 1918 Lloyds had taken over the National; in 1919 Barclays had taken control of British Linen and the Midland of the Clydesdale, followed in 1923 by the North of Scotland Bank. In 1950 the Clydesdale and the North of Scotland Banks were merged. This was followed in 1954 by a merger between the Bank of Scotland and the Union Bank and in 1958 by that of the Commercial and National Banks.[11]

In the 1960s a new spate of mergers changed this structure. In 1962 the District and the National Provincial joined forces and in 1968 merged with the Westminster, creating the National Westminster. The National Bank was sold to the National Commercial Bank of Scotland in 1966 and in 1968 the three London clearing banks, National, William Deacon's and Glyn Mills came under common ownership, following the merger of the National Commercial and Royal Bank and the establishment of the Royal Bank of Scotland. In 1969 the three London clearing banks were combined to form the new Williams and Glyns.[12] In 1969 the merger of Bank of Scotland and British Linen gave Barclays a 35 per cent share in one of the three remaining Scottish banks, while Lloyds had 16 percent of the shares of the Royal Bank of Scotland and Midland owned all the shares of the

Clydesdale.[13] Barclays and Martins merged in 1968 after the Monopolies Commission had refused permission for a planned merger between Barclays, Martins, and Lloyds. The Monopolies Commission refused the proposed larger merger on the grounds that the suggested benefits to the public interest would be little more than marginal. Moreover, these benefits would be offset by the risk arising from the reduction in the number of sources of finance for medium-sized and small businesses, particularly as far as the fast-growing, innovating companies were concerned.[14] The Commission was also not convinced that there existed enough evidence to claim that there were economies of scale in British banking. Nevertheless it raised no objection to the takeover of Martins, the last independent regional bank, by Barclays in order to strengthen its coverage of the north of England.[15]

The amalgamations of the 1960s were approved partly because the Prices and Incomes Board thought that they could reduce costs through the closing down of surplus offices. The argument used was the same as that of the 1918 Treasury Committee of Bank Amalgamations. The size of the banks affected their ability to provide effective lending facilities on the very large scale required by large national and multinational companies and the Board felt that small banks could be at a disadvantage in the provision of services with a high technology content like credit cards or the introduction of computerization.[16] By the time of the Wilson Committee in 1977 there were only six London clearers left: Barclays, Lloyds, Midland, National Westminster, Coutts (owned by National Westminster), and Williams and Glyn (which belonged to the Scottish National and Commercial Banking Group in which Lloyds had a 16 per cent stake). In 1978 Barclays and National Westminster were of a comparable size, accounting for 60 per cent of total British clearing banks' liabilities, while Lloyds and Midland together accounted for less than 40 per cent and Williams and Glyn for under 3 per cent.[17]

In the interwar years, the economies of France, Germany, and Italy had developed, in different ways, a banking system where the size of customers was matched by the size of banks. The existence of local banks was seen as important for two reasons. First because of their function as suppliers of funds to small firms and second because proximity allowed them to use local knowledge to reduce transaction costs. When assessing a small, local firm the bank's perception of the risk involved in making the loan was tempered by its knowledge of the people involved and of the local economy. There is no doubt that locking together the banks to a specific group of customers induced problems of moral hazard and of financial instability, when banks tied their funds too closely to the fortune of the local economy. However, a concentrated banking system, such as the British one, created other problems connected with the cost of assessing smaller customers.[18]

TRANSACTION COSTS: 'A FACT OF LIFE' FOR SMALL FIRMS

When the Bolton Committee was set up in 1969, a number of sectoral reports on manufacturing and services were commissioned from independent bodies. One of these reports was written by the Economist Advisory Group (EAG) and it dealt with the problem of financial facilities available to small firms. The aim of the EAG's study was to discover whether small firms were at a disadvantage relative to large ones because of the existence of an institutional gap in the provision of finance.[19] The main source of information used by EAG was a number of interviews (about eighty-five) with members of various financial institutions.[20]

The conclusion reached by EAG in the report was that the existing structure of the market for finance presented no major defect in the supply of financial facilities for small firms but there were some other general problems that affected small firms and their ability to access finance. The report revealed how small firms were hit harder by credit restrictions and how the transaction costs, connected with the gathering of information about the creditworthiness of small firms, were proportionately higher than for large firms. Transaction costs were higher for small firms as the cost of investigation and administration incurred by lenders varied inversely with the size of the loan. The Committee considered that the existence of higher transaction costs for small firms was a 'fact of life' and, as such, could not be reduced. At the same time it realized that scarcity of knowledge about the affairs of small firms could lead to the possibility of an incorrect assessment of risk and of interest rates not reflecting real risk.[21]

The Bolton Committee confirmed quite clearly that transaction costs constituted one of the main problems encountered by small firms vis-a-vis their relationship with lenders,[22] but it accepted that nothing could be done to reduce these costs. This recommendation owed much to the report by the EAG that stressed that it had not found any evidence that the *availability* of funds to small firms was restricted. According to the EAG the problems of small firms did not result from imperfections in the supply of finance since 'the ability and readiness of the financial institutions to exploit every new legitimate demand for funds is one of the greatest strengths of our financial system'.[23] The banks, however, did admit to two things when asked if they thought that there was a financial gap. The first one was that the credit restrictions were affecting small firms negatively, as large firms pre-empted all available resources.[24] Most importantly the banks also admitted that their dealings with small firms were clouded by their belief that it was uneconomic to handle small amounts (less than £20,000) as the administrative and other transactions costs were too high.[25]

So, in fact, transaction costs were the crucial problem as they led the banks to shy away from those potential borrowers that they considered to be too small to be worthwhile.[26] Transaction costs might have been 'a fact of life' for small firms, but this was a direct consequence of the internal structure of the banks, rather than the nature of small firms themselves.

It is important at this point to look more closely at the internal structure of the banks. It is important to do so because one of the consequences of banking concentration was to create larger, more centralized organizations. The hypothesis made here is that this increased the distance between the banker and the borrower. The more centralized the internal structure of a bank, the higher the number of applications for advances that had to be processed by the centre. To contain costs, information had to be formalized in standardized and manageable formats. Centralization had a negative effect on small firms, because the personal knowledge of local managers was nullified since the head office decision to grant an advance to a business had to be based on standardized requirements, with no reference to the local economic context in which the firm was placed. Denying small firms their context made it more difficult for the banks to assess the firms' ability and competitiveness as the information held by the local network was lost. To reduce information asymmetries the knowledge of the local bank manager would have had to be taken into account, involving the processing of more information (therefore increasing cost) and creating the problem of control. In a situation where the local bank manager has more information than the head office, the head office had to either believe that the bank manager shared the same goal (to minimize the risk of default) or create a system of controls to avoid the bank manager taking undue risks.[27] Therefore centralization meant that small firms were considered by the bank solely within the limits of the standardization imposed by cost containment.

The examples of Barclays and Midland are presented to illustrate this point. At this time these were the two largest banks in Britain, both based in London and with an extensive branch coverage in England and Wales and shares in Scottish banks. These two banks, however, had very different internal structures. Of the London clearing banks Barclays was the one with the most decentralized structure, whereas Midland had the most concentrated one. The following pages show how the two banks dealt with the relationship between principal (head office) and agent (local bank manager) creating organizations that though similar in appearance were, in fact, quite different, due to the differences in how information flowed and in the location of decision-making points. These differences influenced the banks' cost functions when dealing with small firms and the following analysis will show how this shaped the banks' pattern of lending.

THE MIDLAND BANK

The Midland Bank was established in 1836 in Birmingham with the name Birmingham and Midland Bank, and like the other provincial banks of the time, its business was firmly rooted in the local economy.[28] After expanding in the Midlands and Yorkshire through amalgamation with other banks and the opening of branches, the bank moved its headquarters to London in 1891 following its main local competitors, Lloyds, and the Birmingham Banking Company. This move was dictated by various factors, but the main one was probably the fear of saturation of the Birmingham market (it had more banks per head of population than London), and the attractiveness of the London money market. In fact by the end of 1889, Midland's lending at call and short notice to London discount houses and stockbrokers (lending which carried a higher rate of interest than any other type of investment), amounted to 6.1 per cent of its total assets.[29] By the end of the nineteenth century Midland was firmly established as a London bank with a strongly centralized structure and its main board of directors based in London.

Through subsequent amalgamations with other banks, the expansion of the Midland Bank followed the same pattern as that of its competitors. But whereas other banks, like Barclays, created local boards of directors following the amalgamations, Midland would select individual directors and recruit them to the main board while the general managers of the country banks which had been taken over would usually remain as local branch managers. At the beginning of the century the directing core of the bank was constituted by one managing director and three joint general managers. The branches were grouped in divisions, each one allocated to a joint general manager.[30] The joint general managers were assisted by branch superintendents and inspectors. This structure was thought to be the one that would eliminate all differences between the various amalgamated banks and quickly create a homogeneous 'Midland Bank'. This structure did not change in its basic conception of strong centralization until the end of the 1960s.

Apart from the local branch managers, all other managerial functions were based in London. Reports about the economic conditions of the regions flowed from the branch managers to the Intelligence Department in London and from there to the Management Committee. These reports were then used to comment on the changes in deposits and advances occurring in each division. Although information came from the provinces, the top management considered that all relevant knowledge was held by the centre and dispensed from the centre to the periphery as:

Joint General Managers and their Assistants [visited] their branches from time to time and [attended] meetings of branch managers, at which policy [could] be explained, while branch managers [went] to Head Office to discuss their individual problems and to obtain guidance from senior officials.[31]

Thus, while the information concerning the economic conditions of the places from which the business of the bank was generated came from the periphery, all policy decisions emanated from the centre. In 1929 an Executive Committee was formed (later known as the Management Committee). This committee was attended by the chief general managers and the joint general managers. It met daily, and dominated the routine domestic business of the bank with the branches linked to the committee in a structure that offered them little autonomy. This situation continued until 1960.

Decisions about the business of the bank were also centralized. Each application (regardless of size) for a loan or overdraft was examined by the manager of the branch and then sent to London to the branch superintendent for the area in which the branch was located. If the amount of the advance was above the superintendent's limit then the advance was passed on to the general manager's assistant or further up depending on the amount, to the assistant general managers or the joint general manager in charge of the section from which the application had come.[32]

At the end of the 1950s the Midland Bank started losing its position of pre-eminence among the London clearing banks as Barclays Bank overtook it in terms of advances.[33] Among the senior management it was recognized that one of the reasons behind the loss of competitiveness lay in the subjugation of the branches to head office, while the success of Barclays Bank was attributed also to its strong semi-autonomous regional boards and their capacity for attracting local businesses. Therefore, in 1957, a number of area managers were appointed, and sent to the provinces, to act as personal representatives of the general managers in their divisions. These representatives had no executive powers but merely formed a new link in the communication chain between the branches and London. Ten years later the bank decided to acquire a regional structure by giving the regional managers authority over the branches they controlled in matters of lending, staff, and marketing of services, and by creating regional offices. By 1970 there were twenty-one regional offices in operation.[34]

The change in the size and focus of the bank, from the Midlands (the place where the bank had started its activity) to a more national and even international perspective over a number of years, induced variations in the treatment of different types and sizes of business accounts. Large businesses with a broader national outlook won a 'small but discernible advantage'[35] over the local industrial customers who had been so important in the early years of the bank's history. The main advantage for the new large company customers lay in the possibility of negotiating overdrafts and loans directly with the centre of the bank, bypassing any form of localism. The smaller firms suffered the disadvantage of having to deal with a more distant and complex bureaucracy. According to Holmes and Green, the bank's official historians, the disadvantage was not so much that of an increased 'bureaucratic' element in the lending decisions, which meant that applications needing local knowledge were sent to London bankers with no knowledge of regional economies. Instead it lay in the enormous number of accounts handled by the bank, implying that, as the bank grew, accounts were not judged only on the basis of their security and track record but lumped together for the purpose of controlling lending by sectors (and presumably by type of customer).[36]

Until the decentralization of the structure at the end of the 1960s, the movement of information from the branches to head office followed the informal channels of the managers' club meetings and the more formal ones of the reports sent by the branch managers to the Intelligence Department. Because of the very limited power held by the local managers, the bigger businesses negotiated directly with the top management, whereas smaller businesses were filtered up to London through more formalized channels, as described earlier.

BARCLAYS BANK

Barclays' policy towards the amalgamated banks was different from Midland's. After an acquisition, Barclays would appoint the former owners of the local bank as directors of a Local Board in order not to destroy the 'essentially local character of the new acquisition'[37] and to capitalize on local knowledge and existing goodwill. In 1929 Barclays had 1,270 branches divided into thirty-seven districts, with thirty-seven corresponding local head offices. In 1968, just before the acquisition of Martins Bank, the local head offices had been reduced to thirty-one but the number of branches had increased to 1,906 (without including the sub-branches and branches abroad).

Archival evidence from Barclays Bank provides some information on the work of the local boards. In particular there is relatively rich documentation on the Birmingham Local Head Office. In 1950 the business of this district amounted to between 5 and 6 per cent of the entire deposits of the bank (this made Birmingham the most important district, together with Manchester).[38] The Birmingham Local Board consisted of three prominent local businessmen[39] in addition to the chairman (a professional banker). In 1950 an inspection done by London of this district revealed that the business of the district was run with such competence and its record was so good that the inspectors recommended that the Local Board should be granted as much autonomy as possible and that they should be encouraged and given every opportunity of conducting their businesses as is reasonably possible with the minimum amount of reference to Head Office for all those matters concerning advances, premises and staff.[40]

At the end of the 1960s, A. W. Tuke, in his recollections as former chairman of the bank, wrote about the local boards in very much the same terms:

Policy in such fields as lending, staff salary scales, and the opening and closing of branches is a matter for Head Office and very large lendings and senior manager-ial appointments require Head Office approval. Within that framework it is for local directors to manage their District in the light of their knowledge of local conditions.[41]

This evidence shows the high degree of decentralization of Barclays bank structure and the importance and independence of the local boards. The local boards had the power to authorize all advances up to £30,000 (£50,000 from 1953) but these had to be registered and confirmed by the assistant general manager and also be sanctioned by the general manager. All advances above the local boards' limit had to be submitted to the board at London head office.[42] Nonetheless, the limits discussed during local board meetings generally far exceeded the limit allowed[43] and the minutes of the Birmingham Board meetings make it clear that head office consid-ered the Board's opinion on the firms to be final and gave its assent as a matter of course. In fact there were cases when the local board overruled instructions from head office when it felt that head office did not have a clear enough knowledge of the local situation. Furthermore, the local boards discussed and took active part in the affairs of their customers.

This description of the internal structure of the banks shows how communication, and control, between the centre (head office) and the periphery (the branches) was organized. The bank that relied the most on local knowledge and allowed the periphery most freedom seems to have been Barclays, whereas the most formalized and centralized was Midland. Barclays' structure, in theory, made it easier for a small, local firm to gain access to finance as such a firm would have less to show for itself in terms of documentation suitable for transmission to head office. Under the Barclays system, it could instead rely on the local manager's knowledge to reduce information asymmetries and on the authority of the local board.

The shaded area in Table 7.1 shows those decision-making units that operated at a local level; all the others were based in London. Although in theory all of Barclays' advances had to be sanctioned by various managers in London, the autonomy of the local boards often even exceeded its formal discretionary powers. In practice, in 1953 Barclays' local boards had as much authority as Midland's chief general managers.

Table 7.1. Discretionary limits for Barclays Bank and Midland Bank, 1950s, 1960s, and 1970s (£)

Barclays Bank	Midland Bank
Branch: < 3,000	Branch: (n.a.)
Local Board: < 30,000 (50,000 in 1953–1975)	Branch Superintendent: 1–3,000
Assistant GM: < 25,000	GM Assistant: 3,000–7,000
General Manager: < 30,000	Assistant GM: 7,001–15,000
Advances Committee: > 30,000	Joint GM.: 15,001–25,000
Board of Directors: > 50,000	Chief GM: 25,001–50,000
	Management Committee: >50,000[a]

Note: [a] In 1964 the limits for the Midland Bank, starting from the lower level, had changed to £10,000 for the Branch Superintendent, £25,000 for the General Manager's Assistants, £50,000 for the Assistant General Managers, £100,000 for the Joint General Managers, and £200,000 for the Chief General Manager. Advances above this limit had to be authorized by the Board.

Sources: Barclays Bank: BBA, Inspection of Birmingham Advances, 1950; Head Office Instructions and Information, section on Advances, 1928 (used until 1952) and 1953 (used until 1975); London Head Office, Minutes of Directors Meetings, 13/3/1947.
Midland Bank: MBA, Applications and Renewals, 1947 and Board Minutes, 31/1/1964, courtesy of the Group Archivist.

By the mid-1960s, Barclays local boards still had as much power as Midland's assistant general managers. Therefore Barclays, by allowing its regional offices to have autonomous decision-making powers, was the one to minimize the most the distance between the bank and its customers.

The distance between the centre and the periphery can be 'measured' by the number of stops the application for an advance had to undergo from the moment the application was filled in at the branch until it was granted. The stops are represented by the discretionary limits granted to each managerial level. The further an application for an advance had to travel, the more standardized the information had to be, forcing the quantification of the quality of a business, or the potential for development, and reducing the relevance of local knowledge held by local managers and increasing information asymmetry. The more centralized the structure, the larger the number of applications which had to be processed by one person making it expensive (because it was time-consuming) to use information that was not standardized. The need to minimize risk and cost made the banks refuse those customers whose creditworthiness was not easily quantifiable.

LENDING BY ENGLISH BANKS

The description of the structure of the banks and of the various levels of autonomy existing inside these structures provides some insight into how the banks perceived their relation with the periphery, both the internal (branches) and the external one (local economies).[44] The impact of this relationship on the availability of credit to smaller firms is not easily quantifiable. But by looking more closely at the lending patterns of the individual banks during the long period of credit restrictions, it might be possible to identify differences that could be explained by the banks' varying degrees of centralization and involvement with the regional economies.

Table 7.2 shows the percentage annual change in total national advances in real terms (in 1963 prices) for Barclays, Midland, Martins (this bank has been introduced to study the effect of the restrictions on the last provincial bank), and for the London clearing banks as a whole. With different time lags and to a different extent, the credit restrictions affected the advances of all the banks. The degree of reduction, though, was different and seems to follow a pattern.

In spite of the fact that the government, through the Bank of England, started calling for reductions in bank lending in 1946, Table 7.2 shows that, in fact, advances did not decrease until 1952. The decrease which occurred in that year may perhaps be attributed more to the effect which

Table 7.2. Advances in constant terms (yearly per cent increase): Barclays, Midland, Martins, and London Clearing Banks (LCB), 1946–59

	Barclays	Midland	Martins	LCB
1946	13.36	20.44	31.70	15.09
1947	15.09	15.80	18.85	16.13
1948	11.83	9.05	7.89	6.45
1949	0.48	3.32	1.96	7.38
1950	5.71	0.72	5.37	4.02
1951	2.20	4.12	7.83	7.14
1952	−14.88	−15.04	−20.10	−16.87
1953	1.75	−8.13	5.05	−5.01
1954	8.59	14.39	13.08	9.73
1955	−12.40	−7.98	−11.53	−7.30
1956	−1.75	−1.56	−7.71	−1.51
1957	−1.40	−3.43	2.73	−5.02
1958	17.66	15.38	14.09	17.12
1959	41.22	30.63	33.70	28.49

Source: Annual Reports for the banks and Abstract of Statistics for LCB.

rising interest rates had on the demand for credit than to the effectiveness of the Treasury's appeals. Nevertheless, in the following year the advances of Barclays and Martins were already increasing, whereas those of Midland and of the LCB as a whole were not. The different lending patterns of Martins and Barclays can be explained by the fact that Martins Bank was a regional bank and Barclays had autonomous local head offices which were, more often than not, little more than the original local bank. The autonomy of the local head offices allowed Barclays' local directors to make decisions based on first-hand knowledge of the regional economy and on personal relationships with their clients built through the years. This knowledge was of little use to the managers of Midland as the local branches and regional divisions had little or no decisional autonomy as far as advances were concerned. The existence of personal relationships between managers with strong powers of decision and local clients meant that these managers would have tried to reduce the effect of the increase in the bank rate in the period we are observing. Thus, after the first shock of bank rate rise had worn off, customers would go back to the bank confident that a suitable rate could be arranged. Furthermore, both Martins' and Barclays' local boards were directly dependent for their profits on the economies of their district and thus prone to protect their rather small and not very segmented markets. This interpretation would also explain why, after three years of decreasing advances, only Martins managed to increase its advances in 1957. In the case of Barclays the decrease was much lower than that of Midland's, when interest rates had risen from 3 per cent (1954) to 7 per cent (1957) and after the Treasury had intensified credit restrictions in 1955. To consider Barclays as a bank with a more intense involvement with local businesses is also consistent with the greater increase of its advances, compared to Midlands and the LCBs, after the credit restrictions were lifted in 1958 and interest rates decreased from 6 per cent to 4 per cent. The lifting of restrictions meant that Barclays could go back to lending in full to all those customers who for years had been penalized by the restrictions, namely the smaller ones. This is also the year when Barclays became the largest lender in the country, overtaking Midland.

The relationship between the centre and the periphery of the bank was often an uneasy one. In fact, in 1955 Barclays head office started issuing circulars to the local boards asking them to restrict their advances by reducing overdraft limits and more careful scanning of new applicants. These appeals continued throughout the 1950s, with reminders to the local boards that the bank was incurring increasing difficulties in maintaining the 30 per cent liquidity ratio imposed by the government. This ratio was being kept only by continuous selling of investments, which was only possible at progressively lower prices, sometimes involving capital losses. Even after the credit restrictions were lifted, the bank encouraged the local offices to restrict advances to reach a 35 per cent liquidity ratio. These appeals seem to have fallen on rather deaf ears, since in August 1960 head office wrote to the local head offices:

This analysis [of the Classified Return of Advances] is now before us, and compared with mid-May there has been an increase of £20.6 millions. But over 50 per cent of our advances come under the headings of 'Personal and Professional', 'Other Financial', 'Hire Purchase', 'Builders and Contractors' and 'Retail Trade'. With the exception of 'Hire Purchase' which is almost unchanged, all these categories show increases, and frankly we find this disappointing because it was in these categories in particular that we were hoping for reductions.[45]

These categories listed by head office were, except for 'Other Financial', those where small customers were predominant. Thus these instructions reveal how the autonomy of the local boards allowed them to be more involved with local customers than with head office instructions and Treasury policies. These instructions also show the difference in focus between London head office and the local head offices, as one asked for the reduction of advances to small customers while the other maintained its role of local lender.

Thanks to the survival of some data from Barclays Birmingham Local Board it is possible to compare the lending activity of this Board with that of the bank as a whole. Table 7.3 shows the behaviour of advances during the period under analysis both nationally and at a local level. Advances for the bank as a whole decreased more and increased less than the advances authorized by Birmingham Head Office, except in 1957, 1960, and 1962. This difference might be appreciated more by looking at the absolute level of advances. Between 1950 and 1958 advances decreased in real terms, for the bank as a whole from approximately £530 million to

Table 7.3. Barclays Bank and Birmingham Local Board Advances in constant term, 1951–62, yearly per cent increases

	Bank	Local Board		Bank	Local Board
1951	2.2	6.7	1957	−1.4	−12.6
1952	−14.9	−13.9	1958	17.6	22.2
1953	1.7	13.8	1959	41.2	53.7
1954	8.5	23.5	1960	17	0.5
1955	−12.4	−10.5	1961	−1.4	15.7
1956	−1.7	4	1962	4.1	−7.2

Source: For the bank as a whole, Annual Reports, various years; for Birmingham Local Head Office, Barclays Bank Archive, Birmingham Local Board, Returns, Local Head Office Summary, Access 1/95.

about £500 million, whereas the advances of Birmingham Local Board increased, during these years of credit restrictions, from almost £25 million to more than £32 million.

In order to realize the importance of the previous data for the availability of finance to small firms, two things must be considered. First, the Birmingham Local Board was one of the bank's most important provincial boards, accounting, together with the Manchester Board, for the largest regional segment of the bank's business. Second, London Head Office had the power to sanction all advances above the local board's discretionary limit, but not those below. In the light of these considerations, Table 7.3 shows that Birmingham Local Board reduced its advances less and increased them more than the bank as a whole because, as its profits depended on its local advances, it was interested in 'protecting' those advances over which it had direct control, those below £50,000. In other words, these data indicate that at a local level the effect of the credit restrictions on advances for less than £50,000 was felt by businesses to a lesser extent. The combination of these factors meant that for those local firms that were clients of Barclays the credit restrictions had a lesser impact than for those firms that were customers of the other centralized banks. In the late 1960s the source of Barclays, past competitive advantage was still well known, as declared by the *Bankers Almanac*: 'It is more than coincidence that Britain's largest bank is also the most completely decentralised.'[46]

The data available do not allow a direct comparison between the lending activities of Barclays and Midland but they do throw up some interesting differences, connected with the banks' internal organization. In 1951 total manufacturing accounted for 22 per cent of Midland's total advances. Nevertheless, in terms of numbers of accounts, manufacturing represented only 5 per cent of Midland's total customer base, and ten years later this share had decreased to less than 3 per cent.[47] Between 1951 and 1961, the amount of money lent to the manufacturing sector increased by more than 150 per cent, but the number of advances to this sector increased by only 23 per cent, compared to 114 per cent of the 'Other Personal' sector. These figures mean that Midland, though increasing the amount of money lent to manufacturing, did not increase its customer base in this sector. Furthermore, some industries became less important in terms of number of customers, for example motor car manufacturing, shipbuilding, chemical, paper, and furniture makers. On the one hand, it is plausible to assume that Midland's lending to manufacturing simply reflected the trend towards concentration in British manufacturing. However, the following data present more archival material to show Midland's bias against small firms.

The assumption that the bank was shifting towards larger loans and larger customers is confirmed by the fact that for those categories clearly made up of small customers (like the 'small retailers' and 'professional' ones), the average size of advances remained practically unchanged in real terms between 1951 and 1961. If we use the 'Professional' category as a proxy for small firms, between 1951 and 1961 this sector lost importance for the bank not only in terms of money (advances decreased by 12 per cent) but also in terms of customers (the number of advances granted to this category fell by 22 per cent). Overall the customer base of the bank, if the personal sector ('Other Personal' and 'Personal Loans') is omitted, hardly expanded at all between 1951 and 1961, as the number of advances increased from 96,830 in 1951 to only 119,155 ten years later.

A clearer indication of the bias against small firms can be gathered from the lending activity of the bank during the 1950s, before credit restrictions were lifted. Between 1951 and 1957 the total lending of the bank decreased both in terms of money and number of customers, conforming to Treasury and Bank of England directives. Nonetheless, manufacturing as a whole did not register a decrease in the amount of money lent but a rather considerable one in the number of customers (−24 per cent), in all sectors except for aeroplane manufacturing and 'Other Textiles'. Manufacturing sectors which showed a decrease also in the amount of money lent were those where small firms were more prominent: 'Clothing' (−30 per cent), 'Leather' (−38 per cent), 'Food' (−24 per cent), 'Paper' (−24 per cent), and 'Furniture' (−28 per cent). The general decrease in the number of accounts, not matched by a decrease in the amounts lent, is consistent with the evidence presented in Chapter 6, that the banks found it easier to reduce advances by rationing loans to small firms. Between 1951 and 1957 those categories where small customers were predominant, like 'Small Retailers' and 'Professional', suffered a considerable decrease, both in terms of money lent (−38 per cent and −49 per cent) and number of accounts (−30 per cent and −49 per cent respectively).[48]

The number of advances to manufacturing was not only a very small share of the total number of advances but it was also a very low number in absolute terms (9,924 in 1951, decreasing to 7,500 in 1957, and rising up to 12,176 in 1961). As the Midland Bank, together with Barclays, had the most extensive network of branches and the largest share of advances and deposits, and considering that firms tended to have more accounts with the same bank and that in 1960 there were more than 88,000 manufacturing firms in Britain, the data suggests that a significant number of firms did not have an overdraft. The study conducted in 1956 by the Institute of Statistics in Oxford suggested that two firms out of five did not hold a bank overdraft and that, on average, the larger the firm the more often it resorted to banks as a source of temporary finance.[49] It is therefore plausible to assume that Midland's loans to the manufacturing sector were mainly to large firms. The following pages present more evidence to reinforce this impression.

Table 7.4 shows that, between 1954 and 1958, most of Midland's advances were in fact renewals of existing business. Furthermore, after 1955, when the Chancellor called upon the banks to make 'a positive and significant reduction in their advances', the number of new applications accepted decreased drastically, while renewals kept increasing. Even after the restrictions were lifted, the number of new advances increased only to the level it had been before the squeeze. These numbers confirm that Midland's strategy in these years was not one of increasing its market share but of reinforcing its existing one. This strategy was certainly the best one in terms of cost- and risk-minimizing, but not in terms of profit maximization, thus confirming the suggestion that British banks were behaving as satisficers. Further confirmation can be found by looking more closely at the numbers in Table 7.4.

The table shows that the vast majority of advances made were between £1 and £5,000. These loans, however, were unlikely to have been made to small manufacturing firms. The prices of machinery (machine tools for example) suggest that advances for sums below £5,000, even in the case when an advance in this category was made to a small firm, would have been used mostly for working capital, to pay for stock and wages. In 1953 a power press would have cost between £4,000 to £7,000, depending on the size and whether or not it was imported; an optical precision grinder would have cost around £8,000. On the basis of the price of machinery, and assuming that overdrafts must have been used, to some extent, for the purchase of machinery,[50] advances to small firms would have fallen in the category £5,001–£10,000 and Table 7.4 shows how small the number of loans in this category was, compared to the £1–£5,000 one.

The bank suggested to the Radcliffe Committee that its reluctance to lend to small firms was determined by the absence of creditworthy customers.[51] In fact it was due to the fact that the bank thought that lending to small firms was not worth the return it brought, as shown by Midland's foray into term loans. Paragraph 942 of the report of the Radcliffe Committee concluded with the recommendation that banks should be ready to offer term loan facilities, to increase the availability of finance to smaller businesses, as an alternative to a running overdraft. Prompted by the Committee's report, the Midland Bank decided, in 1959, to offer term loans for small businesses. These were heralded as the '*new* way to finance business expansion for small firms'.[52] Term loans were meant to finance plant improvements and machinery purchase and had a duration of three to five years (sometimes even up to ten). Also, as long as the customer kept up repayments, the loan could not be recalled before the expiry of the agreed period.

Ten years later, when the Bolton Committee reviewed Midland's experiment with term loans it came to the conclusion that 'the progress of the scheme and the response from the small firms at which it was aimed

Table 7.4. Midland Bank: number of advances renewed and new applications accepted by size of loan, 1954–58 (£)

Size of loan	1954		1955		1956		1958	
	Renewal	New	Renewal	New	Renewal	New	Renewal	New
1–5,000	67,498	48,442	70,616	35,561	73,439	17,679	40,867	35,137
5,001–10,000	3,936	3,347	4,134	2,559	4,486	1,464	3,373	2,637
10,001–25,000	2,732	2,046	2,937	1,589	3,200	1,002	2,326	1,577
25,001–40,000	944	491	1,056	498	1,089	344	1,084	507
40,001–75,000	984	465	987	403	1,014	270	893	283
75,000+	1,445	567	1,474	499	1,542	343	1,500	407
Total	77,539	55,358	81,204	41,109	84,761	21,102	50,043	40,548

Source: Midland Bank Archive, courtesy of the Group Archivist.

was disappointingly poor. This makes it difficult to sustain the pro-
position . . . that there was a large unsatisfied demand for term loans'.[53]
In other words, the bank had done its best, but small firms just did not
want more money lent to them. However, though the scheme received
quite a lot of coverage by the press it would appear to have been little more
than a public relations exercise, despite the laudatory terms used by the
bank's official historians.[54] Internal memos show that the bank was adamant that the introduction of term loans did not alter the fact that its primary
function in the field of lending continued to be the provision of short-term
credit, repayable on demand, and that the bulk of the bank's business
would continue to be in this field. Thus term loans had to be limited to a
modest proportion of total advances. Head office's instructions to their
branch managers contained the outline of how term loans could be effectively discouraged. Though these loans were for quite small amounts of
money (between £500 to £10,000) the procedure for processing them was to
be no different from that for all other advances. All information about a
customer had to be put on a form, sent to London, and a decision then
taken by the Advances Department. If anything, to avoid 'abnormal
risk . . . the security requirements for Term Loans may well need to be
rather more strict than they would be for "on demand" facilities'[55] (i.e.
for overdrafts). Thus new businesses, or those firms whose worth could
not be easily summed up in an application form, would not have been able
to access this new facility. Furthermore, branch managers were supplied
with a very small number of brochures explaining the scheme in general
terms and were to give them only to those customers who asked for this
service; in other words branch managers were discouraged from advertising this new facility. Figures for 1962 and 1964 (when the scheme was
terminated) suggests that term loans had not been very successful as the
highest number of loans active was 274 in March 1964.[56]

Another reason for the limited success of term loans was that branch
managers had always offered personal advances and the public knew that
this facility existed. Term loans for small businesses were a new product
and managers had not had any experience in marketing it. They would
have had to actively search for customers, as the number of small firms
with an overdraft who therefore might have known of the services
offered, was very small, as suggested by the Oxford Institute of Statistics
study quoted in Chapter 6. Those firms that were already customers of the
bank were more likely to prefer the old system of overdrafts, as these were
in fact cheaper and more flexible. The example of the term loans scheme
confirms what the evidence presented in the previous pages could only
suggest – that the Midland Bank had little real interest in lending to small
firms and expanding their market share in this sector. Although the actual
number of small firms holding an overdraft might have been small,
demand was also determined by the expectation of it being fulfilled.[57]

Chapter 6 shows how demand was being reduced by credit restrictions, and by virtue of the fact that small firms *expected* loans not to be granted and overdraft facilities to be withdrawn. Nonetheless demand for credit was there and banks, or at least the Midland Bank, were acting as satisficers by choosing not to tap into this potentially very remunerative market.

CONCLUSION

At least until 1971, when the Competition and Credit Control policies opened up the market to freer competition, the banks were displaying extremely risk adverse behaviour. They could have lent more and to more lucrative customers, such as small manufacturing firms, but the internal organization of the banks made small loans costly to evaluate and administer in relation to returns. To lend more to small firms the banks would have had to change their structure, in order to be able to reduce costs and change their method of risk evaluation, but their existing high profits did not induce them to such a change to enlarge their customer base. It took the Midland Bank about ten years to change its organizational structure and decentralize, once it realized, in 1958, that Barclays had overtaken it in terms of deposits and advances, and thus becoming the biggest domestic bank. Slow reaction times and a relatively short working day[58] compared to bankers in the 1990s or in the nineteenth century were, after all, the best of monopoly profits.[59]

In the summary of its findings on the difficulties faced by small firms in accessing finance, the Bolton Committee was candid in admitting that small firms suffered from a number of 'genuine disabilities in seeking finance from external sources'. They had been the victims of the credit restrictions; they had fewer sources of finance than large firms did, and finance was more costly. These disabilities, according to the committee, were the result of the higher cost of lending in small amounts and of the higher risk of lending to small borrowers. The committee did not think that the problems of small firms resulted from imperfections in the supply of finance and did not recommend the creation of a new institution for the provision of finance to small firms.[60] The evidence presented in Chapter 6 and in this one, however, shows that in fact all the problems listed by the Committee were the direct consequence of the structure of the banking system. To a large extent the only source of finance available to small firms were the London clearing banks. The near absence of local or regional banks meant that there were no institutions whose economic interests rested with small firms and who could soften the blow of credit restrictions. Moreover, it was the internal structure of the national banks that made administering small loans expensive as these structures made it difficult to assess cheaply the risk of lending to small firms.

The example of Barclays Bank shows how a decentralized structure resulted in more lending at a local level, while providing the bank with a competitive advantage over its rivals. The importance of proximity was recognized by the one institution set up to lend to small firms, the Industrial and Commercial Financial Corporation (ICFC). ICFC's early lending showed massive losses from bad debt and it had to rely heavily on money borrowed from the clearing banks. By 1959, however, it had become strong enough to raise funds on the market.[61] From its inception in 1945, one of the long-term goals of ICFC had been that of opening regional offices and the first provincial branch to open was in Birmingham, in 1950. Birmingham was chosen because the Corporation had noticed that it was receiving fewer applications from the Midlands and it was suggested that this might be because of the reluctance of businessmen to go to London to find finance.[62] Eventually the Midlands was to be the second most successful region after London, accounting for 11 per cent of total investment in 1951 and 16 per cent in 1961.[63] According to Coopey and Clarke, the success of the Birmingham branch was due to the fact that Ernest Ralph, the branch manager in charge, was able to establish a network of local contacts, thanks to his connections with accountants and local bank managers. Through these Ralph was able to access the social and business circles of the region. The contacts established brought business for the Corporation and proved essential in providing informal references. One of Ralph's reports to head office outlines the workings of the network:

The business and professional communities are closely knit within themselves. A great many of the men here were at school together and were brought up within a few miles of each other. They know each other's strengths and weaknesses, and with due discrimination on our part are a source of useful and sometimes valuable information.[64]

This quote shows the crucial importance of local networks and how these could be recognized even by a national organization.

ICFC was the only institution dedicated to giving term loans to small firms and Bolton recognized that this was a safer way for firms to finance capital investment, rather than using overdrafts, as these could be recalled on demand. Ten years earlier the Radcliffe Committee had suggested that the banks offer term loans to small firms but apart from Midland's lukewarm response the other London clearers did not seem to have taken up the suggestion. The Bolton Committee also analysed in some detail the arrangements for term loans in France, Italy, Japan, and the USA. It observed that in these four countries' governments had been active in creating regional institutions as alternatives to commercial banks to provide term loans to small manufacturing firms, as these were seen as an important part of regional development. Bolton's assessment of these institutions was that they had helped small firms improve their productivity and increase their scale of operations.[65] Nevertheless, for fear of distorting the functioning of the market, the Committee did not recommend that the British government emulate these other countries, leaving it to the commercial banks to offer term loans, if they so wished.

Ultimately, even if the Bolton Committee had recommended the creation of regional institutions to lend to small firms, it is unlikely that any government would have acted accordingly. The commercial banks would have been strenuously opposed to any attempt to make the system more competitive and small firms were not worth the political effort required to change the system.

NOTES

1   Radcliffe Committee, *Report*, 48–9.
2   Thompson, 'Chairman's Address', *Annual Statement to Barclays Bank Ltd Shareholders*. The banking cartel's rate for business borrowers was at least 1 per cent above bank rate (minimum 4 per cent, rising to 5 per cent in 1958), with smaller businesses paying 2 per cent above it. See Ackrill and Hannah, *Barclays*, 141.
3   Greenwald and Stiglitz, 'Macroeconomic Models with Equity and Credit Rationing'.
4   Ackrill, Hannah, *Barclays*, 141–2.
5   Ibid., 142.
6   Data courtesy of Edwin Green, Group Archivist, Midland Bank.
7   Ackrill, Hannah, *Barclays*, 142.
8   Ross, 'The Unsatisfied Fringe in Britain, 1930s–80s', 17.
9   Collins, *Money and Banking*, 398.
10 Checkland, *Scottish Banking*, 641.
11 Ibid., diagram of mergers and acquisitions, 640.
12 Ibid., 400.
13 Checkland, *Scottish Banking*, 676–7.
14 Monopolies Commission, *Barclays Bank Ltd, Lloyds Bank Ltd, and Midlands Bank Ltd: A Report on the Proposed Merger*, 44–63.
15 Ackrill, Hannah, *Barclays*, 171–84.
16 National Board for Prices and Incomes, *Report No 34, Bank Charges*, 53.
17 Collins, *Money and Banking*, 401.
18 The relationship between the Scottish banks and industry was different from that of the English banks. The central part played by steel, metal work, and shipbuilding in the Scottish economy meant that banks felt that they could not distance themselves from these industries. The Scottish banks strong objections to the credit restrictions in the 1950s and 1960s, on the grounds that these were bad for manufacturing show that they had a much clearer view of the connection between banks, industrial progress, and regional prosperity that either the British government or the English banks had. See Checkland, *Scottish Banking*, 704 and Saville, *Bank of Scotland*, 646–60.

19   Bolton Committee, 'Financial Facilities for Small Firms', *Research Reports, Report No 4.*
20   The number is reported as approximate because the report itself is vague in this respect. The institutions interviewed were: Clearing banks; merchant banks; overseas banks operating in Britain; discount houses; finance houses; insurance companies; pension funds; stockbrokers; firms specializing in leasing, factoring and export finance; building societies; firms specializing in medium- and long-term finance, like the ICFC firms specializing in finance for technical innovation, including the National and Research Development Council.
21   Bolton Committee, *Report No 4*, 69.
22   Ibid., 192.
23   Idem.
24   Bolton Committee, *Report No 4*, 88–9.
25   Ibid., 92.
26   Interest rates were not the issue: bank overdrafts' interest rates for small business borrowers were normally one percentage point higher than the rates charged to 'blue-chip' customers. This differential was not a risk premium, but reflected the higher cost of dealing with small business loans. Ackrill and Hannah, *Barclays*, 143.
27   Strong and Waterson, 'Principles, Agents and Information'.
28   This localism was reflected in the composition of the board of directors. The first board was made of Birmingham-based businessmen and subsequently the qualifications for directorship demanded that the directors should live within six miles of Birmingham Town Hall. This custom was maintained until the bank's head office was moved to London. See Holmes and Green, *Midland*, 16.
29   Ibid., 81.
30   At the time the districts were London, Lancashire, Midlands, Southern, and Yorkshire.
31   Rouse, 'Midland Bank Ltd', 194.
32   In 1950 England and Wales were divided in five sections (also known as divisions), each under the control of a joint general manager. These divisions were City of London and Overseas Branch; rest of London and suburbs; northern counties; Midlands and eastern counties, southern counties and Wales. See Rouse, 'Midland Bank', 182. H. L. Rouse became one of the two chief general managers of the bank in 1948.
33   In 1959, Barclays Annual Report shows for the first time that the bank had higher advances than the Midland Bank. The dates for profits and deposits are slightly different.
34   Holmes and Green, *Midland*, 223 and 246–7.
35   Ibid., 113.
36   Ibid., 113–15.
37   Tuke, *Barclays*, 78.
38   Barclays Bank Archives (BBA hereafter), Inspection of Birmingham Advances, 1950. Account No 80/1883. These inspections supplemented the role of the Inspection Departments (found in Midland and Lloyds) and were a feature of the rather decentralized structure of the bank.

39 The practice of having local businessmen managing the local boards was peculiar to the Birmingham district. Most other local boards would have been made up of professional bankers. The peculiarity of Birmingham local board was due to its origins as it was the result of the takeover, in 1916, of the United Counties Bank, not a private bank with professional bankers but a joint-stock bank, run by local businessmen.

40 BBA, Inspection of Birmingham Advances, 1950.

41 Tuke, *Barclays*, 78–9.

42 BBA, London Head Office, Minutes of Directors Meetings, 13/3/1947.

43 In one case the limit of the overdraft granted was higher than 1 million pounds (BBA, Birmingham Local Board, Minutes of the Meetings, 6/10/1941, Account No 1/226), and in the case of a very important tea merchant the limit was as high as £2,250,000 (BBA, Birmingham Local Board, Register of Advances, 1954, Account No 1/102)

44 For details on the structure of Lloyds bank and how this compared with that of Midland and Barclays banks see Carnevali, 'Finance in the Regions: The Case of England after 1945'.

45 BBA, Local Head Office Circulars, Account No 29/740.

46 Ackrill and Hannah, *Barclays*, 17.

47 Midlands Bank, Classification of Advances, courtesy of the group archivist.

48 These calculations for the whole of Midland's Classification of Advances are presented in table form in Carnevali, 'British and Italian Banks and Small Firms', appendix to Chapter 5, Tables A5.2 and A5.3.

49 Lydall, 'The Impact of the Credit Squeeze on Small and Medium-sized Manufacturing Firms'. These findings are confirmed in Tew and Henderson, *Studies in Company Finance*, Chapter 6.

50 Bolton Committee, *Final Report*, 161.

51 As the banks suggested to the Radcliffe Committee, *Report*, 48.

52 Quote from a Midland brochure for that year, emphasis in the original. Courtesy of the group archivist.

53 Bolton Committee, *Report*, 169.

54 Holmes and Green, *Midland*, 227.

55 Midland Bank archives, letter from the Chief General Manager to Managers of Branches, 5 November 1959. Courtesy of the group archivist.

56 Midland Bank archives, figures courtesy of the group archivist.

57 Wood, *Commercial Bank Loans and Investment Behaviour*.

58 Senior bankers were expected to work only from 9.30 a.m. to 4.00 p.m. See Pelly, *Loose Change*, 17.

59 Hicks, 'Annual Survey of Economic Theory', 8.

60 Bolton Committee, *Report*, 192.

61 Akrill and Hannah, *Barclays*, 143–5.

62 Coopey and Clarke, *3i: Fifty Years Investing in Industry*.

63 Figures kindly provided by Richard Coopey.

64 Coopey and Clarke, *3i: Fifty Years Investing in Industry*, 42.

65 Bolton Committee, *Report*, 386–403.

8

Germany and the Limits of Organized Capitalism

Chapter 3 highlighted how the relationship between big banks and big firms has dominated the literature on the history of Germany's industrialization, obscuring the connection between local banks and small firms. The chapter repositioned the narrative of Germany's industrialization by moving away from the 'organized capitalism' model based on large firms, large banks, and the economic power of a centralized state. The analysis of the persistence of small firms and of the decentralized industrial order in the period after the Second Word War shows even more strongly the partiality of this model as an explanation for West Germany's post-war economic success. Throughout the post-war period limited companies in Germany have accounted for less than half of total turnover while the proportion accounted for by partnerships and sole proprietorships was much larger in Germany than in Britain. These forms of enterprise depended on local and regional banks in order to raise external finance.[1]

From the late 1970s the crisis experienced by some sectors, typically those based on the mass production of consumer goods, brought small firms back to the attention of political economists. As happened in other countries, small firms made their way back into the literature as alternatives to mass production, such as flexible specialization, were being explored.[2] The strength of the 'resurgence' of small firms in the 1980s and 1990s, however, cannot be explained without understanding the environment from which they had sprung: the political and economic climate of the 1950s and 1960s and especially the connection between local banks and local economies.

The expansion of mass production was the result (and the cause) of the creation of a stable intra-European trading market (in the 1950s and 1960s more than 60 per cent of German exports went to Western European countries), of the very high rates of growth experienced by West Germany and the other European countries, and of the competition of American mass producers. Until 1963 a large influx of skilled labour from East Germany helped keep wages down, without diluting the quality of production. These factors gave producers the incentive and the confidence to undertake the investments required by mass production. In the regions characterized by decentralized methods of production, some manufacturers responded to the challenges presented by American firms by breaking away from decentralized production. Gary Herrigel uses the example of Daimler-Benz to 'illustrate the dynamic of recomposition and invention at work in this period' as decentralization was abandoned in favour of Fordism.[3] Apart from this firm there were others, such as Bosch in household goods, Standard Elektik Lorenz in electrical products, and Liebherr in construction machinery. These firms all followed a pattern that moved them out of decentralized production and the structures of their regions. This can be measured by looking at Württemberg, one of the regions more strongly characterized by decentralized production in the first part of the twentieth century. In 1907 only 6.6 per cent of all industrial employees worked in establishments employing over 500 people and there were only thirty-seven establishments employing more than 500 workers. By 1925, the number of establishments with more than 500 workers had increased to 108 and they employed 16.4 per cent of all industrial employees in the region. In 1950 in the larger region of Baden-Württemberg, 51 per cent of all industrial workers were employed in establishments with more than 200 workers and 21 per cent were employed in establishments with over 1,000 workers.[4]

The expansion of the consumer market thanks to rising incomes led to the growth of sectors based on the mass production of consumer goods. One of the consequences of this was the recruitment from the late 1960s of new types of workers, especially foreigners and women, to make up for the dwindling reserves of skilled immigrants from East Germany. This created a blurring of the distinctive German production system as custom production for exports clashed with the mass production, mass consumption economy. The problems experienced by the West German economy from the late 1970s were the result of the loss of competitiveness due to this shift to the production of standard goods by semi-skilled workers. This decline was reversed by the resurgence of small firms and the decentralization of large ones.[5]

This resurgence was possible because the spread of mass production had not removed small firms. Mass production needed specialized product and operation-specific capital equipment that had to be custom made to fit the specifications of the mass production process. These customized goods were provided by specialist capital goods producers. In Germany, these capital goods producers were well established in the decentralized industrial order and in the post-war period they flourished thanks to the role played by local institutions, such as chambers of commerce and banks. During the years of Germany's fastest growth, the 1950s and 1960s, the 'investment goods' sectors (machinery, electro-mechanical, fine mechanical, and optical industries, for example) were the fastest growing, fuelled by the growth of mass production in Germany and in Western Europe. In 1950 this sector accounted for 29 per cent of total industrial employment and in 1970 this had increased to 45.9 per cent. Consumer goods instead accounted for 27.3 per cent in 1950 and 23.9 per cent in 1970, while steel and chemicals and basic production goods accounted for 22.4 per cent in 1950 and 21.3 per cent in 1970. The weight of small and medium-sized firms in these industries remained substantial throughout the period. For example, the machinery industry was among the largest industrial branches, measured by employment and total sales. In 1951 firms with 500 or fewer employees accounted for 50.9 per cent of all employed in this industry and for 49.3 per cent of sales, while firms employing 1,000 or more people accounted for 34.5 per cent of all employed and for 35.7 per cent of sales. By 1965 establishments with over 1,000 workers had grown in importance, but establishments employing fewer than 500 people still accounted for the equivalent employment, 41.8 per cent and for almost the same amount in sales, 40.6 per cent. Those branches of the 'investment goods' sector with a preponderance of small and medium-sized firms, such as machinery, developed most in those regions characterized by the decentralized industrial order, such as North Rhine Westphalia. There, the machinery industry was the second largest industrial employer (coal mining being the first). In Baden-Württemberg the machinery industry and the electro-technical industry were the two largest sectors in the region. Over 40 per cent of all those employed in the machinery industry worked in establishments employing fewer than 500 people, both in 1955 and 1972.[6]

Herrigel's study of the textile machinery industry shows the important role played by the chambers of commerce and by the banks in fostering the growth of capital goods industries. After the war the main region of textile machinery production, Saxony, was lost to East Germany. The rest of production was concentrated in Württemberg, Bergisches Land, and on the west bank of the Rhine (Mönchengladbach). The textile industry was the largest employer in the country and the boom in demand for clothing and fabric meant a rapid increase in the demand for machinery at a time when the number of producers had declined. This bottleneck in the capacity of existing producers of machinery to supply the growing needs of the textile industry could have resulted in unruly competition, price-cutting, and eventually overproduction. The regulation of the industry was ensured by the textile machinery association, together with the local banks. The trade association was given the task by the government authorities to identify those firms that could be given financial assistance. The association used this power to recommend those firms that agreed to limit the range of their products to the banks for federally guaranteed loans. In this the association sought to coordinate specialization and avoid overcapacity.[7]

From the 1950s up to the early 1970s, the structure of the German economy continued to move towards concentration as the larger firms expanded. This trend stopped after the first oil shock in 1973, and the 1980s were marked by a decrease in the share of employment by firms employing more than 500 people and an increase in the share of the smaller firms. Manufacturing firms employing fewer than nineteen people made a positive contribution to employment showing that new small firms were an important source of economic growth.[8]

Changes in world market conditions in the 1980s negatively affected mass producers and favoured the decentralized regions where small and medium-sized firms were able to adopt new technologies, and to adapt their products to rapidly changing consumer demand. The rise and subsequent fall in the 1990s of flexible specialization in the decentralized regions, especially Baden-Württemberg, has been well documented.[9] It is clear that within this narrative the ability of the economy to renovate itself during periods of crisis has rested on the persistence of the decentralized system of production. This persistence was only partially the result of the support given to small firms by the federal government. The productive links between artisans, small, medium, and large firms which have been a constant characteristic of German industry have been fostered at a local level by strong regional and municipal powers. The post-war reorganization of the West German Federal Republic (FRG) gave local and regional governments strong political and fiscal autonomy. This was divided between the federal government and the other two levels, regional and municipal; the type of taxes and the balance of distribution changed over the period, but local powers maintained a strong degree of autonomy. Throughout the period the maintenance of this autonomy involved conflicts between the centre and the periphery over the structure of finance and administration within the new federal state and over the extent of the power of the *Bundesrat*, the legislative chamber representing regional interests.[10]

Piore and Sabel's flexible specialization model relies very strongly on the notion of the emergence of a new paradigm in response to the crisis of mass production. In Germany (and to a certain extent in France) the crisis of mass production led to a reconfiguration of the relationship between large and small firms. Central to this was the fact that small firms and decentralized production methods had not declined in the 1950s and 1960s and that the political environment had not turned against them. The interaction between large, small, and artisan firms resulted in the development of diversified quality production (DQP), based on the production in small batches of quality goods. Streek maintains that this interaction was not 'new' as Piore and Sabel have speculated but had historical origins and this explains, for example, the establishment in the 1950s of protective legislation in favour of artisan firms. Piore and Sabel's industrial divide can be defined in terms of a break in the historical continuity of industrial society in general. The study of DQP instead places its emphasis more on synchronic differences between social systems, in particular national and regional societies.[11]

The persistence of DQP is the result of the fact that Germany developed as an institutionally rich society where markets were deeply embedded in an array of cooperative, redistributive, and regulatory institutions. DQP and institutional structures were linked by a complex interaction where each sustained the other. Streek writes:

> In particular not only was diversified quality production not obstructed by social institutions, but there was reason to believe that markets and management on their own would be unlikely and frequently unable to generate that pattern, and that if firms were reduced to their own devices the production pattern and prosperity it had wrought would be at risk. In fact the institutional minimalism of neo-classical theory would have harmed them.[12]

A good example of the economic outcome of the links between producers and institutions is that of the machine tools industry. The post-war demand for large-scale mechanical automation systems (LAMAS) meant a change in the traditional demand for machine tools. But German producers were able to adapt to this very rapidly, despite the collapse of the five largest American-style machinery producing companies. In fact the machine tool industry became even less concentrated in the post-war period than it had been before. By 1970 West Germany was both the largest exporter and the largest producer of machine tools in the world. They were able to achieve this thanks to the specific order of the industry. Costs connected to the development of LAMAS, such as training of workers, research and development (R&D), adaptation of technology, did not overwhelm the small producers because they were spread across the range of institutions connected to the industry. The trade association, the *Verein Deutscher Werkzeugmaschinenfabriken e.V.* (VDW), created at the turn of the century, organized training and the development of technology through the cooperation of technical universities and firms through 'precompetitive' research projects. The crisis of the 1970s was also overcome by the existence of this institutional network. The international slowdown of the early 1970s reduced the demand for machine tools and German producers preferred to shift their attention to the less sophisticated East European markets than invest in new technology. When demand started to pick up in the early 1980s, the German machine tool industry was completely unprepared for the competition that came from Japanese producers with their computer numerical control (CNC) equipment to the extent that in 1980, 73 per cent of the domestic demand for CNC equipment was supplied by imports. By 1984, however, the situation had already changed, and this figure dropped to just 30 per cent. This turnaround was achieved thanks to the involvement of firms and institutions in developing CNC technology. The VDW worked together with the Federal Ministry of Research and Technology to develop a subsidy programme that allowed small and medium-sized firms to discount all research and application expenses related to CNC technology on their machines. More 'precompetititve' projects were started with the technical universities, and the trade association and metalworkers union developed a joint programme to train workers in computer programming.[13]

For most of the post-war period Germany was a country of high wages and low differentials across sectors and between small and large firms and a higher employment share of small and medium-sized firms. This combination of external competitiveness and high-wage employment reflected the operation of a distinctive set of socio-economic institutions. These, in turn, were the result of a complex historical compromise between liberal capitalism, as introduced after the Second World War, and two different countervailing forces, Social Democracy and Christian Democracy. This compromise meant that those who wanted to turn Germany into a liberal market economy had to accept the revival of a variety of traditionalist status protections for farmers, civil servants, and the *Mittelstand*, as well as an extensive welfare state and established labour unions.[14] Post-war economic policy was shaped by the different attitude towards capitalism of different political parties and other groups, from the church to academics. The neo-liberals, for example, placed their faith on the benefits of free market capitalism, while the Christian Socialists were opposed to the private ownership of the means of production, as in their view this would lead to the exploitation of workers. In addition the Americans' position towards small firms was to see them as guarantors of competition, in opposition to the emergence of powerful business conglomerates such as those that had developed before the war. The *Mittelstand* could be all things to all people, both in economic and social terms: a more humane version of capitalism, a symbol of the values and aspiration of good German citizens (succeeding against competition, private ownership of home and business, marriage and the family, and savings), and the lubricant of the economy in which the more diversified needs of wealthy consumers were best served and structural change achieved smoothly through the exit and entry of small producers.[15]

However, one of the consequences of this accommodation of interests was to generate wage rigidity. Much of the success of the German economy had been due to the country's industrial relations system. Unions had been responsible for collective bargaining and participation through policies of codetermination in boardrooms, while elected work councils participating in organizing working conditions inside firms.[16] This system had been instrumental in reducing conflict between labour and management. Moreover, the inability of managers to dismiss workers during economic downturns meant that they had to invest in the long-term training of the labour force. This system of strong trade unions and work councils created rigidity but also developed skills and social peace. This process contributed directly to the diversified quality and flexible social system of production that has been the key to Germany's competitive advantage.[17] The system of codetermination (set up at enterprise level by the Works Constitution Act of 1952, renewed in 1976, at plant level in 1972) resulted in a high-wage system, which forced German firms to become engineering and high skills intensive, with diversified and high quality producers. At the same time employer and labour associations developed enterprise-based vocational training and apprenticeship programmes.

THE POLITICAL AND ECONOMIC IMPORTANCE OF SMALL FIRMS

Until the early 1960s the share of small establishments in manufacturing declined more rapidly in Germany than in Britain. This decline affected mostly the very small firms, those employing fewer than ten people, while the decline in Britain affected firms employing fewer than 200 people. Moreover, during the 1960s the share of employment of small establishments in Germany increased. Differences in census data between Britain and Germany make a direct comparison difficult, but in Britain in 1968 small establishments accounted for approximately 30 per cent of employment compared with 44 per cent in Germany in 1970. The total number of small firms (including agriculture and commercial activities) in Germany was substantially greater than in Britain. In 1968–70 there were over 40 per cent more small businesses in Germany than in Britain, a substantial difference even allowing for the differences in population.[18]

Table 8.1 shows how large the share of small firms was, both in terms of establishments and of enterprises and the percentage of large and small firms that defined themselves as *Handwerks*. In the same way as 'small firms' in Germany means not only a small business unit but also a social class, much of the discussion in Germany about 'small firms' has really been about *Handwerk*, or craft. Craft, however, is only an approximate translation. The two government enquiries into the difficulties faced by small firms, in 1895–7 and 1930, focused on *Handwerk*, and much of the *Mittelstandsforschung* (*Mittelstand* research) of the post-war period has in fact examined the conditions of the *Handwerk*. This term signifies more than just small-scale industry, since a *Handwerk* business could employ 1,000 people and this makes *Handwerk* statistics problematic when looking for bona fide small firms. This term developed connotations of

Table 8.1. Germany: employment in all, and small establishments and firms in, manufacturing, including and excluding *Handwerk*, 1967

	Establishments			Firms		
	Total ('000)	Small ('000)	%	Total ('000)	Small ('000)	%
All manufacturing	9,048	3,934	43.5	9,165	3,536	38.6
Handwerk	1,718	1,693	98.5	1,718	1,693	98.5
Manufacturing excluding *Handwerk*	7,330	2,241	30.6	7,447	1,843	24.7

Note: Small firms and establishments are those employing less than 200 people.

Source: Bannock, 1976, 39.

quality, high skills, social embeddedness, tradition, all of which were anchored to formal apprenticeship and quality control. These have all been seen as qualities having a political and social, as well as economic, value.

In Germany *Handwerk* still includes more than 100 different occupations requiring a high level of non-academic skills and formal apprenticeship. Butchers, bakers, carpenters, engineers, tailors, hairdressers, plumbers, car mechanics, opticians, TV and computer servicepersons all fall into this category and get their certificate of qualification from the local or regional Craft Chamber.[19] Specific *Handwerks-kammer* (Chambers of Craft Industries and Trades, CIT) for *Handwerk* firms set up in every large town provide skill centres for running apprenticeships. Membership to the local CIT was made compulsory for all local firms and they provided other services as well, including information about local, urban, and regional planning, environment safety and other regulations, on markets, marketing, and trade exhibitions; and advice on how to set up businesses, labour law, technical design, accountancy services, bookkeeping, taxation, and payroll systems. One of the most important roles fulfilled by CITs was to represent and defend members' interests vis-à-vis local, regional, and federal authorities. The cost of the services of the CITs was only partially met by levies from members as federal government grants paid between 60 per cent and 80 per cent of the cost of information, training, and advisory services. There were also Chambers of Trade and Industry that provided small firms with services.[20]

The legal protection and support given to the *Handwerk* firms is reflected in the much greater number of firms employing fewer than ten people in Germany than in Britain. In 1963 there were nearly twelve times as many manufacturing firms in this category in Germany than in Britain, about 366,000 compared with 31,000. At the same time market concentration was higher in Britain than in Germany, where there was also a lower level of merger activity. The reasons for the higher number of small firms in Germany were a less progressive tax system with lower levels of direct taxation and lower rates of income tax,[21] the faster growth of the German economy (as slow growth encourages concentration), a different banking system, and public policy, in particular the support given to the *Handwerk* sector.[22]

In 1946 the American occupation authorities appointed Ludwig Erhard as Minister of Economic Affairs for Bavaria, and in 1948 he was made head of the new German Economic Council. Most of the people who worked with him belonged to the Freiburg school of neoliberal economists and lawyers. Erhard's policies placed strong emphasis on competition and increased productivity achieved through large-scale industrial units, considered as the most efficient way of increasing production and mass consumption.[23] In the USA, the post-war debate on the future of the German economy settled on a model that replicated the USA's corporate structure.

Decartelization and deconcentration were to be pursued not with the aim of destroying Germany's industry but rather to break up excessive power and create competitive oligopolies, as in the case of the restructuring of IG Farben into three large companies, Hoechst, Bayer, and BASF and a number of smaller ones.[24] This anti-cartel legislation, finally ratified by the Bundestag in July 1957, outlawed cartels and restrictive practices. However, to satisfy German industrialists Erhard had to accept that exceptions could be made in those cases where agreements would increase efficiency, productivity, or competitiveness on export markets. In practice the law was extremely mild in relation to mergers, with the Cartel Office having little power to act against them.[25] At the same time the prohibition of cartels, and the danger of concentration, were balanced by *Mittelstandspolitik*, the positive encouragement of small and medium-sized firms. This policy was formally started as part of the political programme in 1957 when the government declared:

it is absolutely necessary that we should have a middle stratum. We do not want the people to be divided into a small class of economic overlords and a vast mass of dependants through the ever-increasing concentration of the economy into large firms. We require independent medium and small units in the crafts, trade business and agriculture.[26]

This quotation highlights how the government thought that the encouragement of the 'middle estate' was desirable not only for economic but also for political and cultural reasons.

Germany's post-war political leaders, Chancellor Konrad Adenauer and his Minister of Economics, Ludvig Erhard (later to be Chancellor), saw the crucial role of small firms in the social market economy. Their importance was measured not just in terms of their direct contribution to

GDP, but also in terms of increasing the overall efficiency of the economy by contributing to the productive efficiency of bigger firms as competitors and subcontractors. Small firms were also seen as playing a profoundly important role in the stability of post-war German society. New firm formation was therefore facilitated by providing low-cost funds to small firms. Originally these funds came largely from Marshall Aid under the European Recovery Programme but later subsidized loans continued to be provided from both the federal and regional levels of government.[27] In the post-war period three policies were initiated to facilitate the viability of small firms. Apart from low interest loans, small firms were allowed to group together to compete against large firms, a particular type of cartelization justified on the grounds that it increased the total amount of competition. Also, in 1953 the Basic Law on Skilled Crafts and Trades was passed, requiring new entrants to hold proficiency certificates before they were allowed to practise. This was seen as an important way to ensure standards of quality of production and of the efficiency of small firms and was reinforced by the activities of the trade associations, which provided professional training and information services.[28] Direct financial assistance was added to the deliberate attempt to give preference to small and medium-sized firms in placing public contracts. Between 1956 and 1964, of all the defence contracts that could be placed with smaller firms, 46 per cent went to firms employing fewer than fifty persons. During the same period, over 40 per cent of the total value of building contracts placed by the Federal Treasury were given to the craft sector. Small firms also received tax concessions. Institutionally, *Mittelstandspolitik* found expression in the special *Mittelstand* committee of the *Bundestag*, as well as a *Mittelstand* department in the Ministry of Economics and the Institute for *Mittelstand* research at the Universities of Bonn and Cologne, both set up in 1958.[29]

By the late 1960s the German government was noticing with concern the contraction in the number of small businesses, especially in the *Handwerk* sector, and this was feared to reduce competition. The 1970s saw a number of government initiatives intended for the smaller firms, such as the encouragement of the creation of new businesses by trained craftsmen in structurally weak areas, and in new housing estates, through financial assistance and advice. Between 1970 and1978 the government gave about DM1,055 million of European Recovery Programme money to the *Handwerk* sector. In addition several *Bundesländer* had their own schemes and gave an average of DM100 million per year to the *Handwerk* sector. Considered together, regional and national money increased from about DM55 million in 1970 to DM600 million in 1978 and benefited one in four of the 33,000 new businesses set up in 1978.[30]

The Competition Law of 1958 was also modified in 1973 to strengthen its ability to check mergers as the process of concentration in the economy had accelerated. The Federal Cartel Authority was given powers to disallow any mergers that would result in a group with a market share of 20 per cent or more, 10,000 employees or more, or an annual turnover of DM500 million. The following year in its instructions to the Cartel Authority, the Federal Government stated:

In view of increasing structural change in the economy it is a pressing task of competition policy to guarantee on a long-term basis, a multiplicity of sizes and types of firms as an important condition for the functioning of competition. As experience has shown, even in a recessionary climate, efficient small and medium-sized firms can hold their own, even against large firms, because of their greater flexibility and adaptability. What is essential, however, is that those competitive advantages which large firms have only by virtue of their size should be adjusted in favour of small and medium-sized firms.[31]

BANKS AND DECENTRALIZED PRODUCTION

What follows here is a continuation of the analysis stated in Chapter 3 to assess the role played by state regulation and banks in lifting barriers to the growth of small firms in the post-1945 period. Germany's industrial strategy, as perceived by businesses, banks, and the state, has been one based on the promotion of DQP. This strategy has required extensive cooperation in production and development between large and small firms and institutions to encourage firms to deliver this strategy of high diversity and quality. DQP, however, could only be pursued if firms could access long-term capital to invest in R&D, and labour force training and this required long-term, stable relationships with banks, so that firms could pursue long-term objectives. In this way firms were able to avoid the preference for short-term profits inherent in market-based finance systems. The German state played a very important role in creating and sustaining a system of long-term industrial finance indirectly and directly, by controlling a large part of the banking sector and by providing financial aid.[32]

The initial consideration is that the federal structure of the West German republic was reflected in the organization of the central bank. The *Deutsche Bundesbank* was created in 1957 by restructuring the central banking system that had been instituted after the end of the Second World War by the Allies. It was given a decentralized structure, with a main office in every *Land* (*Landeszentralbanken*), and branches in all the main regional centres for industry, commerce, and banking. The council of the *Bundesbank* was headed by its board directors and by the presidents of the eleven *Landeszentralbanken* (these chosen by the governments of the various *Länder*). The decisions taken by the central bank have thus been strongly influenced by the regional outlook of its council.[33]

Tables 8.2 and 8.3 show, first, that compared with Britain after the Second World War the German banking system remained a much more segmented one with a much lower tendency towards concentration and a much larger number of banks. Second, the distribution of assets confirms the pre-war trend that savings banks held an increasingly large share of the market than the commercial banks. Over the period the market share of savings and cooperative banks increased while that of the commercial banks decreased.[34]

Chapter 3 illustrated how from the end of the nineteenth century German banking developed as a system based on three major banking groups: one made of commercial banks dominated by the large national banks, one of savings banks, and one of cooperative banks. These last two were organized as associations. This system can be defined as a federal model of bank organization characterized by autonomous units operating in local, regional, national, and international markets. The success of any unit depended on regular cooperation with other units operating at other

Table 8.2. Germany: number of banks and bank branches, 1957, 1967, and 1979

| | 1957 | | 1967 | | 1979 | |
	Banks	Branches	Banks	Branches	Banks	Branches
Commercial banks						
Big banks	8	787	6	2,103	6	3,104
Regional banks	96	1,020	107	1,686	101	2,463
Private banks	245	104	189	217	89	277
Savings institutions						
Central Giro	14	191	14	311	12	317
Savings banks	871	8,192	862	13,433	603	16,752
Cooperative banks						
Central institutions	19	89	19	101	10	49
Credit cooperatives	11,795	2,305	9,312	7,877	4,443	15,117

Source: Bannock, 1981, 49.

Table 8.3. Germany: assets of the various banking groups, 1950–79 (%)

	1950	1957	1960	1970	1979
Commercial banks	36.7	27.7	24.4	24.9	24.7
Savings institutions	32.1	36.1	35.7	38.5	38.3
Cooperative banks	10.4	8.5	8.6	11.5	14.6

Note: These figures do not include the contribution to the total of mortgage banks, hire purchase banks, and the post offices.

Source: Bannock, 1981, 51

levels within the bank or bank association. One of the consequences of this federalist model of organization was that it promoted strong competition in all segments of the financial market. At the same time cooperation between large and small banks within the same group allowed savings and cooperative banks to combine the advantages of decentralization, such as closeness to the customer, with the scale advantages of larger banking units. In this way small banks were able to compete with the large commercial banks, for example in activities such as export finance, while large commercial banks, because of their national branch network, competed with savings and cooperative banks for firms in the *Mittelstand* sector. Large commercial banks had to compete with local savings and cooperative banks, because state regulation prevented them from buying them. Throughout the post-war period all the banks, regardless of size or geographical coverage, competed head-to-head in all financial market segments, in all geographic markets, and with all categories of firms. Thus each major commercial bank and the two association banking groups were constantly seeking to finance the needs of virtually any firm or craft, small, medium, or international conglomerate.

The historical development of the savings banks sector created a system divided into three tiers, all associated with each other. The first one was made of legally independent banks owned and supervised by city governments. They had to make a profit that could be invested in commercial markets, but as they were also public institutions they had to support local policy initiatives. The second level of savings banks were the regional savings banks associations known as *Landesbanken* (or *Girozentrale*). There was normally one *Landesbanken* for each federal state and this was owned by the *Land* government and the regional savings banks association in that *Land*. A *Landesbank* served as the *Land*'s banker but it also competed in the commercial sector with other banks outside the savings banks group and it assisted local savings banks by providing banking services they could not afford to operate. The third level consisted of a national association with strong political weight in the federal government and a national central bank (DGZ Bank). The cooperative banks also had a three-tier associational structure. The first tier was made of member-owned credit cooperatives. On the secondary level there were regional cooperative banks and associations. Compared to the regional savings banks, the cooperative regional banks were relatively few and not as important within the group. On the third level were the national cooperative banking association and the national cooperative bank (*Deutsche Genossenschaftsbank*, or DG Bank). Both the DG Bank and the national association played a leading role within the cooperative banking sector, providing services and policy guidance. The three big commercial banks had a national network of branches but from the 1970s these were organized to resemble the association banking groups (rather than as a hierarchy) as local and regional branches were given much more autonomy. The headquarters and specialized subsidiaries provided an internal capital market and specialized financial services to autonomously operating regional and local branches.

The post-war period was marked by group competition. With help from their associations the small banks were able to compete successfully with local branches of the commercial banks. From 1952 to 1981, the combined assets of the three major commercial banks declined from 16.9 per cent to 8.8 per cent of total bank industry assets, while the combined asset share of the savings banks and *Girozentrale* (*Landesbanks*) rose from 32.7 per cent to 38.6 per cent, and the cooperative sector's share increased from 8.5 per cent to 15.2 per cent.[35] The state played an important role in the promotion and regulation of competition with the aim of maintaining a segmented system. State intervention was crucial not only for the reorganization of the three banking groups in the post-war period but also for maintaining the segmented nature of the system. In 1958 the decision to lift the branching restrictions instituted in the 1930s meant the beginning of competition between groups, as the banks started a branch opening frenzy, to capture the growing pool of savings.[36]

After the war the Allies broke down the major commercial banks into thirty independent regional banks to avoid concentration, but during the 1950s the banks were allowed to reconsolidate and the process was completed by 1957. An attempt was also made to break up the savings banks organization by eliminating the *Girozentrale* (*Landesbanks*) but the intervention of the *Land* government in most regions by becoming the main shareholder in the regional *Girozentrale* saved it. In 1953 the regional associations re-established the central association, the *Deutscher Sparkassenund Giroverband*, or DSGV, and in 1954 the central savings bank was allowed to resume its activities. Despite the continued protests of the private banks, such as the cooperative banks, the Banking Law of 1961 maintained the savings banks' privileges as banks with a public status including their tax exemptions, though these were lifted in 1967.[37] The Competition Commission reported in 1968 that although the savings banks should lose their tax-free status, public banking would continue to play an important part in the economy, ensuring that all social groups and the *Mittelstand* could have access to banking services at competitive prices. The state's actions can be seen therefore as essential in ensuring competition. At the 1969 national congress of the savings banks, the Federal Economics Minister, Schiller, declared his belief that because the savings banks were regionally anchored institutions they could counter economic concentration and animate competition.[38]

The state also intervened in the reorganization of the cooperative banks by contributing 50 per cent of the capital to create the new central bank for the cooperative banks, the *Deutsche Genossenschaftskasse* (DG Kasse). The state's intervention reflected the strong institutional nature of the cooperative sector, with this serving a public-interest function, promoting economic prosperity among its membership rather than seeking profit maximization. In the reconstruction period the DG Kasse was used by the state to channel funds to rebuild the *Mittelstand*.[39]

The growth of the cooperative banks led, after 1967, to a number of bank mergers in the search for cost efficiency to better compete against the other banking groups. The big banks instead sought to fight the encroaching competition of the savings and cooperative banks by pursuing a strategy of decentralization. The collapse of Germany's second largest private bank (*I.D. Herstatt*), in 1974, prompted the establishment of the Gessler Commission, to examine the merits of universal banking, and in particular the big banks' social and economic role. By the 1970s the competition from the other banking groups was starting to reduce the profitability of the big banks, while the rise of international capital markets meant that large firms had alternative sources of industrial finance. This, in turn, meant that lending to the *Mittelstand* became very important. Such a strategy was pursued first by *Dresdner Bank* in 1972, and later by *Deutsche Bank* in 1974 by increasing the lending power and autonomy of regional offices and of their branches (*Deutsche* made its regional offices independent profit centres).[40]

The much larger number of small firms in Germany is both a function of the more segmented banking system and a consequence of it. In 1970 bank advances to the *Mittelstand* were estimated to be 44.1 per cent of total bank advances and the biggest subtotal of lending was in manufacturing.[41] By comparison the Bolton Committee estimated that in Britain in 1968 total advances to small manufacturing firms accounted for about 10 per cent of advances to the total manufacturing sector.[42] The segmented nature of the system also ensured a high degree of specialization in small lending between different categories of banks. The commercial banks, a group which included the three big Berlin banks, regional and other commercial banks, had, in 1979, the largest share of total advances to the business sector but the smallest share of advances to the *Mittelstand*, while the savings and giro banks had the largest share of the latter. At the end of the 1970s, the role of the commercial banks in lending to the *Handwerk* sector was relatively smaller still, while the savings banks had the largest share. The explanation for this is that the smaller banks tended to concentrate their limited resources on the smaller customers and were more deeply rooted in the local community. Furthermore, the savings banks were obliged by law to restrict their lending to the local authority area in which they were located, while, until 1974 cooperative banks could only lend to their members.[43] By contrast, in Britain bank lending to small businesses has been much more concentrated among fewer and much larger institutions. While in Germany at the end of the 1970s the three Berlin banks accounted for less than 30 per cent of lending to the *Mittelstand*, the four London clearing banks accounted for less than half that proportion. At the same time, while in Germany there were several thousand independent banks most of which made advances to small firms, in Britain there were only a few hundred of these independent banks, most of which were savings banks prevented by law from making loans to businesses.[44]

Apart from these structural differences, public policy towards small firms was also different as the German state involved itself in creating favourable conditions for small firms through credit guarantees and state subsidized bank lending both at a federal and *Länder* level. Credit guarantees for medium- and long-term bank loans were supplied by credit guarantee associations (CGA), located in every *Land*. These were private limited companies created in the early 1950s by the business community (including banks) as mutual assistance organizations for the purpose of helping small firms which were unable to obtain bank loans due to the lack of sufficient collateral. The smaller savings and cooperative banks were the ones that took the initiative and provided the initial funds, together with chambers of commerce and trade associations. These funds were supplemented by loans and grants from the regional government and (by loans) from the ERP Guarantee Programme. The CGA could make loans for a period of twelve years (twenty-three for buildings) but had a limit on the amount they could lend per customer to ensure that their lending was restricted to small firms. The request for a credit guarantee was normally made by the bank that had decided to turn down an applicant, either wholly or partially. The CGA would then ask the local chamber of commerce for an assessment of the borrower, and the borrower's trade association for an assessment of the outlook for the trade in the area in question. The interest rate charged was in principle at the market rate, but could benefit from a subsidy from the *Länder* or the government, under one of the state sponsored schemes. The CGA required security but would accept collateral that a bank would not take, such as a second mortgage or stock. Once a borrower was accepted by the CGA this would grant 80 per cent of the loan, while the rest had to be provided by the borrower's bank.[45] While loans backed by the credit guarantees accounted for quite a small percentage of total lending to small firms, some regional examples suggest that in 1976 this amounted to approximately 1 per cent of total advances to the *Mittelstand*. All in all, about 4 per cent of bank advances to the *Mittelstand* enjoyed some form of subsidy or guarantee from the federal or *Länder* governments.[46] The loss experience on guarantees was very low, under 1 per cent in 1976.[47] Banks benefited from the scheme because the loans they granted were assessed by trade associations and chambers of commerce experts who provide free consultation and monitoring during the life of the loan, so that the banks' overall transaction costs were reduced. The subsidy associated with the credit guarantee institutions benefited almost exclusively the entrepreneur, who would otherwise have been rationed out of the market. The banks, however, profited to the extent that overcoming such rationing brought them the follow-up business of the newly established firm and therefore these subsidies cannot be seen as reducing general welfare.[48]

The details of the credit guarantee scheme are interesting, first because they show the state's involvement with small-firm finance from the very early post-war years. Second, the scheme demonstrates how the existence of local actors such as banks, chambers of commerce, trade associations, and government created an alternative solution to the problem of financing small firms. In Britain, apart from the absence of local banks to engineer such a solution, there were no provisions for subsidized bank lending to small firms. The Scottish and Welsh Development Agencies and the Council for Industry in Rural Areas made subsidized loans to small firms and low interest loans were available through the Industry Acts, though these loans were predominantly for large firms. These loans, however, were available to a much narrower range of small businesses than in Germany and could not be accessed through application to the banks, making it much more difficult for the firms to apply. The scale of subsidy was also much smaller than in Germany.[49]

CONCLUSION

From the 1950s and 1960s, *Mittelstand* firms' ability to grow and participate in the development of DQP was conditional on long-term finance. This was made available primarily through the savings and cooperative banks. What ensured the supply of long-term loans to small and medium-sized firms was the combination of strong bank competition and of state regulation. The establishment of regional and national bodies to collect and redistribute the deposits of savings and cooperative banks ensured both the supply of finance to regions and that small banks could continue to exist, supplying funds to smaller, local firms.

Throughout the post-war period the savings banks had the largest share of commercial lending and this put pressure on the other banking groups to compete. Furthermore, regulation gave savings and cooperative banks unique incentives to provide small and medium-sized firms with long-term funds. These banks had to operate in a limited market and their success was dependent on the long-term economic health of the area in which they operated. Moreover, these banks' charters and statutes determined that they should pursue profit, but only as a means to other goals. Savings banks were mandated with the promotion of the local economy, while cooperatives had to serve the interests of their members. For this reason these banks have been characterized as being rent-seeking institutions, rather than as profit maximizers.[50] Probably rent-seeking behaviour lead to the provision of too many services to firms, because these created jobs and managerial rewards. These rents in the case of savings banks also included the satisfaction of the local political leaders who governed these banks, as local firms' investment projects were financed.[51] Nevertheless, rent-seeking did not make these firms uncompetive. Since the early 1950s their ability to increase and maintain their market share of commercial lending validates this assertion.

The producers in the decentralized industrial systems that grew in the boom years were able to respond successfully to the challenges of the 1980s and continued to be supported by a vast range of institutions at the local level. The production, development, and marketing needs of these producers were supported in this very turbulent period by local network, reducing costs.[52] Regional banks provided capital and consulting advice to their small and medium-sized customers. By 1982, savings and cooperative banks, those closer to the *Mittelstand*, provided half (50.7 per cent) of all loans to industry (from 37.4 per cent in 1972). These banks also started offering advice on business strategy and technology as well as acting as an intermediary between small firms, to reassure potential partners of mutual reliability. Regional banks, including the savings banks, also set up 'capital participation corporations' (KBGs – *Kapital-* or *Unternehmensbeteiligungsgesellschaften*) in conjunction with regional governments to allow small and medium-sized firms to increase their indebtedness. These KBGs invested funds in firms but in the form of equity, owning a portion of the firm and receiving dividends, but without assuming any managerial role. By 1988, in North Rhine Westphalia savings banks had established twenty-six of these KBGs, involving 224 small firms. In the whole of the Federal Republic by 1989 there were almost sixty of these organizations, investing a total of DM2.7 billion in nearly 2,000 firms.[53]

The British government started pro-small firms' policies only in the late 1970s. Ten years later it spent about half a billion pounds of dedicated resources on the promotion of small and medium-sized firms.[54] The German government just before unification spent 1.8 billion pounds. Such a difference cannot be accounted for only by the fact that Germany had a larger population and a larger income per capita. In fact the two central governments spent similar figures, the big difference was the amount spent by the regional governments, an institution missing in Britain. While policies for small firms had been an integral part of economic policy in Germany since the end of the Second World War, in Britain they became important only in the late 1970s, although a Small Firms Department was established by the Department of Trade and Industry after the publication of the Bolton Report in 1971. The philosophy of the British government in its dealings with small firms was informed by its free market stance, and intervention to promote small firms was based on the notion that it should remove, or compensate for, market imperfections. Therefore, incentives for enterprises were really aimed at 'minimising taxation, regulation and red tape and providing commercial services... to improve their access to finance, information, professional advice and training'. The law to promote small and medium-sized firms in Baden-Württemberg, in contrast, included the provision of regional funds to, for example, promote technological innovation.[55]

During the period studied here, the German state has been instrumental in maintaining the segmentation of the banking system that ensured small firms had local supplies of finance. At the same time competition between different types of firms meant those firms that could grow could find a supplier to match their financial needs. There have been cultural, social, and political reasons why the German state has intervened in the economy in support of small firms. These reasons placed small firms at the heart of German cultural identity. This centrality explains the apparent contradiction of two parties, the CDU and the SDU, both pursuing very similar policies with regards small firms. Apart from these cultural reasons, neither party could afford to neglect these firms as their numbers gave their owners a substantial political voice.

NOTES

1   Edwards and Fischer, *Banks, Finance and Investment*, 83–5.
2   Piore and Sabel, *The Second Industrial Divide*.
3   Herrigel, *Industrial Constructions*, 149.
4   Ibid., 163.
5   Piore and Sabel, *The Second Industrial Divide*, 151 and 230–4.
6   The choice of regions is dictated by the information available. Herrigel, *Industrial Constructions*, 164–5.
7   Ibid., 167–8.
8   Fritsch, 'The Role of Small Firms in West Germany', 38–54.
9   Cooke and Morgan, *The Associational Economy*, 83–113.
10   Herrigel, *Industrial Constructions*, 257–62.
11   Streek, 'On Institutional Conditions of Diversified Quality Production', 35.
12   Ibid., 27.
13   Herrigel, 'Industry as a Form of Order', 120–2.
14   Streek, 'German Capitalism: Does it Exist? Can it Survive?'.
15   Beyenburg-Weidenfeld, *Wettbewerbstheorie, Wirtschaftspolitik und Mittelstands-foederung 1948–1963*.
16   Hollingsworth and Boyer, *Contemporary Capitalism*, 286.
17   On this point see also Streek, *Industrial Relations in West Germany*.
18   Bannock, *The Smaller Business*, 38–43.
19   Wengenroth, 'Small-scale Business in Germany',133.

20   Sauer, 'Small Firms and the German Economic Miracle', 84.
21   Bannock, *The Smaller Business*, 67 and 73. Although tax support for small firms improved after 1979 in Britain, see Bannock and Albach, *Small Business Policy in Europe*, 38.
22   Bannock, *The Smaller Business*, 37–57.
23   Djelic, *Exporting the American Model*, 109.
24   Berghahn, *The Americanisation of Western Germany*.
25   Djliec, *Exporting the American Model*, 168–71; also Denton, Forsyth, and Maclennan, *Economic Planning and Policies in Britain, France and Germany*, 59–60.
26   Ibid., 62.
27   Sauer, 'Small Firms and the German Economic Miracle', 85.
28   Ibid., 79.
29   Denton, Forsyth, and Maclennan, *Economic Planning and Policies in Britain, France and Germany*, 63–4.
30   Beckerman, *Das Handwerk in der Bundesrepublik Deutschland*.
31   Bannock, *The Smaller Business*, 51.
32   Deeg, *Finance Capitalism*, 22–4.
33   Bannock, 'Finance for Small Firms', 88–9.
34   For a description of the structure of ownership, names of banks and such like details see Owen Smith, *The German Economy*, 319–43.
35   Deeg, *Finance Capitalism*, 45.
36   Ibid., 47.
37   Ibid., 49.
38   Henze, *Grundriss für die Sparkassenarbeit: Grundzüge der Geschichte des Sparkassenwesen*, 120.
39   Deeg, *Finance Capitalism*, 47.
40   Ibid., 54.
41   This per cent declined steadily through the 1970s, to 31 per cent in 1979. However this decline could be the result of inflation as the data are compiled on the basis of total of business loans which do not exceed a DM1 commitment to any single firm; Bannock, 'Finance for Small Firms', 237–40.
42   Bolton Committee, *Report*, 142.
43   Bannock, 'Finance for Small Firms', 247–51.
44   Ibid., 252.
45   Ibid., 257.
46   Ibid., 266–7.
47   Francke and Hudson, *Banking and Finance in West Germany*.
48   Harm, *The Financing of Small Firms in Germany*, 15.
49   Bannock, 'Finance for Small Firms', 267.
50   Allen and Gale, 'A Welfare Comparison of Intermediaries and Financial Markets in Germany and the US'.
51   Deeg, *Finance Capitalism*, 116–17.
52   Herrigel, *Industrial Constructions*, 186.
53   Ibid., 187.
54   Bannock and Albach, *Small Business Policy in Europe*, 23.
55   Ibid., 34.

9

The Permanence of Small Firms in France

Before the 1970s, French economic history had been ready to recognize the central role played by small firms for most of the nineteenth century in terms of their contribution to technical progress, their capacity to satisfy a very diverse and fragmented demand, and their support role vis-à-vis large firms.[1] For the period between 1880 and 1950, however, historians have written about the survival of small firms mostly in negative terms. This survival has been attributed to the permanence of an imperfect, poorly integrated market, to the practice of large firms to decentralize some of their production to smaller firms to maintain flexibility in times of low demand, and to the protective role played by governments, interested in preserving small firms for political and social reasons. In this interpretation small and medium-sized firms lost any dynamic element, provided no positive contribution, and were relegated to the periphery of a dual economy. In the main, the historiography on the economy of post-war France has focused on the development of large-scale, integrated firms and on how French business adapted itself to the American model. Much of this literature has concluded that French business was 'backward' in its adoption of modern methods of manufacturing.[2] In this perspective the modernization and growth of the economy in the post-war period has been attributed fully to the role of the state in fostering strategic sectors and to the opening up the economy to world markets.[3] This historiography has not considered small and medium-sized firms as central to this process.

However, since the crisis of large firms in the 1970s, small firms' contribution to France's economy has been revised in much more positive terms.[4] This historiography has shown that, rather than being archaic leftovers, small firms in the inter-war period were central to the economy. Moreover, their permanence meant that during the expansionary years between 1950 and 1973 they were able to supply increasing levels of demand oriented towards diversified products with a short 'shelf life'.[5]

Although statistics show an increase in the trend towards the concentration of the French economy up to the late 1970s, these figures are misleading.[6] The nineteen sectors of the economy where concentration was at its highest, such as mining, electricity generation and distribution, defence, and synthetic fibres, accounted for 10 per cent of the people employed and for 14 per cent of turnover. Even by including those sectors where concentration was lower, such as iron and steel, glass-making, and electrical equipment (where four firms accounted for 30–49 per cent of total employed and turnover), these firms accounted for 22.5 per cent of the employed and for 28.5 per cent of turnover, leaving more than two-thirds of the working population and more than 70 per cent of turnover to be generated by sectors where concentration was very weak, even non-existent. Thus, while large firms were certainly important in some sectors, their impact on the economy as a whole was modest. For most of the century the share of the largest firms in manufacturing output did not increase, not even during the boom years from 1955 to 1963. In fact output by large firms was decreasing in those sectors which experienced the fastest growth, for example in electrical and mechanical engineering and in pharmaceutical industries.[7] Moreover, many of the largest firms did not grow thanks to market forces but because of state intervention and their activities have not always been successful, as in the case of aeroplane production. Some of the sectors where small and medium-sized enterprises were predominant in the late 1970s were some types of chemical production, farm machinery, machine tools, high-precision instruments, building material, pharmaceuticals, metal working, food, textiles, clothing, leather, and wood. A few of these sectors can be defined as 'traditional' but the others are clearly characteristic of a modern economy.[8]

Table 9.1 shows that far from being marginalized, small and medium-sized firms remained a central feature of the economy. In 1962 France had 61.4 per cent of its labour force in firms employing fewer than 500 people, while this figure was 54 per cent in Germany and 33.2 per cent in Britain.[9] Moreover, the most authoritative study of France's post-war economic performance by Carré, Dubois, and Malinvaud, shows how during the 1950s and 1960s small and medium-sized firms performed better than

Table 9.1. France: distribution of the workforce according to industrial plant size, 1936–66 (%)

	1936	1954	1962	1966
0–4	33	19	16	14
5–10	6	6	5	6
11–20	6.1	6	6.3	6.4
21–100	16.5	21	22.1	23.2
101–500	18.3	23.3	25.3	26.4
500+	20.1	24.7	25.3	24
Total	100	100	100	100

Source: Lescure, 1999, 146.

large ones in terms of growth of turnover and profitability. The firms that experienced the highest rates of growth of turnover were the medium-sized ones employing between 20 and 500 people.[10] This suggests that small firms in France were able to make the transition to medium-sized firms without experiencing the same barriers to growth that their British counterparts did.[11] Small firms grew thanks to the strategy of innovation and of occupying niche markets that enabled them to occupy leading positions in new and large consumer markets (e.g. *Camping-Gaz*, *Bic*, *Poclain*, and *Rossignol*). In the 1970s, successful small firms moved to the supply of those parts of the market not reached by mass producers through batch production. In other words the key to their survival was specialization.[12]

THE ENVIRONMENT FOR SMALL FIRMS

The growth of small and medium-sized firms in France up to the mid-1970s took place in a political climate of apparent hostility. The men who took over the management of the economy in the post-war period saw small firms as anachronistic and believed that a modern economy should equip itself with large production units. The investment programme of the Monnet Plan (1945–52) was oriented towards large-scale firms (mostly newly nationalized) in the staple industries such as coal, electricity, steel, transport, cement, and farm machinery. Until the Seventh Plan of 1973, the plans that followed Monnet's promoted mergers and industrial concentration.[13]

During the 1950s and 1960s the French economy experienced its fastest rates of economic growth. Growth was lower than that experienced by Germany and Italy but higher than in Britain. Post-war growth took place without a substantial change in the degree of concentration of industrial production that had been in effect at the beginning of the century.[14] From the beginning of the century to the depression of the 1930s the very large firms grew bigger still, though this trend slowed down after 1930, until the end of the Second World War. Between 1946 and 1955 this trend reappeared mostly as a consequence of nationalization[15] but was interrupted until 1965, after which the trend in concentration seems to have involved the medium-sized firms rather than the larger ones. By the mid-1970s the concentration of establishments (excluding the nationalized industries) was less advanced in France than in other major industrial nations.[16]

Until 1973 the planners' intention was that the process of concentration should accelerate as this was seen as the best way to make French industry more competitive internationally. Mergers were encouraged through loans, bonuses, and tax concessions.[17] Until the Seventh Plan of 1973 the planners did not doubt the capital and technological advantages that large scale would bring or that mass production would allow France to compete in the Common Market. Mergers took place alongside the policy of encouraging the creation of shared subsidiaries to replace the interwar cartels, more difficult to sustain in the new legislative framework of the Common Market. However, even though the state's incentives helped, it is likely that this process of concentration would have taken place anyway, thanks to the opening up of markets in the post-war period.[18] In sectors considered strategic by the government, such as steel, an effort was made to force the creation of national champions, firms equipped on a scale for international competition. Mergers were encouraged because more concentrated sectors made it easier to select 'winners'. Although the aim of these mergers was to create multidivisional companies, they often resulted in poorly organized structures with much more resemblance to the financial holdings of the interwar period.[19] In steel, for example, the government forced waves of mergers but rational internal management was never established effectively. The state's technocrats had no clear idea of how a modern competitive corporation ought to be managed and as a result they encouraged business–state links that were more suited to the purposes of government procurement than to creating structures capable of competing in international markets.[20] By the early 1970s, the poor performance of the state's 'champions' led to a drastic shift in policy. The Seventh Plan in 1973 insisted on the need to take measures which would favour the growth of small and medium-sized firms[21] and these firms came to be seen as an innovative and necessary counterpoint to the excessive power of multinationals. Small firms were not a 'relic of the past' anymore.[22]

Chapter 4 showed the nature of the political and economic climate that allowed small firms to prosper in the interwar period. Before the Second World War French businessmen, and even business leaders, such as Eugène Schneider, who owned one of France's largest steel companies, saw small and medium-sized firms as guarantors that 'economic and social relations would not become unbearable and inhuman'.[23] The permanence of French industrial structures before 1939 was a reflection of the rigidity of the social order, where the social stigma attached to bankruptcy dwarfed ambition and eliminated risk-taking behaviour, thus preventing change from taking place. The state's role in this was to act as a further stabilizing element, allowing cartels and ententes to grow. At this time the policies of the French state and the interests of the business community were perfectly matched as a consequence of the relatively homogeneous character of the French elites. The men in charge of economic and financial policy were the sons of the bourgeoisie, linked through social networks and marriage to the captains of industry. Therefore it is hardly surprising that political institutions adapted their policies to create the stability that the industrial community desired.[24] Those who looked to America as a source of inspiration in terms of production and management innovation were unable to diffuse their ideas because they were not part of the decision-making process. At the time the USA was perceived as a country where the economy shaped social institutions and cultural values and not the other way round; a country where the 'materialist religion' was predominant. Mass production was seen as sacrificing quality for quantity. One of the most influential books of the time, *Les Etats Unis d'aujourd'hui*, written in 1927 by André Siegfried, then dean of the school that trained civil servants and politicians, the *École Libre des Sciences Politiques*, rejected the American model on social, cultural, and political grounds. He argued that mass production and consumption reduced the individuality of workers and consumers, inducing human homogenization and heralding the triumph of the mass, threatening bourgeois values.[25]

The experience of the Second World War, marked by the loss of the war followed by German occupation and by the collaboration of the Vichy government, induced a profound sense of national identity crisis. As a consequence post-war France came to be shaped by a small group of modernizers who saw the American model as the most likely to succeed. The coalition led by De Gaulle defined itself in terms of opposition to the previous regime and its structures, including economic ones fostered by that regime. In particular the structure of French industry was blamed for the country's crushing defeat and America's system of production became the only possible model for the modernization of the economy.[26]

By the end of 1947 a small group of men linked to the American allied forces had gained control of key institutions. The French modernization drive started from the core of the state and only later spread to French industry. Jean Monnet created and ran a new body, the *Commissariat Général du Plan* to establish and coordinate the State's intervention in the economy. The *Commissariat*, modelled on the American War Production Board, was the first attempt at institutionalizing an American interpretation of Keynesian thought. The men who worked with Monnet had been carefully selected for their familiarity with American models and their belief in the necessity of economic and industrial modernization based on the large, mass-producing industrial corporations and high levels of labour productivity. Economic planning in the guise of the first *Plan de Modernisation et d'Equipment* in 1946 was to achieve the allocation of resources and the renovation of productive structures to increase productivity by launching vast investment programmes in basic industries, especially in the nationalized enterprises.[27] The *Commissariat* was able to become a central institution thanks to its links with the Treasury (the sort of link that the British planning body, the National and Economic Development Council, never had). This traditional administrative body was pushed to adopt a more positive role in the restructuring of the French economy by its new chairman François Bloch-Laîné, appointed in 1947.[28] The need to provide the state's administration with civil servants who would promote the creation of a new France led to the establishment in 1945 of the *École National d'Administration*, soon taken over by the modernizers of the *Commissariat* and of the Treasury. The nationalization of basic industries and of credit institutions between 1945 and 1946 gave the French state the power to have direct influence on the economy and on the shape on industry.[29]

The pervasiveness of the American example can be seen in the popularity achieved in the 1960s by Servan-Schreiber's book *Le Defi Americain*. The book asserted that Europe and France were in decline and that this decline could only be arrested by looking at America's methods of production. At the time the book's huge popularity derived from the fear that the American 'way of life' was taking over France because of its depiction as a dynamic society dedicated to social mobility, equality, and individual responsibility. America was represented as a country that invested in human beings through the promotion of education. All these things were clearly perceived as being absent in French society and as the elements that gave America its competitive advantage. The American challenge could only be met by creating a European federation where companies could build giant factories, as European (and especially French) companies were too small. Servan-Schreiber pointed at Britain as the only country that was making the right investments, in electronics, nuclear energy, and aviation.

It would be, however, a mistake to see the post-war period as one where the transformation of the economy was a linear trajectory involving rejection of small-scale enterprise and adoption of the multidivisional corporate firm. After the war, the French political executive had to achieve economic growth while containing the political opposition from sectors of the economy and society which felt threatened by the modernizing agenda.[30]

The project of the French modernizers, based as it was on large-scale enterprises, implied the disappearance of the traditional small family firm. The promotion of mergers to ensure the creation of large-scale production units run by managers rather than owners became one of the priorities of the First and Second Plan. This strategy, however, was not without opposition. The most prominent federation of business associations, the *Conseil National du Patronat Français* (CNPF), created in 1945, despite consisting mostly of large firms, was opposed to the modernizing agenda as it feared too much government intervention and the threat of nationalization. Its divided views made the CNPF an ineffective instrument of collective action.[31] Instead the *Confédération Génerale des Petites et Moyennes Enterprises* (CGPME), created in 1944 under the leadership of Léon Gingembre, had a much clearer and united opposition to the modernization agenda, seen as a direct threat to the survival of family capitalism. The CGPME represented 50 per cent of French industry, 95 per cent of the retail trade, and employed 48 per cent of French labour.[32] They saw themselves as representing not just a substantial part of the economy, but also French social order. The political power of small businesses was particularly strong after 1947 as the high proportion of working-class voters who supported the communist party reduced the potential con-stituency on which governments depended and therefore made petit-bourgeois voters more important.[33]

In the early 1950s the CGPME started a violent campaign against the *Commissariat du Plan* using the control it had over a number of local and national newspapers or magazines. The Plans were attacked as being socialist and anti-democratic, harmful to the thousands of workers who would be affected by the closure of small and medium-sized firms. The political strategy of the CGPME was to use its substantial weight as a pressure group to bring to power a man who would defend family capitalism, exploiting the fragility of the coalition government. In 1952 the election of Antoine Pinay as prime minister, himself a small business-man, was a victory for the CGPME, as Pinay represented the France of farmers, family firms, and craftsmen.[34] The opposition of the National Assembly to the restructuring of French industry and to the end of family firms, and the fragility of the government (the Pinay government fell at the end of 1952) meant that the Second Plan was modified to include some concessions for small firms.

Although small firms had lost the political position and weight that they had had before the war, their opposition reached into the very core of the 'republican synthesis'.[35] The revolt movement that formed in the 1950s around Pierre Poujade, a small businessman, and which in 1956 attracted two and a half million electors provides a good example. The Poujadists portrayed the Plans and their emphasis on large-scale corpor-ate business as attempts to uproot the country's tradition. The Plans' 'progressive' efficiency manifesto was just propaganda aimed at elimin-ating small firms, shops, and farms, they argued. The Poujadists instead used the language of individualism and freedom that included crafts-manship and the personal service of small shopkeepers.[36] Although the movement quickly subsided, this was not a sign that the 'republican synthesis' had collapsed in the wake of the modernizers' success in reducing the weight of the more traditional sectors in the economy, as claimed by Stanley Hoffman in 1963.[37] Instead the French state found a way of resolving the conflict between 'modernizers' and 'conservatives' by directing financial resources to both groups. This meant that economic planning with its bias towards large-scale concentrated industry coex-isted alongside financial incentives for small firms, guaranteeing their survival.

From 1948 onwards the special taxes on business mergers were progressively reduced. In 1954 a tax incentive was introduced for firms reaching specialization agreements designed to encourage the mass production of a more limited number of articles.[38] In the same year a number of funds were established to give loans at lower interest rates to firms to encourage concentration of production units and to decentralize.[39] At the same time, however, small firms received preferential loans at subsidized rates and were taxed differently and less than large businesses because the forfeit system which small firms could adopt (instead of income declaration) lent itself to the underassessment of their incomes.[40]

The State used financial institutions as instruments of economic growth to deliver financial incentives to different categories of firms and to achieve its various economic goals, including the protection of the middle classes. A distinctive feature of France's 'state capitalism'[41] was the creation of specialized credit institutions such as the *Crédit Agricole*, the *Crédit Populaire*, the *Caisse des Dépôts*, and the *Crédit National*. The *Caisse des Dépôts* held all the funds accumulated in local savings banks, the pension funds of the nationalized industries and any unspent tax revenue. Its main function was to turn these highly liquid savings into medium-term credits for industry in collaboration with the *Commissariat du Plan*. In contrast, the *Crédit National* was a semi-public bank created to supervise medium-term credit. Its activities filled the gap left by the banks, who were unwilling to hold large amounts of fixed assets. The *Crédit National* guaranteed medium-term loans up to five years (extended to seven years under the Fifth Plan in 1970) to clients of the commercial banks. The commercial bank then proceeded to grant an automatically renewable short-term credit which could then be discounted at the *Crédit National*.[42] The *Crédit Populaire* and the *Crédit Agricole* became the banks that lent to small and medium-sized enterprises locally.[43] To favour growth while mediating and reducing political conflict, the state used finance as a weapon. As Zysman has written: 'The government might have adopted "To each his subsidy" as its motto.'[44]

Financial incentives, however, were not simply tools used by the state to 'neutralize' the political opposition of small-scale business. Viewed in this way what happened in France in the 1950s and 1960s would be just the story of a battle between a modernizing, centralized state and a traditionalist periphery, when in fact the picture is more complex. When de Gaulle returned to power in 1958, the nationalist conservative coalition that ran the country represented small business while simultaneously the concentration of power in the hands of a strong executive excluded them. The political leaning of most small businesses trapped them (and their representatives) inside a conservative majority, but they also held the fate of the conservative alliance in their hands. Conservative victories came to depend on the votes of those economic marginals, representatives of a traditional France that the modernizing forces within the state were supposedly committed to displace.[45] As a result nobody won a clear victory and small businesses were protected. Stephen Cohen has pointed out that the state's protection of small business meant that 'Once-powerful social groups were held in line politically so that they could not dismantle the growth machine.... Gaullism kept the powerful but vulnerable forces of the French past politically impotent, while the market displaced them.'[46] However, while politically small firms did go quiet after the Poujade events there is very little evidence that the market displaced them.

After 1972 small establishments acquired a new importance in manufacturing industries. Between 1972 and 1982 plants employing between ten and forty-nine people increased their volume of employment but also their share of the total. Large plants instead suffered a decreasing share of industry employment. By 1982 the distribution of employment by size of plant was the same as it had been twenty years earlier. The resurgence of small firms took place across the board as the smallest plants increased their share of employment in seventy-seven of forty manufacturing sectors. Plants with ten to forty-nine employees increased their share by more than 10 percentage points in six sectors, and in four of these sectors small plants had suffered a substantial decrease in employment share between 1962 and 1972. The pervasive vitality of small firms is consistent with Sabel and Piore's hypothesis that the world had entered a period of decentralized technological change.[47]

Moreover, 'Americanized' planning on the part of Jean Monnet and his men did not result in a wholesale adoption of American methods of production, as shown in the case of steel production. In the First Plan of 1946 the steel industry, through its producer associations, received the largest single share of public investment in the private sector (16 per cent).[48] Nevertheless, the industry modernized following its own impulses. The Wendell steel group refused to install a continuous strip mill for fear of overproduction. Instead the adoption of large-scale American style production was the result of the actions of a few optimistic entrepreneurs, such as René Damien of Usinor and the head of Renault, Pierre Lefaucheux. The other producers followed reluctantly. The 'modernizers' had a specific perception of the American model, and it is their interpretation of American production technology, management methods, and market order that shaped how these were adapted to the French context.[49] The same process of adaptation can be observed to have taken place with another one of the Plan's champions, Pechiney the aluminium-makers.[50] Planning had made individual enterprises structure themselves in such a way as to facilitate the capture of government's funding and support. This was done most efficiently by concentrating production in a few enterprises. In the reconstruction period this strategy was market compatible, as expanding markets seemed able to absorb mass production goods. But by the 1960s the pursuit of competitive advantage suggested a strategy of deconcentration, however much the persistence of government initiatives encouraged the opposite.[51] Government compensation for poor economic performance, the very source of its early success, was now the chief obstacle to France's adaptation.[52]

PERMANENCE OF STRUCTURES AND SUPPORT FOR SMALL FIRMS

Although between 1945 and 1973 the State's economic priority expressed by the various Plans was to promote the growth of the corporate sector, this did not exclude efforts to improve the productivity of small firms. The policy of regional development launched in the 1950s had also the aim of helping small and medium-sized enterprises to modernize their management and equipment. In 1955, the *Fonds de Développement Économique et Sociale* (Funds for Economic and Social Development) were established to provide loans to firms who wanted to modernize their equipment. The policy was designed specifically to help small and medium-sized enterprises and fill the gap left by the weakening of small local banks.[53] Between 1955 and 1961, fifteen regional development companies were created to acquire minority interest in regional small and medium-sized enterprises and to grant them long-term loans.[54] However, the impact of these organizations was limited and their operations grew slowly. They were also rather unprofitable as the banks (who held 45 per cent of their capital), tended to see them as potential competitors and limited their growth by selecting their clients among firms that they did not want because they were too risky.[55]

As shown in Chapter 4 the Depression hit local and regional banks hard and many had to close. After 1945 the number of local banks declined more rapidly, mostly through a process of concentration as they pursued a strategy of associating and in some cases affiliating themselves to one of the national banks. In 1947 there were still 209 local banks, but by 1971 there were only sixty-nine left.[56] In 1957 the French banking system included the four largest deposit banks, the *Crédit Lyonnais*, the *Société Générale pour favoriser le développement du Commerce et de l'Industrie en France*, the *Banque National pour le Commerce et l'Industrie*, and the *Comptoir National d'Escompte de Paris*. All these four banks had national networks of branches and were all nationalized in 1945. The other two large deposit banks, the *Crédit Industriel et Commercial* (CIC) and the *Crédit Commercial de France*, were not nationalized. Both were Parisian banks, but the CIC headed a large group of regional banks and the branches of the group covered the larger part of the country, while the second one had a smaller coverage. Of the twenty-two regional banks left the largest one was the *Crédit du Nord*, a regional bank but also the fifth largest in France. The *Crédit du Nord* grew to such an extent even without becoming a national bank, thanks to the region in which it operated. Apart from Alsace and Lorraine there was nowhere else in France with such a wealth of resources and diversity of economic activity. During the years of rapid economic growth the bank lent to coal mining, metallurgical industries, textiles, chemicals, and a large number of smaller industries, including food processing as this was also a rich agricultural region.[57]

The strength of the other regional banks also reflected the strength of their regions. There were some other very large regional banks, such as the *Société Lyonnaise de Dépôts*, the *Société Marsellaise*, the *Crédit Industriel d'Alsace et de Lorraine*, the *Société Nancéienne*, the *Société Générale Alsacienne de Banque*, the *Crédit de l'Ouest*, the *Banque L. Dupont et Cie*, and the *Banque Scalbert*. Apart from the *Société Marseillaise* none of these, however, were independent like the *Crédit du Nord*, but were all associated with the CIC, apart from the *Société Générale Alsacienne*, which was associated to the *Société Générale*. Alsace and Lorraine had two large regional banks and a number of smaller local banks. This was a region with a varied economy, supplied with power, coal and iron, iron and steel, and a large engineering industry. There was also a well-established textile industry and clothing and leather goods were produced locally as were glass and ceramics. Timber, wool products, and paper were also important. There were also a large number of food processing industries, brewing, distilling, sugar refining, confectionery, tobacco, wines, and fruit. Lyon had its silk industry but also important were metallurgical and chemical products, and mining and engineering centres, and the Rhone Valley with its wine. The *Crédit Lyonnais*, one of the national banks, had its origins here, but the region's economy was served by a regional bank, the *Société Lyonnaise*. The Marseilles area also had its own independent regional bank and many smaller, local banks. Apart from being the leading seaport in France, Marseilles had many local industries, the main one being the manufacture of edible oils and soap. Most of the firms making these goods were small concerns which resorted to local bank credit. The Valley of the Loire was served by the *Banque Regionale de l'Ouest*, by the *Crédit de l'Ouest* and by the *Banque Hervet*, while the *Crédit Nantais* operated in Nantes and mostly in Britanny. The Valley of the Loire, as one of the most fertile in France, had a large food processing industry, while in Nantes there was shipbuilding and engineering. Another agricultural region, Normandy, also had its own regional bank, the *Crédit Industriel de Normandie*.[58] Unlike English banks, French banks granted a substantial proportion of their total credits in the form of discounts even for medium-term loans as these were seen as more liquid. The overdraft was used much less frequently than in Britain and it was customary for French businessmen to use more than one bank and for banks to associate to cover larger than usual loans. Had it not been for the re-discount facilities, the French banks would have been unable after 1945 to meet the growing demand for credit from all sectors of the economy.[59]

Apart from the twenty-two regional banks, in 1957 there were still 158 local banks, most of which were very sound. This was thanks to the strong hold they had over the local market, a consequence of French individualism and local patriotism. This was well understood by the CIC group, and its strategy was to associate with regional and local banks rather than take them over. Most importantly, the local and regional bankers had been able to survive thanks to their special knowledge of the locality and their willingness to grant credit to local businesses, which to the large Parisian banks, without local roots, seemed too risky. In 1957, observing the activity of the French banks, a contemporary commentator remarked that

The local man, with his special knowledge both of the parties and of the local economy would be able to judge these risks more surely. Many of them granted medium and long term credits to assist the development of local industries that may have seemed too small to attract the interest of the large banks.[60]

The state's increased intervention in the economy after the Second World War included the role that the semi-public and public banks had to play to stimulate investments. In this context the Popular banks became the suppliers of medium-term funds to the middle classes, and to small and medium-sized enterprises. In 1947, Léon Gingembre, the founder and leader of the *Confédération des Petites et Moyennes Entreprises*, was also a member of the board of the *Caisse Centrale de Crédit Hôtelier* (this collected the funds of the Popular banks for medium-term lending) while at the same time the representative body of the banks, the *Chambre Syndicale,* had very strong links with the *Confédération* based on shared aims and interests.[61]

The *Chambre Syndicale* played a very important role in the negotiations between the Popular banks and the government at the beginning of the credit controls after 1948. The autonomy and decentralized character of the banks made it difficult for the *Conseil National du Crédit* (CNC) to force the restrictions and lengthy negotiations between the *Chambre* and the Treasury eventually led to an admission that the credit restrictions went against the banks' role as supporters of small and medium-sized enterprises and that these harmed the small firms.[62] Throughout the 1950s, as the measures imposed on the banking system to curb credit became harsher, the *Chambre* mediated between the CNC and the Popular banks that refused to comply with the restrictions. By presenting themselves as the champions of small firms, and with the support of Léon Gingembre, the banks obtained a relaxation of the restrictions with regards to the supply of medium-term funds to small firms.

The other channel used by small and medium-sized firms to access credit was through the *Sociétés de Caution Mutuelle* (SCM). These were placed under the control of the *Chambre Syndicale*. The main role of the SCM was the supply of medium-term credit to the members of the same economic group who provided each other with guarantees. By virtue of these mutual guarantees this organization had a strong local and regional character and they guaranteed medium-term credit for small and medium-sized firms through the creation of a number of groupings such as that for steel, chemical, metalwork and building industries. In 1946 there were sixty SCM and their number had increased to 288 in 1973.[63]

The Popular banks' success in defending their interests and those of their clients was due to the favour with which they were looked on by the Ministry of Finance, and in particular by its Minister, Valerie Giscard d'Estaing, despite the opposition of the *Banque de France*. It was thanks to Giscard d'Estaing that the Popular banks were able to extend their activities when in 1962 a change was made to their statute, allowing them to extend deposits and medium-term credit to all the *'professions libérales'* (defined by the Treasury as doctors, lawyers, architects, dentists, midwives, pharmacists, accountants, and vets). This change really made the Popular banks the banks of the middle classes and greatly increased their resources. The Popular banks, however, did not meet with the favour of the *Conseil National du Crédit* (CNC), the body run by the Ministry of Finance and by the *Banque de France* to supervise the entire credit system. This can be seen in the control that the CNC imposed on the extension of branches during the 1950s. Each request had to be passed from the bank to the CNC through the *Chambre* and more than half the requests were turned down. The composition of the CNC was the main reason for these vetoes, as it was controlled by the big Paris banks. This veto was lifted only in 1966 with the Debré law. By 1969 the number of Popular bank branches had increased to 1,250 from 697 in 1945.[64]

LOCAL BANKS AND SMALL FIRMS: A CASE STUDY

The case study of Annonay (Ardéche) after the Second World War provides some indication of the nature of the link between local banks and small firms and the role played by banks in the restructuring the local productive system. In Annonay in 1864 more than 4,100 people worked in manufacturing, mostly in leather, but also in paper and textiles. This was a strong case of 'induction technique' as leather could be used in the manufacture of bonnets and by-products of tanning allowed the production of glue and gelatines used for cardboard-making, while there were also connections between paper and cloth-making. In addition a number of local firms made machinery for these industries.[65] The local banks were the *Banque Béchetoille* and the *Ets. Mercier*, both created in the nineteenth century by local textile merchants. Up to the 1960s Annonay was a town dominated by small, family firms with a high degree of integration between them. Of the forty-seven firms employing more than ten people, twenty-seven had been founded before 1920 (and of these seventeen before 1900) and thirty-five before 1940. These thirty-five employed 95 per cent of the 5,500 industrial workers in the town. However, in the 1950s a process of restructuring started that led to high levels of concentration as many firms joined with others outside the region to safeguard their place on the national market. Many of the tanneries closed, while the textile industry increased in size. The mechanical sector became the dominant employer in the area in 1975, especially after Renault took control of Saviem in 1965. As a consequence the size distribution of firms changed. In 1964, 15 per cent of those employed worked in firms with fewer than forty-nine people, 52 per cent in firms employing fewer than 499 people, and 32.9 per cent in firms with more than 500 employees; in 1975 these figures had changed to 4.1 per cent, 43 per cent, and 52.9 per cent respectively.[66]

The leather industry had also undergone a process of concentration in the post-war period and most firms had been united as *Tanneries Françaises Réunies* (TFR). In 1974 the TFR announced that the Annonay factories would have to close because of international competition and bad management following the process of concentration. After the announcement the workers occupied the Town Hall and the municipality constituted a *Groupe d'Étude de la Tannerie* (GET) to work out a stragegy to save the tanneries. The GET was made up of the president of the Annonay Chamber of Commerce, the other major economic actors, industrialists, and representatives of the local banks *Béchetoille* and *Ets. Mercier*. The bankers were necessary to study the financial situation and contact the TFR banks. The end result of a complicated situation was the creation of the *Société des Tanneries d'Annonay*, a public limited company allowing 128 of the 500 workers to keep their jobs.[67] This case shows how 'a common local interest' united political forces that had been traditionally conservative and not especially involved in economic matters and local economic actors. This episode also prompted the Chamber of Commerce to redesign itself and take on a much stronger industrial role with a strong local emphasis, but connected with national bodies. The Chamber and the municipality moved from a passive defence of the status quo to become gatekeepers of the local economy.[68]

A later study conducted in Annonay analysed a sample of small firms of different ages and in different sectors, such as clothing, paper, mechanical, subcontractors to the car industry, and leather, all representative of the traditional district.[69] The aim of the study was to understand what forces aided these firms even after the intense process of concentration that had occurred in this area during the 1970s. Among other things the study showed the importance of the local banks for the firms, though internally generated funds were still the most important source of capital. Banks played an essential role in allowing these firms to survive the pressures of concentration especially in the case of the newer firms. To the extent that money was advanced even in the absence of guarantees, based on the entrepreneur's reputation. Even in the case of those firms that were most adamant not to lose their independence by using outside capital, during a difficult period *'ce sont les banques qui ont sauvé l'entre-prise'* (it was the banks that saved the firms), as one of the businessmen interviewed for the study stated.[70]

CONCLUSION

The reason why there was a revival of small and medium-sized enter-prises in France after the recession of the 1970s was that they had been very strong in the interwar period and after the Second World War. In 1931 French industry showed little evidence of concentration. The market capitalization of the largest firms of the time, Saint-Gobain and Alsthom, was no more than a fifteenth part of ICI or IG Farben.[71] At the same time two-thirds of all wage earners belonged to firms with fewer than 100 employees and 40 per cent to firms employing fewer than ten.[72] France's industrial structure was the result of a deliberate policy aimed at avoiding overproduction. In this climate small firms were seen as better for the economy than large ones, and with the state organizing agreements to fix prices and quotas there was no incentive to merge.

Instead, the post-war modernizing state perceived small and medium-sized enterprises as backward. Their political and economic importance, however, could not be dismissed as they covered many industries and many areas: textile centres in the Vosges, paper and leather systems in Annonay in the Ardéche, cutlery in Thiers, shoemaking in Fougères or Romans, small-scale metallurgy and the watchmaking industry in Franche-Comté, and the Lyon silk industry. Some small and medium-sized enterprise systems also became more visible in the post-war period, such as those in Brittany, Anjou, Choletais, Jura, Savoy, and Monts du Lyonnais.[73] It is not clear whether at the time the planners were able to perceive the contribution made by small firms to the economy. However, a retrospective assessment of the impact of the various Plans and of the performance of large firms suggests that the boom of the 1950s and 1960s was in large part sustained by small and medium-sized firms. To present the period from the economic boom to the oil crisis as one characterized by the clash between decentralized systems of production and the state's 'modernizing' attempts through its various Plans would be misleading.

The political voice of small firms meant that these had to become part of the state's management of the economy. Through public and semi-public institutions the state became the economy's banker, including small firms. Moreover, the association representing small firms allied itself with the Popular banks to reduce the impact of the credit restrictions.

The permanence of local systems of production was also supported by regional and local banks. Although these banks were often associated with larger banking groups they were not taken over by the Parisian banks because these understood the strength of local feelings and how these feelings gave local banks a competitive advantage.[74]

The recession of the 1970s showed that small and medium-sized enterprises had more resilience than major enterprises. The arrival of the Left in power in the 1980s with a new Plan which denounced the 'crippling gigantism' of large industrial groups recommended small and medium-sized enterprises as the 'leading edge of the economy'.[75]

NOTES

1 See, for example: Bergeron, *Les Capitalistes en France (1780–1914)*; Fohlen, *L'Industrie textile au temps du Second Empire*; Fohlen, 'Entrepreneurship and Management in France in the 19th Century'.
2 See, for example: Lévy-Leboyer, 'Le patronat français, malthusien?'; Lévy-Leboyer, 'The Large Corporation in Modern France'; Landes, *L'Europe Technicienne*, chapter on France; Lévy-Leboyer, *Histoire de la France industrielle*; Daviet, 'Some Features of Concentration in France'.
3 See, for example: Chadeau, *L'industrie aéronautique en France (1900–1950)*.
4 For an extensive bibliography see: Aniello and Le Gales, 'Between Large Firms and Marginal Local Economies: The Making of Systems of Local Governance in France'.
5 Lescure, *PME et croissance économique*, 7.
6 Chadeaux, 'La permanence des petites et moyennes enterprises en France au XXeme siecle', 22–3 and 26.
7 Caron, 'L'évolution de la concentration des entreprises en France au XXème siècle', 145.
8 Chadeaux, 'La permanence des petites et moyennes entreprises en France ou XXeme siècle', 24–32.
9 Lescure, *PME et croissance économique*, 146.
10 Carré, Dubois, and Malinvaud, *French Economic Growth*, 221.
11 Ibid., 336; between 1954 and 1966 for an increase of about a million in the number of industrial employees, 35 per cent worked for small establishments, 45 per cent for medium establishments, 20 per cent for large, and only 3.3 per cent for the very large establishments. Caron, *An Economic History of Modern France*, 280.
12 Lescure, *PME et croissance économique*, 150–1.
13 Lescure, 'SME in France, 1900–1975', 143.

14   Carré, Dubois, and Malinvaud, *French Economic Growth*.
15   Nationalization created either monopolies or oligopolies in mining, electricity, gas distribution, tobacco, iron and steel, while state intervention created private-public oligopolies in defence, shipbuilding, aeroplanes, oil and natural gas. See Chadeau, 'La permanence des petites et moyennes entreprises', 26.
16   Caron, *An Economic History of Modern France*, 166.
17   Caron analyses in depth the seven plans in chapter 13 of *An Economic History of Modern France*.
18   Ibid., 305.
19   Lévy-Leboyer, 'The Large Corporation', 118.
20   Zysman, *Governments, Markets and Growth*, 148.
21   Firms employing less than 499 people, and these at the time accounted for 40 per cent of industrial sales.
22   Caron, *An Economic History of Modern France*, 362.
23   Djelic, *Exporting the American Model*.
24   Ibid., 48–9.
25   Siegfried, quoted in Djelic, *Exporting the American Model*, 50.
26   Ibid., 71–4.
27   Kuisel, *Capitalism and the State*, 243–6.
28   What distinguished the 'modernizers' from their predecessors was not that they belonged to a younger generation, because Monnet was born in 1888, Sauvy in 1898, Bloch-Lainé in 1912, but that they held a different conception about the role of the state, seen by these men as an active promoter of growth, rather than as an arbiter between different factions. For biographical details and analysis of the economic philosophy of the men in charge of the modernizing agenda see Gueslin, *Nouvelle histoire*, 61–3.
29   Djelic, *Exporting the American Model*, 97–101.
30   Zysman, *Governments, Markets and Growth*, 101.
31   Djelic, *Exporting the American Model*, 238–9.
32   Ibid., 239.
33   Vinen, *France*, 120.
34   Djelic, *Exporting the American Model*, 241. Also Gueslin, *Nouvelle histoire*, 36–7.
35   Ibid., 63.
36   Kuisel, *Capitalism and the State*, 271.
37   Hoffman, *In Search of France*, 62.
38   Baum, *The French Economy and the State*, 237.
39   Although the size of the funds was quite small; ibid., 242–4.
40   Denton, Forsyth, and Maclennan, *Economic Planning and Policies*, 157–8.
41   Bouvier, *Un siecle de banque française*.
42   Denton, Forsyth, and Maclennan, *Economic Planning and Policies*, 159–66.
43   Bonin, *L'Argent en France depuis 1880*.
44   Zysman, *Governments, Markets and Growth*, 135.
45   Berger and Piore, *Dualism and Discontent in Industrial Societies*.
46   Cohen, 'Twenty Years of the Gaullist Economy', 241.
47   Adams, *Restructuring the French Economy*, 32–3 and 276–8.
48   Zysman, *Governments, Markets and Growth*, 108.

49 Kipping, 'A Slow and Difficult Process: the Americanisation of the French Steel-producing and Using Industries after the SWW', 233.

50 Cailluet, 'Selective Adaptation of American Management Models'.

51 Adams, *Restructuring the French Economy*, 247–8.

52 Ibid., 248.

53 Concentration had taken place among financial institutions as well and it had affected mostly local banks. Lescure, 'SME in France', 144.

54 Lévy-Leboyer, *Histoire de la France industrielle*, 378–9.

55 Lescure ' SME in France', 160–1.

56 Caron, *An Economic History of Modern France*, 296.

57 Wilson, *French Banking*, 27.

58 Ibid., 31–8.

59 Ibid., 96.

60 Ibid., 49.

61 Albert, *Les Banques Populaires en France (1917–1973)*, 315.

62 Ibid., 315–16.

63 Ibid., 330–4.

64 Ibid., 317–28.

65 Ganne, *Gens de cuir, gens du papier*.

66 Ibid., 7–16.

67 Ibid., 168–75.

68 Ibid., 174. Other examples of this process can be seen taking place in other regions such as Anjou and the Choletais. See: Minguet, *Chefs d'entreprise dans l'Ouest*.

69 Ganne, 'La Mutation récente de PME annonéennes'.

70 Ibid., 101–2.

71 Ganne, 'France: Behind Small and Medium-size Enterprises Lies the State', 119.

72 Kuisel, *Capitalism and the State*.

73 Ganne, 'France', 121–3.

74 Verdier, *Moving Money*, 24.

75 Ganne, 'France', 127.

10

Small Firms and *Made in Italy*

In the last decade, research on Italian economic growth has increasingly recognized the importance of the role that small firms have played.[1] The constant difficulties of the country's private and public industrial groups have further legitimized the view of those who see small and medium-sized firms and industrial districts as the heart of *Made in Italy*, the building block of a post-Fordist society, and creators of growth and exports.[2]

As in the case of the other countries in this study, Italy's small firms were not born overnight. However, their importance has only recently been incorporated into historical narratives that reject the notion of convergence of industrial systems towards one best way of production. A central part of this alternative view of industrialization has been the notion of the industrial district as a social and economic community of firms within a specific geographical area.[3] The success of Italy's small firms has been attributed to the existence of these localized economies specialized around the production of similar goods,[4] where firms cooperate in the productive cycle and benefit from external economies. By the end of the 1990s there were more than 200 industrial districts in Italy, specializing in the range of products that are at the core of *Made in Italy*: fashion, furniture, designer goods, from tiles to spectacles, but also machine tools and other engineering products, accounting for more than 40 per cent of total industrial employment.[5] The realization of the connection between locality and small firms came from the observation that between the 1970s and the 1980s industrial employment had increased predominantly in those areas not connected to the industrial triangle (Milano, Genova, Torino) and where small firms were a predominant feature. This observation resulted in a number of studies, pioneered by Arnaldo Bagnasco's *Le Tre Italie*, published in 1977.[6] This and other studies highlighted both the economic vitality of regions like Toscana, Marche, Emilia, and Veneto, which were engaged in the production of goods that had been considered traditional, and the legacy of the country's dualistic industrial structure.

Before these studies the permanence of small firms had been explained by economists and politicians as simply the result of the rapid growth of the country's large firms. Small firms were relegated to a place in the niches of the economy and to a supporting role as pools of employment and recipients of large firms' strategies of decentralized production to reduce the level of unionization. Italy's large number of small firms was seen as proof that the economy had not yet reached a comfortable level of maturity. By the end of the 1960s the growth of capital intensive sectors such as iron and steel, chemicals, cars, and oil refining suggested to some commentators that the days of Italy as a country of small firms were numbered.[7]

Table 10.1 shows how at the beginning of the 1950s Italy's industrial structure was polarized between large firms, those employing more than 500 people, and very small units of production. Over time this polarization became less marked because of a number of reasons. The main one is that in the 1950s and 1960s, far from occupying a marginal role in the economy, small firms had been producing consumer goods, those same goods that in the 1990s developed into *Made in Italy* products. Small firms were producing these goods independently from large firms, benefiting from the 'economic miracle', the fast growth of the Italian economy from

Table 10.1. Italy: employment by size of manufacturing firm, 1951–91 (%)

Number employed	1951	1961	1971	1981	1991
1–9	32.3[a]	28.0[a]	20.2	22.8	26.2
10–19	5.4[b]	7.3[f]	8.7	12.4	15.3
20–49	8.7[b]	11.6[g]	13.1	13.7	16.3
50–99	8.1[c]	10.1[c]	10.8	10.2	10.0
100–199	11.8[d]	12.4[h]	10.4	10.1	9.1
200–499	8.6[d]	9.1[i]	12.8	11.1	10.1
499 >	25.1[e]	21.5[e]	24.0	19.7	13.0

[a] Between 1 and 10 employed.
[b] The 1951 industrial census listed the size group 'between 10 and 50 employed'; the figure presented here is an estimate on the basis of the hypothesis that this category is divided in '10 to 20' and '20 to 50' in the same way as they were in the 1961 census.
[c] Between 51 and 100.
[d] The 1951 industrial census listed the size group 'between 100 and 500 employed'; the figure presented here is an estimate on the basis of the hypothesis that this category is divided in '100 to 200' and '200 to 500' in the same way as they were in the 1961 census.
[e] More than 500.
[f] Between 11 and 20.
[g] Between 21 and 50.
[h] This number is an overestimate as the 1961 census listed the category 'between 100 and 250 employed'.
[i] This number is an underestimate, as the 1961 census listed the category 'between 250 and 500 employed'.

Source: Barca, 1997, 270.

1951 to 1963, but also an integral component of that 'miracle'.[8] Moreover the growth of small firms during the 'economic miracle' was also in the capital goods sectors, on the back of the expansion of large capital intensive firms such as cars, steel, oil, rubber, chemicals, cement, and white goods. These firms all needed networks of subcontractors to expand production very rapidly without having to build even larger integrated plants. Small and medium-sized firms were able to expand production thanks to loans from banks which were available also because of the visible existence of demand from these big firms in full expansion. The 'economic miracle' also meant that compared to previous periods Italians ate better, dressed better, and could spend more money on furnishing their homes and on a building boom. All this implied increasing levels of consumption of consumer goods and the growth of the market for the country's light goods. During the 1960s the industrial sectors that grew faster in terms of numbers employed, apart from cars and rubber manufacture, were engineering, furniture, and shoes, all sectors with very high numbers of small firms.[9] These sectors also experienced increasing levels of exports. In 1970 Italy's share of world market in sectors where small firms were predominant such as leather products was 16 per cent, for textiles it was 10 per cent, 17 per cent for furniture, 24 per cent for clothing, and 54 per cent for shoes.[10] The successful activities of small firms during the 1950s and 1960s meant that after the crisis that enveloped the country's large industrial groups in the 1970s small firms were there to come to the rescue because they were already a dynamic part of the economy. From 1971 there was an increase in the number of the smaller units and of those employing less than fifty people, while all the other categories, especially the largest ones, reduced their importance in numerical terms. This was also the result of the crisis of mass production and of the process of decentralization pursued by the larger firms.[11]

THE POLITICAL ECONOMY OF SMALL FIRMS

During the interwar period the country had moved in the direction taken by the other industrialized countries with the (limited) development of large-scale, capital intensive firms. Nevertheless, the debate as to whether this was the best way for the country to industrialize had not abated. The argument flared up again in 1947 during the sessions on industry of the Economics Commission of the *Assemblea Costituente* (this was the body in charge of setting up the operating parameters of the new Republic). The evidence presented by industrialists and economists to the Commission shows the existence of a camp strongly critical of the state's constant support of industries such as iron and steel that could only survive thanks to this support.[12] This camp maintained that the alternative to large enterprise was development based on the type of industries in which the country had a competitive advantage in terms of capabilities, well-established agglomerates of small firms, and domestic and international markets.

After the war, the economic ideology of the leading political party, the *Democrazia Cristiana* (DC, or Christian Democratic party), was liberal but tempered by the values of Catholic solidarity. This group opposed the Americans' plans for a complete renewal of the country's economic structures, motivated by the need to avoid confrontation and conflict between the different social and economic groups which it represented, from the *Confindustria* (this body represented the interests of the larger industrial groups) to small artisan firms.[13] Even the opening up to the international economy was full of difficulties and conflicts between the central bank in the role of the 'modernizer' and the *Confindustria*, opposed in first instance to the abolition of tariffs.[14] The victory of those who wanted to open up the economy to the positive influence of foreign competition was rewarded by the spectacular performance of the country's exports. Exports to the European Community increased by 30 per cent every year between 1958 and 1963 and by 13 per cent every year to the rest of the world, with mechanical engineering goods and chemicals as the main exports.[15]

The structure of the Italian economy in the post-war period did not change markedly compared to the previous period, in the sense that the preponderance of small and medium-sized firms and low levels of concentration remained its main feature. In fact, the years of the 'economic miracle' between 1951 and 1963 saw a further reduction in the level of concentration thanks to rising levels of demand, increasing levels of technological innovation,[16] and the opening up of new markets. These factors led to an increase in the number of medium-sized firms and of oligopolistic competition between the larger companies.[17] Nevertheless, it would be misleading to present Italy as a case of 'capitalism without concentration'. In fact a more accurate picture would be one of polarization between hugely segmented and fragmented industrial sectors and an 'oligopolistic core' made of the country's largest groups, who have exercised huge economic and political power over the country's economy.[18] A substantial part of this 'oligopolistic core' was made of state-owned enterprises such as steel, chemicals, and energy.[19]

The state's management of the economy in the post-war period followed a model of centralized control of decentralized organizations (with the exclusion of the state-owned enterprises). In practice this meant the granting of special fiscal regimes for artisan firms and subsidized credit to industry, on condition that firms joined local associations and other regulatory bodies, such as chambers of commerce. In turn these bodies became weighty pressure groups, but also the conduit of the state's industrial policy.[20] The example of artisan firms illustrates this point clearly.

As in Germany with *Handwerk,* Italy's 'artisan' sector brought together a much more varied spectrum of firms than the simple notion of 'craft' would suggest. In the post-war period the *Associazioni Artigiane* (artisan associations) exercised a very important role in shaping the structure of Italy's industry. In 1956 the Law 860 recognized the existence of this sector, and in 1957 artisans were given access to health care and in 1959 to pension rights. These laws recognized the existence of small firms and of hundreds of thousands of workers who had set up their own activity in the years immediately following the end of the war. The reasons which led to the institutional establishment of small firms were in the first instance cultural and ideological. The importance of the smaller firms had been argued by some economists already at the beginning of the century, as a counterbalance to the proletarianization created by factories and as an alternative to the rigidity of large-scale production units. These ideas became the bedrock of the DC's attitude towards small firms in the post-war period. At the same time the country's second party, the *Partito Comunista Italiano* (PCI, the communist party), recognized the importance of small firms as part of its strategy to bring the *ceti medi* (the middle classes very broadly defined) closer to the party. In terms of their relationship with small firms, the main difference between the two parties was that the PCI saw them as the necessary counterbalance to the power of oligopolies, but nevertheless as terminally inefficient. It was only in the 1970s that left-wing economists started reassessing the positive aspects of small-scale production. These were not the only reasons for the support of small firms. In the immediate post-war period the government's monetary policy to stabilize the value of the currency was one of the factors that aggravated unemployment and social unrest. The newly created DC could not afford to follow a strictly liberal line and forgo the support of the mass of potential small entrepreneurs. The need for consensus led it to develop a responsive strategy that meant that the state became the vehicle to provide various social and economic groups with help,[21] hence the support given to the artisan firms with the law of 1956.[22] The reactive attitude of the state can be seen also in the fact that over the years the help given to the 'artisan' firms was extended as the definition of 'artisan' became fluid to include firms and not just the self-employed, so that more and more small firms came to benefit from increasing forms of tax relief and special dispensations in terms of the regulation of labour practices.

With the establishment of artisans as a category, artisan associations developed along party lines with the Communist association providing services in the 'red' regions and the Christian Democrat in the 'white' ones. The services offered, however, were similar: administrative services such as the registration with the local chamber of commerce and with the pension office, accounting and the preparation of tax documentation, requesting permits, registering patents, analysis of production costs, and legal assistance. In addition the associations acted as intermediaries with the banks.[23]

The political decision made by the DC to support small firms has been explained by Susan Berger, Alessandro Pizzorno, and others in terms of the 'uneasy stratum' thesis. This thesis sees small firms as not only backwards and inefficient but also reactionary, unstable in their alliances, and always ready for a Fascist adventure. Christian Democrats, they argue, have therefore supported small firms to appease them.[24] However, Linda Weiss maintains that while the so-called Fascist tendencies of small firms have yet to be proven, a more positive argument can be made to explain the support given to small firms. Also, the policies that have been implemented by the DC (and by the Communist administrations in the 'red' regions) have not just allowed small firms to survive but have made this sector expand and become stronger, not a policy consistent with the notion of the 'uneasy stratum'. Apart from the Artisan Statute of 1956, policies for small firms have included exemptions from income tax, subsidized loans, and regional development policy. Subsidized loans are a very good example to show how these have been instrumental in *increasing* the number of small firms. From the start of the loan scheme to artisan firms in 1953 to the end of the scheme in 1976, 2,388 billion lire of subsidised credit were invested in this sector, allowing more then 300,000 artisans to invest in new workshops, machinery, and equipment. Loan finance covered about 64 per cent of total investment requirements. At least 31 per cent of the loans allocated over the entire period led to the creation of new workshops, while the loans granted for machinery also led to the establishment of new workshops, as many artisans worked from their own homes and therefore only needed machinery to start their activity. As much as 80 per cent of soft loans to small and medium-sized firms was granted to firms employing fewer than 100 people and Weiss has calculated that seventy soft loans were granted for every 100 small industrial firms at the end of 1971. As a result of these incentives, Weiss has estimated that about 12,000 new small firms were established over the 1960–70 period. This figure is particularly significant if one considers that between the two census dates of 1961 and 1971, the number of small manufacturing firms increased by 16,000 units, from 42,700 to 58,700. This meant that 75 per cent of the increase in this sector was financed by government loan schemes, mostly located in the centre–north. Government policy towards small firms led to their promotion, not their being propped up. The fact that most of the loans went to those north-centre regions where small firms were preponderant shows that government support was not motivated (only) by getting votes or by appeasement. Weiss has called this motivation 'a more fundamental concern', the preservation of a particular class structure whose disappearance would have polarized Italian society between the industrial proletariat and a very small class of large business owners. An expanding *ceto medio* allowed the DC to occupy a large 'middle ground', which also included the expanding public sector and of course the growing state-owned industrial system. The DC's cultural preference for small ownership was in direct response to what was seen as the problem of the working class and of the rise in power of the Communist party. In the 1950s when most policies in favour of small firms were created, the rise of the Communist party made the support of a property-owning class, or a class of potential property owners a very desirable thing. Thus the DC in its 1946 programme for the new constitution declared that capital and labour must be brought together to 'deproletarianize' the workers and remake the middle class, by inducing as many as possible to become property owners. The party slogan declared: 'Non tutti proletari ma tutti proprietari' (Everyone property owners, not proletarians).[25] The Artisan Statute, for example, opened the door of the *ceto medio* to many unemployed or salaried workers, by giving them the means to become small entrepreneurs. Petit bourgeois producers, according to Weiss, acted as crucial stabilizing agents in a country where capital and labour had been sharply divided and where this division, in the years after the end of the war, seriously threatened the political system.[26]

Another reason for the growth in the number of potential entrepreneurs can be found in the inversion in the process of industrial concentration that had started in the interwar period. The employment share of firms with more than 500 workers had increased between 1927 and 1951 from 19 per cent to 25 per cent. By 1961 this share had gone back to pre-war levels, while the share held by small and medium-sized firms had increased. One of the reasons for this change during the 1950s was the restructuring which many large firms had to undergo in the post-war years, which led to large numbers of unemployed. These were men (mostly) who had acquired a solid experience of factory work and could, under the right circumstances, start their own activity. One of Bologna's largest mechanical firms, the ACMA (*Anonima Costruzioni Macchine Automatiche*), had faced the problem of reconversion to peace production by sacking a large number of its workforce but had subsequently developed subcontracting relations with those men who had set up their own activity. In Modena the crisis of Fiat Grandi Motori led to the creation of a large number of small mechanical engineering firms. In Castelgoffredo, near Mantova, the closure of one of the area's largest hosiery-making firms, employing more than 1,000 workers, led to the creation of many small firms, as former employees received knitting machines as part of their severance. Apart from these examples, the factor that created the pre-conditions for the growth of the small firm sector was the expansion of domestic demand. Between 1951 and 1961 domestic consumption increased by almost 5 per cent every year, and by more than 6 per cent in the case of consumer durables, such as furniture and white goods. With the creation of the European Economic Community (EEC) in 1957 exports increased as well and between 1959 and 1963 increased by more than 16 per cent every year. Small firms could benefit because most of them were part of local systems of production where different firms contributed to a different phase of production.[27]

BANKS AND SMALL FIRMS

The restructuring of the banking system after the war to create a decentralized system to strengthen local banks was part of the same set of policies devised to help the creation of the *ceto medio*. By providing this 'class' with its own financial channels the DC aimed to create a sort of 'decentralized capitalism' which would act as a counterbalance to the power of the large private business groups, which the DC wanted to avoid being too close to, or too reliant upon. The central bank, the *Banca d'Italia*, played a decisive role in this, as the governor of the Bank, Donato Menichella, saw the defence and strengthening of local banks as a way to balance the power of the larger banks and to spread risk. Decentralization and a segmented banking system were seen as elements that would increase stability, while a concentrated banking system would hinder economic growth.[28] Giuseppe Conti and Giovanni Ferri show the connection between the growth of the local banks and of the small firms in those parts of the country that have been defined as industrial districts.[29] Throughout the post-war period the national banks within industrial districts had a much lower share of the local market than in other areas.[30] Lower assessment, monitoring, and enforcement costs and economic and political connections between bank managers and local entrepreneurs suggest that within industrial districts credit has been abundant.[31]

Nevertheless in some cases these connections generated opportunistic behaviour, as in the case of Prato's savings bank at the end of the 1970s.[32] In other cases, the absence of 'virtuous' economic behaviour and of strong social networks has led those local banks entrenched in the local community, especially in the south, to charge higher interest rates than those of the national banks.[33]

Table 10.2 shows how after the Second World War the segmentation of the banking system persisted and that it was marked by a very low level of concentration. In 1946, when the Bank Law was updated, the view of the *Banca d'Italia* reflected that of the pre-war economists. The Bank believed that growth could be attained only if firms could access the credit market and that the role of the banks was to promote economic development (and full employment) through the granting of credit to concerns committed to increasing production.[34] The banking structure inherited from the 1930s, with its large number of institutions of various types and sizes, had to be defended as it guaranteed the diffusion of credit.[35] Therefore the Bank concluded that it was not advisable to privatize those banks which had been put under state control in 1936.[36] The connection between Italy's rapid economic growth and the role played by the banks was assessed by a rather critical observer, Raffaele Mattioli, the chairman of one of the largest banks, the *Banca Commerciale Italiana*. According to Mattioli the banks contributed to Italy's 'economic miracle' in the 1950s through the financial support given not so much to large firms but mainly to small ones.[37]

A consequence of this belief in the banks as agents of economic development was the shaping of regulations to restrain bank competition in order to protect the medium-size and small banks from the large national banks. The *Banca d'Italia* thought that the existence of small banks was important because of the assistance they gave to small and medium-sized firms which, it was felt, would otherwise be overlooked by the larger banks.[38] Therefore controls were needed to preserve a structure in which small banks, operating at regional or local levels, could coexist with the larger banks. Thus bank competition was restricted to prevent an increase in industrial concentration since it was felt that if the small firms were deprived of necessary credit they would be forced to merge with the larger firms.[39] The aim of the *Banca d'Italia* in granting permits to open new branches was to 'ensure a balanced distribution of various categories of banking institutions, such as to make room for the coexistence of decision centres at different removes from government power and

Table 10.2. Number of Italian banks by juridical type, 1938–74

	1938	1948	1956	1966	1974
Public law banks	5	5	6	6	6
Banks of national interest	3	3	3	3	3
Ordinary commercial banks	170	151	145	152	131
Popular banks	294	227	210	206	177
Savings banks	97	84	89	90	89
Rural and artisan banks[a]	1,151	756	730	787	663
Total	1,720	1,226	1,183	1,244	1,069

[a] The *Banca d'Italia* includes foreign banks in this figure.

Source: Banca d'Italia, *Bollettino Statistico*, various years.

thereby to avoid the drawbacks of excessive concentration'.[40] Further-more, the monetary institutions believed that it was against the public interest to permit competition that would eliminate banks by causing bankruptcy because of the social cost implicit in the loss of confidence in the system and because of the state's obligation to protect depositors' money.[41]

Unlike the British system where regulation rested on the banks' will-ingness to watch the 'governor's eyebrows', in Italy controls on the banks could easily be imposed by the monetary authorities thanks to the struc-ture of ownership of the banks and of the central bank. Following the Bank Law of 1936, the *Banca d'Italia*[42] was nationalized and its shares given to the savings banks, the Popular banks, the banks of national interest, and the state-owned insurance companies.[43] The bank was run by a board of directors and by the governor. The members of the board were representatives of the main provincial branches of the Bank[44] and were elected by the local shareholders (i.e. by the local banks which owned the shares of the *Banca d'Italia*), while the governor was appointed by the board following formal approval by the prime minister.

The Bank Law, apart from linking the *Banca d'Italia* to the banks and to the regions, also regulated the structure of ownership of the banks in such a way as to create a system of interlocking controls. The banks were either owned directly by the state (i.e. the three banks of national interest owned by IRI) or indirectly controlled by it through the shares owned by the banks of national interest.[45] The Popular banks also issued shares to their customers, though one individual could own only a very limited number of shares and in any case had the right to only one vote. The only banks that could be controlled by private industrial or financial groups were the ordinary commercial banks. Except for the boards of directors of the ordinary commercial banks, the other banks' boards usually comprised bankers from other banks and members of the municipal, or provincial, authorities, creating institutional links with the local community.

The main controls imposed on the banks were those limiting their credit activity to short-term lending and restricting competition, both by limit-ing the creation of new banks and opening new branches, and by pre-venting the merger of pre-existing credit institutions. At least until the end of the 1950s, the *Banca d'Italia* when granting the authorization to open new branches favoured credit institutions of a local or provincial-regional character, while at the same time pursuing the policy of limiting the further expansion of the bigger institutions to a few large or medium-sized centres.[46] In 1948 there was a total of 7,403 bank branches and by 1960 this number had increased to 9,157. Of these, 83 per cent were concentrated among the type of banks most accustomed to operating in small centres and with small customers, whereas only about 8 per cent of the authorizations were granted to the largest banks which, in the early

1950s, accounted for about 35 per cent of the deposits of the entire Italian banking system.[47]

The allocation of new branches among competing applicants was one of the biggest problems faced by the *Associazione Bancaria Italiana* (ABI—Italian Banking Association), which in the early 1950s was called in to give advice to the *Banca d'Italia*. One of the most important factors that had to be taken into account was the potential of the area. If the area could support another bank or branch the ABI was inclined to authorize the new entry, even when it prejudiced an existing bank. Another consideration was the branch status of the applicant. For example, if two banks wanted to open a branch in the same area, and one already had a branch in that area, the ABI was inclined to give the other bank a chance in order to avoid the presence of only one bank in a single place. The size of the firm applying was also an important consideration. If one bank was large and the other one small, the ABI considered whether the area had primarily large or small banks, and then made the allocation so as to redress the balance. The nature of the business demand in the community and the comparative ability of each of the applicant banks to satisfy this demand was also taken into account.[48] Though this system regulated competition by restricting the opening of new branches, it also promoted competition by ensuring the presence of more than one bank and of more than one type of bank in the same area.

Competition was controlled also through the limitation of the territorial area in which the banks could operate. The assumption on which the *Banca d'Italia* based its regulation of territorial expansion was that the granting of credit should be confined to a very specific area. This varied according to the size of the bank and on where its head office was. The banks of national interest (those directly controlled by IRI) were the only ones to have a nationwide organization. The other large banks (defined as such by the extent of their deposits) could operate in a whole region only if their head office was established in the regional capital, otherwise they could operate only in the province in which their branches were concentrated. The other banks could collect deposits and make loans in the province only if their head office was based in the main provincial town, otherwise their territory was limited to the municipality in which their branches were located.[49] For bank customers the area from which they could borrow was determined by the place of residence (personal borrowers) and by the legal domicile (firms). Banks were allowed to lend to a customer outside their area of competence only if the customer ran at least part of their activity within that area or if the intervention of the bank did not harm the banks situated in the area in which the lending operation took place and thus contravene the conditions of 'healthy competition'.[50]

Another important regulation of the activity of the banks was the imposition of a limit on the size of advances. The banks had to be authorized by the *Banca d'Italia* before they could grant a loan to a single customer which would bring that customer's total liability to the bank to over one-fifth of the paid-up capital and reserves of the bank. This regulation linked the size of the advances to the size of the banks, segmenting the market as small banks could only cater for small loans. The regulation of competition included also the regulation of prices to avoid price wars that would have eliminated the smaller banks. To control prices the Bank Law made the creation of a banking cartel compulsory. This practice although it created oligopolies was acceptable as it prevented the smaller banks having to offer rates on deposits that they could not afford in order to keep customers. In fact banks did go against the law and regularly broke the cartel, but this point will be discussed later in the chapter.

Alongside the genuine belief in the importance of small firms and small banks for economic development, it is reasonable to suppose that the monetary and political authorities had a more disingenuous reason for supporting these two sectors of the economy. Local banks could be used as political tools as the elected municipal authorities participated in the selection of the local banks' boards. The support given by those banks to small firms had an important political significance as the survival of the small firm was seen as a way of preventing people from leaving peripheral areas and changing local balances of power. This process was particularly evident in areas like Veneto and Piemonte, controlled by the Christian Democrats, or regions such as Toscana and Emilia Romagna controlled by the Communist party.[51]

The *Banca Commerciale Italiana*, the *Credito Italiano*, and the *Banco di Roma* were given the title of Banks of National Interest following the Bank Law of 1936. These were, and are, joint-stock companies and had branch networks which covered most of the peninsula. Until the privatizations of the 1990s their capital was owned directly by the state through the holding company IRI. These three banks occupied a position of preeminence as bankers to the very large industrial concerns, and also thanks to their foreign banking business. Until quite recently, these banks were reluctant to enter the field of small commercial and personal loans, which meant that the average size of their lending operations was higher than that of the other banks. In 1959 the average size of their advances, more than 10 million lire, was about nineteen times the average figure for the savings banks.[52]

The public law banks were foundations or public corporations that were between 50 and 400 years old. The largest of them, the *Banca Nazionale del Lavoro* was (until the 1980s) the only one to have a national network, whereas the other four, the *Banco di Napoli, Banco di Sicilia, Monte dei Paschi di Siena*, and *Istituto Bancario San Paolo di Torino*, were regional or at most interregional banks. Each of these banks had Special Sections, themselves organized as public corporations, which specialized in lending at medium- or long-term for special purposes (real estate, agriculture, public works and utilities, and industrial concerns), as will be described further on in the chapter.

The ordinary commercial banks were joint-stock companies and were the only banks in Italy to be controlled by private industrial and financial concerns. The ordinary credit banks varied greatly in size, from small units with a few offices to concerns with a hundred branches spread over many regions. The consolidated figures for the group show that their loans consisted of a large number of relatively small operations: the average size of advances was about a fifth of the figure for the banks of national interest. Until the middle of the 1970s the four most important of these banks were the *Banca Nazionale dell'Agricoltura*, the *Banca d'America e d'Italia*, the *Banco Ambrosiano*, and the *Banco di Santo Spirito*.

The differences in size within the Popular banks sector were even more striking than in the preceding group, as this group includes one of the country's largest banks, the *Banca Popolare di Novara*. No substantial difference exists between the activities of the ordinary commercial banks and the Popular banks, save for the preference the latter have shown for smaller deposits and the extensive granting of personal advances, remaining faithful to their traditional function as collectors of small savings and lenders to small enterprises.[53]

The savings banks were public bodies governed by special regulations. They were chartered corporations whose object was to promote the formation of savings and find suitable uses for them. The local authorities presided over the selection of the members of their boards. These banks were grouped together by law in regional or interregional federations. The object of the federations, which were corporate bodies with full legal status, was to coordinate the activity of the member banks, to fix their respective spheres of action, and grant assistance to the savings banks that were most in need of help. The savings banks carried out a great many small lending operations; at the end of 1959 they accounted for only 20 per cent of total loans and advances, yet they covered about 55 per cent of the total number of credit relationships over the whole banking system.[54] The largest savings bank was the *Cassa di Risparmio delle Provincie Lombarde* (CARIPLO).

The rural and artisan banks were cooperative banks in the form of either unlimited liability partnerships or joint-stock companies. They enjoyed particular popularity in small country towns and villages. In addition to clearly defined short-term lending operations, such as the discounting of bills, the opening of current accounts secured by government or equivalent securities or by bills of exchange, they were authorized to handle medium-term operations not exceeding five years in the form of unsecured and mortgage loans. These banks could also perform subsidiary transactions more in the nature of loans among farmers than of bank loans, such as purchasing farm machinery, tools, and products on behalf of members and acting as farm syndicate agencies for supplies to members.

As mentioned earlier, the banks within each group were not very homogeneous. Nonetheless, as the standard deviation around the mean of each group is not very large, they can be grouped by size of deposits and judicial nature. The group with the largest banks includes the banks of national interest and the public law institutes. This group is followed by that of the ordinary commercial banks, the only privately owned banks; and the last group comprises the smaller banks, the Popular banks, the savings banks and the rural and artisan banks. Table 10.3 shows the lending activity of the six groups.

The table shows how in 1960 the larger banks granted the largest average loans and accounted for most of the lending to the manufacturing sector. The smaller banks had the highest percentage of customers and the smaller average loans. The first group of banks conducted its business on a national scale but with a branch system limited to the capital towns of the regions and the busiest centres. The second and third group comprised much smaller banks but with a network of branches extending to the smaller urban and rural centres.

Table 10.4 shows the state securities held by the three groups of banks as a percentage of total assets in three benchmark years. The table shows that the group holding the highest concentration of small banks, group three, invested a lower proportion of its assets in state securities. This behaviour is consistent with the hypothesis that banks solely involved with local economies were more prone to invest in the private sector. This propensity also indicates that local banks were risk-takers to a higher degree than

Table 10.3.   Italy: bank lending to manufacturing, 1960

	Total lending (%)	Number of accounts (%)	Avererage size of loan (millions)	Number of banks	Number of branches
Group 1	53	26	18	9	2,097
Group 2	24	25	9	146	2,078
Group 3	23	49	5	1,112	4,845

Group 1 = Banks of national interest + public law banks.

Group 2 = Ordinary commercial banks.

Group 3 = Popular banks + savings banks + rural and artisan banks.

Source: Author's calculations from data in Banca d'Italia, *Bollettino Statistico*, 1960.

Note: The choice of 1960 for this table is for presentation purposes only as the picture does not change in other years.

Table 10.4. Italian banks, state securities as a share of total assets, 1950–70 (%)

	1950	1960	1970
Group 1	16	17	9
Group 2	18	15	8
Group 3	15	11	4

Group 1 = Banks of national interest + public law banks.
Group 2 = Ordinary credit banks.
Group 3 = Co-operative people's banks + savings banks + rural and artisan banks.

Source: Author's calculations based on data in Banca d'Italia, *Bollettino Statistico*, 1950, 1960, 1970.

the national banks. Another explanation could be that the larger banks were more involved in the financing of public debt, probably because their connection with the state was closer. Lending to manufacturing remained consistently above 40 per cent of the banks' total lending, changing from 60 per cent in 1949 to 44 per cent in 1972 as the country changed from being an industrializing economy to a fully industrialized one.

The shape of the modern Italian banking system has its origins in the Bank Law of 1936. Nonetheless the *financial* structure of the country emerged in the post-1945 period as the result of the intense debate that was sparked in 1946 by the Ministerial Committee of Inquiry on Finance and Insurance.[55] This debate concerned, among other issues, the separation of short-term loans from medium- and long-term ones and the distinction between equity and debt finance in the context of the pre-war 'pollution' of the two which had led to the banking and industrial crises of the 1930s. The decision taken by the *Assemblea Costitutente* on the strength of the recommendations of the Committee of Inquiry, dictated the structure of Italy's financial system.

One of the most important findings of the Committee, reached through interviews with the representatives of the country's various financial institutions, was that they thought that the separation between banks and the provision of medium- and long-term finance to firms should persist. They did not see the stock market, however, as an important alternative source of capital for industry. Though lip-service was paid to the importance of a well-functioning stock market, little was actually proposed to promote it, apart from a more favourable fiscal treatment for firms that issued shares.[56] Rather, it was felt that the funds held by investors should be passed on to firms through the mediation of the *Istituti di Credito Speciale*, (ICS or Special Credit Institutes) as these would lend to firms and finance their activity through the sale to the public of industrial bonds.[57]

The relegation of the stock market to a subsidiary role and the creation of institutions connected to banks to channel and control funds from investors to firms has been seen in the historiography as anomalous in the context of the pro-market attitude that animated the post-war debate.[58] Nevertheless, this 'anomaly' made perfect sense from the point of view of the government, the monetary authorities, and the banks. Though Luigi Einaudi, the Finance Minister, and Donato Menichella, the Governor of the *Banca d'Italia*, were firm in their belief that the market should function without hindrance, they were also equally committed to the stability of the country's currency and to promoting Italy's industrial development. In this context a financial system in which funds were channelled through institutions was seen as more easily manoeuvrable than a system left to the vagaries of individual firms and investors.[59] Thus, while nothing was done to *hinder* the development of the stock market, little was done to promote it. Most importantly the authorities also believed that the smaller industrial and artisan concerns would be left out of the transfer of money, if the supply of credit was left solely to the workings of the market.[60]

As the 1950s progressed, a more Keynesian approach to the economy was adopted, following the *Schema di sviluppo dell'occupazione e del reddito nel decennio 1955–64* (Plan for the growth of employment and incomes in the decade 1955–64), also known as the 'piano Vanoni', from the name of the minister who drew it up. This plan was the first attempt to adopt Keynesian policies by declaring that state intervention and planning in the economy were essential to sustain economic growth and maintain employment, especially in the southern part of the country. Accordingly the banks and the ICS were to be the linchpin of the state's financial intervention.[61] The banks were more disingenuous in the matter of their promotion of the stock market. The banks had little to gain from the development of the stock market except an increase in competition. But they could reap substantial profits through the sale of ICS bonds to the public. The banks also used the direct purchase of these bonds as a way of investing deposits, as ICS bonds carried a higher return than state securities and were risk free.

Guido Carli, who replaced Menichella as the Governor of the *Banca d'Italia* in 1960, was conscious of the need to develop the stock market to avoid firms suffering from an imbalance between debt and equity. One proposal was to transform part of the credits held by the ICS into shares to be placed on the market, as these credits represented the majority of funds used by industrial firms to finance new investments.[62] If this proposal had become operative it would have had the effect of enlarging the stock market and might have prevented the development of that connection between banks and firms that was to become pathological in the 1970s.[63]

From the point of view of this book, among the most important ICSs were the regional institutes, the *Mediocrediti Regionali*, for the financing of small and medium-sized firms created in various stages from 1950 by consortia of local banks. The aim of these institutes was to assist small and medium-sized firms to finance the modernization and mechanization of plants in order to improve the competitiveness of these firms in local markets and abroad and to encourage the building of plants in less-developed areas of the region.[64] Depending on the firms' circumstances the loan could be granted at a subsidized rate.[65] These institutes were created at a regional level for two reasons. The first was that their funds were derived from the sale of bonds to the local banks. The second was that in order to avoid excessive transaction costs the institutes operated close to the firms and to the banks these firms usually dealt with, so as to be able to operate on the basis of trust and reputation. A local institution was also better equipped to evaluate both the market in which the firms operated and their real prospect for development. This seemed particularly important in view of the fact that these institutes were to grant medium- and long-term loans for capital investments.[66] Despite the formal separation of short-term lending (done by banks) and medium-term (done by the *Mediocrediti Regionali*), most small firms used their bank for loans that were used only nominally as working capital. The reason is that the *Mediocrediti* were involved mostly in supplying subsidized loans and these required lengthy procedures.[67]

AN INEFFICIENT BANKING SYSTEM?

The banking system that was shaped by the Bank Law of 1936 was tightly regulated so that competition would not eliminate the smaller and more local banks. As described in the preceding pages, local banks were seen as very important sources of finance for small firms and their role was fundamental in the context of a Keynesian approach to economic development. Nevertheless, as the country industrialized the segmentation of the banking system and the virtual absence of other financial institutions led to the efficiency of the system being questioned, especially from the mid-1970s onwards.[68] The debate that followed brought about the progressive lifting of many of the territorial restrictions and the abolition of controls over interest rates and, in the 1990s, to the merger of some banks.

Within this debate the role of small banks was recognized as having been very important in the earlier stages of post-war economic development, but their permanence, in a modern, international, financial environment was questioned. Small banks were considered inefficient because of their inability to achieve economies of scale, provide modern services,

and use advanced technologies. Furthermore, it was claimed that
regulation stifled competition and that local banks exploited monopoly
positions in their relationship with local customers.[69] At a local level the
market of the smaller banks in Italy was composed of personal borrowers,
small retailers, and small and medium-sized firms. These, because of
perceived higher risk and/or limited bargaining power, were subject to
high interest rate differentials, more than 2.5 per cent. By virtue of the fact
that most of their customers were small, small banks had control of the
sector of the market that brought the highest returns. Nevertheless, this
did not exclude competition inside this market. In practice the Italian
banking system was characterized by the type of oligopolistic competition
among interconnected groups traditionally called 'chain' competition.[70]
Interbranch competition (between branches of different banks) was at its
most intense between adjacent branches and weakened as the distance
between branches increased; the larger banks competed for customers
that the smaller banks were unable to attract, but the passage along the
scale was gradual. Finally the various categories of banks specialized in
fields that were neither entirely separate nor entirely coincident, and
where each bank tended to compete in different ways and to a differing
extent with the others. Also, there was imperfect competition between
banks and other financial intermediaries: the post offices for deposits, the
ICSs for some types of lending, insurance companies for investments in
securities, and so on. Competition among local banks was often ferocious,
seriously eroding profit margins, at least in some areas with a high banking density like most of the industrial north of the peninsula. Competition
was particularly strong among the smaller banks in urban centres and
often brought about the breach of the interbank agreement, as deposit
rates were increased and lending rates decreased to 'poach' customers.
Therefore, though the existence of discrimination in terms of price differentials against small firms cannot be denied, a 'fact of life' for Italian small
firms as much as for British ones, it would seem that the criticism that the
regulation that protected small banks killed off competition can be
rejected.

Critics have also suggested that small banks had higher costs, not being
able to achieve economies of scale, thus making them less profitable.
A study done by the *Banca d'Italia* on a sample of 375 banks in 1980
showed that average total operating costs decreased as the size (in terms
of assets) of the banks increased.[71] This indicated that larger banks did
enjoy economies of scale, probably due to higher degrees of automation.
Other studies have not been able to establish with certainty the existence
of economies of scale, other than the supply on the part of larger banks of
more services.[72] Nonetheless, small banks were shown to be more profitable, as the ratio of interest received on advances to total assets decreased
with the increase in the size of the banks. The reason for this was that

small banks, as described earlier, tended to have customers who brought higher returns and also because the composition of assets changed as banks increased their size. In fact the ratio of loans to assets declined sharply with increasing bank size, as large banks tended to invest more in government securities than small banks did, as shown in Table 10.4. Local banks also had lower transaction costs as they could use their close relationship with customers to reduce information asymmetries.[73] They could also use the investment information that is contained in local networks to assess new customers.[74]

Furthermore, a study done in 1990 on the profitability of banks in the 1980s showed that small and medium-sized banks (defined as such on the basis of capital needs, deposits, loans, number of branches, etc.) with a regional dimension were the ones with the lowest unit costs (measured as total costs over total business transacted), while larger banks had the highest unit costs.[75] These findings are in line with research done, albeit for a different period, on American banking. These studies showed how costs decreased with the increase in size up to $5 million (worth of deposits held by the bank), while costs remained virtually the same for banks in the $5 million to $50 million bracket. For banks with more than $50 million in deposits costs decreased only slightly as size increased.[76] Other studies have shown the existence of increasing economies of scale up to $50 million, but only very small changes in larger banks.[77] Further studies showed how if a bank were to increase by 100 per cent the number of its deposits and loans and if all other elements that might influence costs were kept constant, all other costs directly connected with the increase in size, such as rent of processing machinery, rent of larger premises, more personnel, and postal costs would increase by 92 per cent.[78]

THE CREDIT RESTRICTIONS OF 1963

The segmentation of the banking system also meant that during those phases when monetary policy required credit restrictions small firms did not suffer the brunt of them.[79] This was particularly evident from the end of 1963 when the expansionary policy of the *Banca d'Italia* came to an abrupt end following the deterioration of the balance of payments, worsened by increasing inflation, and capital flight as confidence in the lira decreased. Monetary policy was tightened in September 1963 when the freezing in the net debtor position vis-à-vis non-residents was announced. This action restricted the banks' liquidity, de facto imposing a reduction on their capacity to grant credit.[80] The aim of this policy was to reduce the borrowing capacity of individuals and firms, therefore reducing internal demand and inflation. The impact of the credit restrictions is hard to evaluate as the ratio of advances to deposits kept increasing, reaching

81 per cent in December 1963. The squeeze became more drastic in the first half of 1964 as, although the increase of advances had slowed down,[81] the balance of payments was still in deficit and prices were still rising. Capital flight and speculation worsened the position of the lira to the extent that in March 1964 the International Monetary Fund had to intervene with a loan and speculation was checked. By May 1964 the balance of payments had gone back into surplus and exports increased by 40 per cent compared to the previous year. Some commentators have attributed this rise to the effect the credit restrictions had in reducing demand, therefore freeing products for the export market.[82]

Investments in manufacturing declined from 2,500 billion lire in 1963 to 1,500 billion lire in 1965, and the indexes of industrial production of most manufacturing sectors decreased. Almost 140,000 workers lost their jobs between 1963 and 1965 (employment returned to 1963 levels only in 1967).[83] Notwithstanding the reality of these data, it is hard to establish how much this recession was due to restrictive monetary policies or to a general negative conjuncture, or partially due to the country's loss of competitiveness as wages rose. It is also difficult to assess which category of firms suffered most from the credit restrictions and which category of bank was the most hit by the reduction of liquidity. It might have been easier for the larger firms to maintain their lines of credit, as their contracting power with the banks was stronger. On the other hand the large banks were those whose foreign indebtedness was largest. Advances to many sectors of the economy were reduced in 1964, following the onset of the credit restrictions. In manufacturing only the 'metalwork' and 'paper' sectors did not suffer a reduction in advances. Though the total amount of money lent decreased between 1964 and 1965, banks in fact *increased* the total number of advances made to most manufacturing sectors. This indicated that though the banks were lending less they were still trying to meet demand coming from firms who were suffering due to the negative conjuncture—just the opposite of what the British banks were doing, as shown in Chapter 7. By looking at lending by type of bank more interesting facts are revealed which support the hypothesis that a segmented banking system will defuse the impact of credit restrictions.

Table 10.5 shows that in real terms each type of bank reduced its advances between 1963 and 1964, though only the largest banks, the three banks of national interest, continued to reduce their advances in 1965.

Table 10.6 shows that the banks which did not reduce the *number* of advances granted to the manufacturing sector were the savings banks and the public law banks, banks with a strong regional identity. These data confirm that though in money terms advances were reduced the fact that there were local banks allowed the number of firms receiving funds to increase, tempering the effect of the economic downturn. Furthermore,

Table 10.5. Italy: advances to the manufacturing sector by type of bank, 1961–5, Constant values—1955 (Millions of lire)

	1961	1962	1963	1964	1965
National	990	1,197	1,443	1,395	1,366
Public law	709	923	1,087	1,071	1,088
Ordinary	775	931	1,039	1,012	1,060
Popular	395	466	511	491	515
Savings	343	410	483	433	438

Source: Author's calculations on data in Banca d'Italia, *Bollettino Statistico*, various years.

Table 10.6. Italy: number of loans to the manufacturing sector by type of bank, 1963–5 (000)

	1963	1964	1965
National	74	75	72
Public law	95	96	101
Ordinary	161	160	166
Popular	116	115	120
Savings	179	188	192

Source: Author's calculations on data in Banca d'Italia, *Bollettino Statistico*, various years.

the segmentation of the banking system had another positive effect since, while the banks reduced their advances between 1964 and 1965 the Special Institutes did not.

Tables 10.7 and 10.8 show that, throughout the credit squeeze, the Special Institute continued to supply all firms, including small ones with medium- and long-term credit, thus diminishing the long-term effect of the restrictions on investment. Again this can be compared with what

Table 10.7. Italy: advances by Special Institute to all sectors, 1963–5, Constant values—1955 (Millions of lire)

1963	4.355
1964	4.811
1965	5.219

Source: Author's calculations on data in Banca d'Italia, *Bollettino Statistico*, various years.

Table 10.8. Italy, advances by Special Institutes to small manufacturing firms, 1963–5,
Constant values—1955 (Millions of lire)

1963	259
1964	330
1965	387

Source: Author's calculations on data in Banca
d'Italia, *Bollettino Statistico*, various years

happened in Britain, where there was no institutional alternative to the
commercial banks for supplying finance to the smaller firms.

CONCLUSION

The Italian banking system has not been without its critics. Recently
Marcello de Cecco considered that governments' decisions to favour a
decentralized system, decisions motivated according to him by the fear of
not being able to control the three big banks (*Comit, Credito Italiano*, and
Banca Nazionale), hindered the development of an efficient banking system. He believes that if no barriers had been placed to the growth of these
banks Italy would have a banking, and an industrial system, more similar
to that of its competitors. A segmented banking system allowed small
firms to survive and this prevented Italy from being an industrial power
and a full member of the EEC.[84] This interpretation implies the existence
of an 'ideal-type' of development and that successive Italian governments
failed to see it. There is no question that like many governments in other
countries like the Italian ones were far from perfect in their management
of the economy. In particular Italy has suffered from governments' un-
willingness to reform the public administration which we know now has
led to corruption and rent-seeking.[85] The other big problem experienced
by the Italian economy has been the persistence of the divide between the
north and the south and the slowness of endogenous growth in the
southern regions.

Just as in Germany and France the reasons for fostering small firms
were economic, political, and social. However, of the four countries
surveyed in this book Italy presents the most intense case of banking
regulation and subsidies with the explicit aim of actively promoting the
growth of small firms. Since the interwar period this protection has
eliminated a significant barrier to the growth of this part of the economy.
This was one of the factors, after the Second World War, that led to the

development of strong industrial districts made of highly efficient and internationally competitive small firms.

NOTES

1   For an extensive bibliography see Colli, *I volti di Proteo*, 20.
2   For a definition of *Made in Italy* as representing those goods in which Italy has an international competitive advantage see Curzio and Fortis, *Il Made in Italy*.
3   The use of the notion of industrial district applied to the Italian case was made for the first time in 1979 by Giacomo Beccattini in 'Dal "settore" industriale al "distretto" industriale. Alcune riflessioni sull'unita' d'indagine dell'economia industriale'.
4   Industrial districts specialize around the production of similar goods connected either by the raw material used, or by the local capabilities developed by workers in the area. For example, although Vigevano, in the north-west, has come to be best known for its shoes, the area produces also a number of leather articles and in recent years also the machinery for making these goods. See Crestanello, 'La Trasformazione in 10 distretti Industriali durante gli anni '80'.
5   Curzio and Forti, *Made in Italy*, 46–7.
6   Bagnasco, *Le Tre Italie*.
7   Colli, *I volti di Proteo*, 29–35.
8   For a recent overview of the Italian 'economic miracle' and economy after the Second World War see Rossi and Toniolo, 'Italy'.
9   Colli, *I volti di Proteo*, 84.
10 Ibid., 235. For a more general overview of Italian exports see Guerrieri and Milana, *L'Italia e il commercio mondiale*.
11 Brusco and Paba, 'Per una storia dei distretti industriali dal secondo dopoguerra agli anni novanta', 270–1.
12 Ministero per la Costituente, *Rapporto della Commissione Economica presentato all'Assemblea Costituente. II: Industria, II, Appendice alla relazione (interrogatori)*, Poligrafico dello Stato, Roma, 1947.
13 Segreto, 'Americanizzare o modernizzare l'economia?'.
14 Battilossi, *L'Italia nel sistema economico internazionale*.
15 Falcone, 'Effetti dell'integrazione economica Europea sulla struttura delle esportazioni Italiane'.
16 Giannetti, *Tecnologia e sviluppo economico Italiano*.
17 For an extensive summary and analysis of the data available on concentration in the post-war period see Battilossi, 'Mercati e concentratione', 291–345.
18 Sapelli, *Storia economica dell'Italia contemporanea*, 106–7.
19 For steel see: Osti and Ranieri *L'Industria di stato dall'ascesa all'degrado*; for energy Sapelli and Carnevali, *Uno sviluppo fra politica e strategia*; for more general overviews see Padoa-Schioppa Kostoris, *Italy, the Sheltered Economy*; Amatori, 'Growth via Politics: Business Groups Italian Style'.
20 Arrighetti and Seravalli, 'Istituzioni e dualismo dimensionale dell'industria Italiana', 343.

21   See also Weiss, *Creating Capitalism: The State and Small Business since 1945*.
22   Arrighetti and Serravalli, 'Istituzioni e dualismo dimensionale', 357–8.
23   Ibid., 366. The advantages given to artisan firms in terms of tax and labour costs started being eroded from the mid-1970s following the economic crisis, and also because the smaller firms were losing their political and economic importance, as the state's focus shifted more onto the larger small firms and medium-sized ones.
24   This argument is developed by Berger and applied also to France and its *petit bourgeoisie*: Berger, 'D'une boutique à l'autre; Berger, 'Uso politico e sopravvivenza dei ceti in declino'; Berger and Piore, *Dualism and Discontinuity in Industrial Societies*; Alessandro Pizzorno has applied this notion to explain government intervention in the south: Pizzorno, 'I ceti medi nel meccanismo del consenso'.
25   Democrazia Cristiana, *Atti dei Congressi*, 54.
26   Weiss, 'The Italian State and Small Firms', 223–37.
27   Amatori and Colli, *Impresa e industria*, 232–57; for examples of the many firms such as Zanussi which thanks to the growth of private consumption grew from small workshops to market leaders, see 257–62.
28   Menichella, 'Intervento al convegno nazionale delle casse rurali ed artigiane' 84–5, and also, Banca d' Italia, *Relazione annuale 1961*, 97.
29   For an extensive definition and list of districts at different points in time see Brusco and Paba, 'Per una storia dei distretti industriali Italiani, 265–333.
30   Conti and Ferri, 'Banche locali e sviluppo economico decentrato', 443–52.
31   Corti and Ferri also give the examples of various areas such as Marche, Prato, Carpi and, Montepulciano, 454–8. See also Dei Ottati, *Tra mercato e comunitá*. For a very well-documented analysis of the development of a local banking system, that of the Marche and the shoemaking industry, from informal credit arrangements before Unification to the beginning of the Second World War, and its connection with the modernization of local industry see Sabbatucci Severini, 'Circuiti creditizi per la manifattura', 237–63. For an in-depth analysis of the impact of financial subsidies and of bank finance on industrial districts see Spadavecchia, 'State Subsidies and the Sources of Company Finance in Italian Industrial Districts, 1951–1991' (Unpublished PhD thesis, University of London, 2003).
32   Capparelli, *Il ruolo della banca locale*.
33   Conti, 'Le banche e il finanziamento industriale', 493. On this last point see also Faini, Galli, and Giannini, 'Finance and Development: The Case of Southern Italy', 158–214.
34   Menichella, 'Intervento all'assemblea annuale dell'istituto centrale per le banche popolari' 5 February, 1959. The extracts from Menichella's speeches can be found in Lunghini, *Scelte politiche e teorie economiche in Italia 1945–1978*.
35   Menichella, 'Discorso all' assemblea dell'associazione fra la banche ordinarie di credito Italiane', 8 November 1957. In Italian in the original.
36   Menichella, 'Discorso all'assemblea dell'associazione bancaria Italiana', 23 June 1955.
37   Mattioli, *Relazione sull'esercizio della Banca Commerciale*, 248.

38 Menichella, 'Il sistema creditizio fattore di stabilita' monetaria e di sviluppo economico'.
39 The government's concern about the impairment of competition in industry led to a parliamentary inquiry in 1959. See: 'Testo del disegno di legge per la tutela della liberta' della concorrenza-relazione ministeriale e parere del CNEL', *Rivista internazionale di scienze sociali*, 15 (1960).
40 The Governor of the Bank, Guido Carli, Banca d'Italia, *Annual Report for 1961*, 97.
41 Ibid., 10–11.
42 The Banca d'Italia was founded in 1893 as the result of a merger of three of the six banks of issue then in existence. It was given sole right of note issue in 1926.
43 In 1959 the Bank had ninety-eight shareholders of which seventy-seven were savings banks. See Lutz, 'The Central Bank and the System of Credit Control', 154.
44 Because of the regionally fragmented structure of the banking system and of the country, the Bank adopted from its inception a decentralized structure to monitor the activity of the banks. Therefore, in addition to a head office in Rome, the Bank instituted main branch offices situated in the main provincial capitals, sub-branches in other main towns and agencies to cover the rest of the territory. In 1970 the Bank also created Regional Economic Observatories attached to most of the main branches in order to have a clearer view of the economies of the various regions.
45 The banks of national interest owned the majority shares of the public law banks and of the savings banks. The rest of the shares were held by other banks and by the municipalities of the towns in which the banks had their head office.
46 Banca d'Italia, *Relazione 1956*, 440, and *Relazione 1948*, 216.
47 Ceriani, 'The Commercial Banks and Financial Institutions', 126.
48 Associazione Bancaria Italiana, 'L'intervento dell'Avv. Siglienti ai Lavori della Commissione d'Inchiesta sui Limiti della Concorrenza'.
49 Banco di Roma, *The Italian Banking System*, Chapter 2, section 2.2; Barca and Manghetti, *L'Italia delle Banche*, 215.
50 Banca d'Italia, *Annual Report for 1952*, English version, 429. The amount of lending authorized outside the area of territorial competence was usually quite a small proportion of total bank lending, see Lutz, 'The Central Bank', 158.
51 An example of the connection between political power and banks can be found in the fact that in 1975, seventy of the eighty-nine savings banks had presidents belonging to the Christian Democratic Party. For an informative view of the relationship between politics and banks see Barca and Manghetti, *L'Italia delle Banche*, 19.
52 Ceriani, 'The Commercial Banks and Financial Institutions', 134.
53 Banco di Roma, *The Italian Banking System*, Chapter 1, section 1.3.
54 Ceriani, 'The Commercial Banks and Financial Institutions', 137.
55 Ministero per la Costitutente, *Rapporto della Commissione Economica presentato all'Assemblea Costitutente, Relazione su Credito e Assicurazione*.

56 For a more detailed analysis of the proposal made to promote the stock exchange see Pace and Morelli, *Origini e identita' del Credito Speciale*, 374.

57 Ministero per la Costituente, *Relazione sul Credito*, 446–53, *Questionario*, n. 18, answers in the *Appendice*.

58 Bagella, *Gli Istituti di Credito Speciale e il mercato finanziario (1947–62)*, 47. For a detailed analysis of the political environment that led to the creation of the Special Institutes see Piluso, 'Gli Istituti di Credito Speciale', 507–50.

59 Bagella, *Gli Istituti di Credito Speciale*, 88.

60 Banca d'Italia, *Relazione del Governatore*, 371–2.

61 For further reading on the 'piano Vanoni' see Balducci and Marconi, 'L'Accumulazione del capitale', 72–9;for the implementation of the plan and its reception by the monetary authorities see Menichella, 'Espansione economica in regime di stabilita' monetaria'; Saraceno, 'Riesame del piano Vanoni al fine 1957'; Shonfield, *Modern Capitalism*, 180–5.

62 Carli, 'Trasformazioni reali e trasformazioni finanziarie', 23.

63 Bagella, *Gli Istituti di Credito Speciale.*, 60–1. For the 1970s and the increasing role of the banks in the financing of firms see Onado, *Il Sistema finanziario Italiano*, 13–20 and 91–100.

64 Camilleri, *Industrial Medium-term Financial Institutions in Italy* (London, 1966), 64.

65 Spadavecchia, 'Financing Industrial Districts in Italy, 1971–91. A Private Venture?'.

66 De Marchi, 'Osservazioni critiche sull'attuale legislazione Italiana', 251.

67 Nardozzi, *Tre sistemi creditizi a confronto*, 62.

68 See for example Alifuoco, *Il sistema creditizio locale in un'economia periferica. il caso del Veneto*.

69 Ciampi, *La politica creditizia e l'innovazione finanziaria*.

70 Banca d'Italia, *Italian Credit Structures. Efficiency*, 66–7.

71 Ibid., 19–23.

72 Marchesini, 'Gli Effetti delle fusioni bancarie', 59–81.

73 Verdier, *Moving Money*, 16–20.

74 For an analysis of the structure of one of these networks and how a local bank used it to assess borrowers see Carnevali, 'Between Markets and Networks: Regional Banks in Italy'.

75 Landi, *Dimensioni, costi e profitti delle Banche Italiane*, 61–6.

76 Alhadeff, *Monopoly and Competition in Banking*, 83.

77 Schneiger and Moole, 'Chicago Banking', 325.

78 Bell and Murphy, 'Economic Scale in Commercial Banking'.

79 Lack of space prevents a detailed examination of post-war Italian economic policy. For an in-depth analysis see Frattiani and Spinelli, *A Monetary History of Italy*, 157–233.

80 Mengarelli, *Politica e Teoria*, 44.

81 Mengarelli, 'La politica monetaria in Italia (1960–1975)', 79.

82 Ibid., 82.

83 Graziani, *L'Economia Italiana*, 81–2.

84 De Cecco, 'Splendore e crisi del sistema Beneduce', 539–47.

85 Cohen and Federico, *The Growth of the Italian Economy*, 105–6.

11

Conclusion

At the end of the nineteenth century, as a consequence of the growth of the international economy and of financial markets, British banks moved away from 'insider lending', while relationship banking was replaced with the more impersonal transaction banking.[1] This process also involved big banks in France and Germany but what distinguishes the British experience is that as local banks disappeared, nothing replaced them to make use of the investment information possessed by local networks. Instead, the French, German, and Italian banking systems remained segmented and the state intervened with the promotion of additional public and semi-public lending institutions. In all the four countries big banks and small firms had, at best, an uneasy relationship, but on the continent the variety of alternatives suggests that the potential fringe of unsatisfied borrowers was smaller. The downside of this situation was that during the interwar period regionally dispersed continental banking was inherently more unstable than the concentrated British one. The comparison between these four countries shows that there is more to banking history than trying to establish which system was better.

British banking developed as it did, concentrated and centralized, also because of the absence of interests strong enough to demand alternatives. In Germany, France, and Italy, cooperative and savings banks changed their nature over time, developing closer links with local business communities in response to changing demands. As shown in the previous chapters this process was met with opposition from the commercial banks. Nevertheless, conflict resulted in adaptation, thanks to state intervention. Although large in terms of deposits, British savings banks were prevented by law from lending their funds for commercial purposes, even when they were strongly connected with the local business community, as in the case of the Birmingham Municipal Savings Bank.[2] The dialectical process that took place between the state and social and economic groups representing small firms in France, Germany, and Italy did not happen in Britain, at least not until the late 1970s. When seeking for the causes of the decline of small firms in Britain it is to the absence of this process that one must turn. The comparative story on the Continent shows that conflict was the factor that shaped the state's response towards the competition between different types of banks, ensuring the permanence of segmentation. Moreover, the banks created, or promoted, by the state were the expression of the will to ensure the fulfilment of the credit needs of those smaller firms whose borrowing power from the capital market did not match their political power. Throughout the twentieth century small capitalists on the Continent were in the position of arbitrating the conflict between the capitalist Right and the working-class Left, and they used their position to put pressure on the state to protect local banks and/or create public credit institutions.[3]

In the relationship between banks and customers, information asymmetries can never be totally avoided and this makes adverse selection inevitable. To some extent, therefore, banks will always ration their loans. But a segmented banking system allows different types of banks to specialize in different types of customers in different geographical areas. The regional and local Continental banks studied in this book all specialized in different segments of the market, as did the public and semi-public credit institutions created by the state. Specialization was one of the preconditions for the reduction of information asymmetries, as lending to the same type of customer made risk assessment easier thus reducing the impact of credit rationing on the population of local firms. The experience of the three Continental economies studied here shows that specialization either by local and regional banks, or by public and semi-public institutions, also led to a long-term commitment to their customers. This was particularly true in the case of those banks that were deeply embedded within local economies. Relationship banking could be seen here in its strongest manifestation, where the long-term relationship between borrowers and lenders allowed assessment and monitoring costs to be lowered. The downside of this form of relationship, as shown by the examples in this book, is that banks were less able to spread risk, although the creation of national associations went some way towards reducing this hazard.

The conflicts that shaped the banking systems analysed in this book, and the state's response towards small firms, were not only between different social and political groups. Governments themselves were split in their reaction towards small firms and even within different political groups these attitudes were never clear cut. The examples of France, Germany, and Italy show that small firms occupied such a place in the cultural identity of these countries that even 'modernizers' could not completely exclude them from their plans. In all three countries small firms were seen as preservers of social stability and as valuable pools of votes; not so in Britain. Neither the Conservative, nor Labour party developed policies explicitly directed at the protection and fostering of the growth of this sector of the economy. Therefore, in Britain small firms had little lobbying power and very little political representation, in marked contrast with the Continental experience.

THE END OF RELATIONSHIP BANKING?

From the mid-1970s onwards most economies experienced varying degrees of banking deregulation as governments attempted to make this sector more responsive to the pressures of international competition. High and volatile rates of inflation, coupled with the increased changeability of interest and exchange rates, stimulated European banks to reassess their attitudes towards risk and uncertainty. The liberalization of the banking system took the form of increased price competition and changing government attitudes towards the type of business activities in which banks and non-bank financial institutions could engage. As a consequence the traditional barriers that used to segment financial and banking business came down. In the 1980s in countries like France, for example, where there had been a very rigid legal separation between banking and the securities business, new laws enabled banks to participate in the capital market business.[4] At the same time the policy reaction to the increased liberalization of both financial and banking markets was to increase the supervisory regulatory response. Banking supervision became international as regulators became increasingly concerned with systemic risk, heightening attitudes towards solvency, liquidity, and the profitability of financial institutions. In Europe, monetary and financial cooperation leading to unification was implicit in the 1957 Treaty of Rome which established the European Community (originally composed of Belgium, France, Germany, Italy, Luxembourg, and the Netherlands). However, it was only in 1978 that the member countries of the Community (joined by then by Denmark, Ireland, and Britain) decided to create a European Monetary System (EMS) to stabilize exchange rates via an exchange rate mechanism and to improve monetary integration.[5] Although the EMS was introduced as an exchange rate regime, the system had important implications for commercial banking because it provided a framework that affected several markets in which commercial banks were active, such as foreign exchange markets, the loan and deposit markets, and bond markets.[6] Furthermore, at the end of the 1980s, the Bank for International Settlements introduced proposals to unify capital requirements for all banks in the industrialized world.

The combined forces of liberalization and increased supervision that were brought to bear on financial and banking systems in the run-up to the establishment of monetary union in 1992, and in the years that followed, have led to increased levels of banking concentration, bringing the Continental banking system closer to the British one. The implications of this trend for small firms could prove very negative.[7] As banks grow larger they abandon lending to small business as the distance between the bank and the borrower widens. This increases the need for an arm's length relationship, based on standardized information. Standardization impoverishes the quality of the information and the long-term knowledge of the local banker is lost. Quantitative evidence of this can be found in a study of US banking. In 1995, Berger et. al. found that large banks tended to lend to large and medium-sized businesses, while small banks specialized in lending to smaller borrowers. The bank mergers that had taken place in the United States from the beginning of the 1990s had led to a contraction in lending to small firms.[8] The negative impact of this was offset only if there were other local banks to which the small firm could transfer its long-term relationship.[9]

From the early 1990s the German banking system experienced a profound change, exemplified by an intense merger activity involving large private banks but mostly cooperative and savings banks.[10] The number of independent banking institutions dropped by about 40 per cent and mergers were accompanied by the closure of branches. Between 1998 and 2001, more than 10,000 bank branches were closed.[11] While the intense merger activity of the 1990s can be seen as a consequence of liberalization and of the changes in the European and international financial markets, they also reflected an adjustment process in an 'over-banked' market. Even by 2000 Germany had more banking institutions than France, Italy, and Britain, mostly because of the size of the cooperative and savings banks sectors strongly entrenched in their local markets.[12]

The restructuring of the banking sector affected the *Mittelstand* in a number of ways. In preparation for the Basle II Capital Accord, banks started considering risk-adequate credit pricing more accurately and this shaped their lending business away from the smaller firms.[13] The closure of branches reduced the scope for relationship banking; small firms saw a worsening of service quality alongside increased credit shortages. These were particularly damaging for the overall competitiveness of the German economy given the reliance of *Mittelstand* firms on bank debt.[14]

Until the end of 1996, France experienced a similar move towards consolidation as banks within the same banking groups merged. In 1996 the first merger between banking groups took place with *Crédit Agricole*'s takeover of *Indosuez*. This was followed in 1997 by the mergers of *Crédit du Nord* with *Societé Générale*, *Crédit Industriel et Commercial* (CIC), and *Crédit Mutuel*, followed in turn by the merger of *Paribas* and *Banque Nationale* in 1999. By 2000 there were seven key banking groups in France as opposed to four at the beginning of the 1990s: the Popular banks, the savings banks, *Crédit Agricole–Indosuez*, *Crédit Lyonnais*, *Crédit Mutuel–CIC*, *Société Générale* and *BNP–Paribas*. Banking consolidation, however, did not increase concentration in the business loan market and in fact lowered the top four bank asset concentration level. The groups made up of mutual banks, such as the savings banks, increased their share of the market and this probably explains why the share of small and medium-sized firms in the loan market increased during the 1990s. The changes in the structure of French banking also meant that with the exception of very small firms, French businesses increased the number of intermediaries from whom they borrowed. This increased the availability of credit, especially for medium-sized firms. Contrary to expectations, the consolidation of French banking did not lead to restrictions in the supply of credit to small firms, but this is because the increase in competition between different types of banks led small and medium-sized firms to start relationships with more than one bank and also to lengthen the duration of the relationship. Multibanking was the factor that allowed these firms to increase their bank credit.[15]

Following increased levels of financial integration with the other European countries, Italy also started experiencing increased levels of banking competition. To face this competition the new Bank Law of 1993 allowed the liberalization of branch opening, mergers between banking groups, and opened the way to privatization. As European financial integration increased, many of the incentives provided to firms by the state had to be dismantled, as in the case of the subsidized loans provided to small firms. Similar to the French case, lengthy, multibank relationships became a feature of Italian banking in the 1990s, ensuring the supply of credit to small and medium-sized firms. Unlike French firms, however, Italian ones continued to have a local bank (defined here as one with headquarters in the province where the firm is located) as their main bank. The overwhelming majority of banks that acted as main lenders to small firms were local, indicating the small banks were still matched with small firms.[16] Following a period of consolidations during the 1990s which led to increased levels of banking concentration, local banks, especially the Popular banks, have shown better performance indicators than the national banks, thanks probably to the solidity of their corporate governance structures.[17]

Despite the consolidation process that has taken place in Continental banking since the 1970s, the banking sectors of the countries considered in this book are still characterized by variety in terms of size, geographical spread, and specialization. One of the consequences of increased levels of competition between banking groups has been the development of multibanking relationships on the part of small and medium-sized firms. The reconfiguration of the relationship between banks and small firms can be seen as the periphery's response to the forces that are pushing for financial agglomeration. Moreover, small firms are still using their political power to put pressure on the government to reduce the negative consequences of the forces of financial globalization. In Germany, for example, in September 2002 the government led by Gerhard Schroder opposed the Basle Accord II on the grounds that it made it harder and more expensive for small firms to raise loans. The opposition of the German government led to a modification of the Accord and to special concessions on loans to small firms.[18]

The situation in Britain developed differently. In 1971 Edward Heath's government *Competition and Credit Controls* document opened up the British banking system to market forces, followed in 1979 by the abolition of foreign exchange controls on capital movements. As sterling lending to domestic customers could now move offshore, regulatory controls became superfluous and ineffective. Credit controls were abolished in 1980, hire purchase controls in 1982, and the building societies cartel restrictions in 1985. One of the consequences of increasing international financial integration was that British banks, like their European counterparts, were allowed to become more like universal banks, offering their clients a range of financial services.[19] Although concentration in financial and banking services in Britain declined thanks to changes in regulation and the entry into the market of many foreign banks (culminating in 1992 when HSBC took over Midland bank) this did not lessen the hold of the 'Big Four' over small business customers. In 2002, despite the first signs of new competitors such as HBOS (the new bank created from the merger of Halifax and Bank of Scotland), Alliance and Leicester and Abbey National, four banks—Barclays, Royal Bank (owner of NatWest), HSBC, and Lloyds TSB—still controlled 90 per cent of the smaller firms' banking market. In an interview in October 2001, the representative of the Federation of Small Businesses, Stephen Alambritis, was critical of what the Federation saw as a complex monopoly of the big four, with identical charging structures. In such a situation multibanking was not an option for small firms.[20]

In 1992 the Bank of England established a separate division whose role was to monitor small firms and publish a yearly report on the sources of finance available to them.[21] Small firms had come to the fore of the Bank's attention following the recession at the beginning of the 1990s. The commercial banks had started targeting small firms from the mid-1980s to expand their customer base, but a combination of poor credit assessment techniques and the onset of the recession led to high levels of bad debt followed by a credit crunch for small and medium-sized firms. The Bank of England stepped in to restore a better relationship between banks and firms. The Bank's first report highlighted the fact that small firms were too reliant on overdrafts (which could be recalled on demand) and on other short-term finance, and that the banks needed to develop more sophisticated and systematic risk management techniques, including credit scoring systems. Over a decade the commercial banks invested considerable resources to improve their credit assessment techniques. These techniques judge a credit applicant's risk of default or delayed debt repayment by performing statistical analysis on the correlations between past account behaviour and the applicant's eventual repayment performance and use this as a basis to predict likely future performance.[22] While this system of credit assessment has enabled banks to manage risk better, small firms' representatives complained to the Bank that scoring systems worked against particular firms, because 'non-standard' information that could support their case was not taken into account by an automated system. Credit scoring systems were perceived by small firms as remote and difficult to influence.[23]

Despite the banks' development of more sophisticated methods of credit scoring access to finance in the twenty-first century remains a problem for small firms in Britain.[24] While the Bank of England in its final report in 2004 declared that this was no longer a concern for small firms, the Federation of Small Businesses still listed finance as one of the barriers to growth. Overdrafts remain the main source of external finance and although more firms are switching banks, there is no evidence of multibanking.[25]

Globalization and international competition are putting great pressure on the banking systems of most countries to agglomerate. Regulation at supranational level (such as the Basle Accords) is moving towards the development of standardized approaches to risk assessment based on credit ratings that can smooth out competitive inequalities between banks from different countries. In this process of agglomeration and standardization, relationship banking and local information are lost. The future will determine whether this will harm small firms and the regeneration of local economies. The evidence from the past, however, suggests that abandoning local banks would be a mistake.

NOTES

1 Collins and Baker, 56.
2 Horne, *A History of Savings Banks*; on Birmingham see Hilton, *Britain's First Municipal Savings Bank*.
3 Verdier, *Moving Money*, 130–2.
4 'Un tout petit boum', 95–9. For a more general overview see Frazer and Vittas, *The Retail Banking Revolution*.
5 Although Britain joined the EMS it did not participate in the Exchange Rate Mechanism (ERM).
6 Abraham, Abraham, and Lacroix-Destree, 'EMS, ECU and Commercial Banking', 7.
7 Since the report by the Bolton Committee the definition of a small firm has changed only slightly, including new firms employing up to 250 people.
8 Berger and Udell, 'Relationship Lending and Lines of Credit in Small Firm Finance'.
9 Berger, Saunders, Scalise, and Udell, 'The Effects of Bank Mergers and Acquisitions on Small Business Lending'.

10   Bundesverband Deutscher Banken, *Neue Strukturen für die Zukunft—Wandel in der Deutschen Kreditwirtschaft*.
11   Hommel and Schneider, 'Financing the German Mittelstand', 73.
12   Hardach, 'Banques régionales et banques locales en Allemagne', 41–3.
13   The 1988 Basle Accord stipulated the banks had to back the total amount of their loans to corporate clients with a capital charge of 8 per cent of own funds. This rule did not take into account that some corporate clients, such as small firms, might be riskier than others. As a result the amount of own funds that Basel I required for a loan to a corporate client may not have corresponded to the actual risk. The Basle II Accord proposes to partially correct this mispricing by allowing banks to set capital requirements as a function of a firm's credit rating.
14   For more details on this see: Hansmann, and Ringle, 'Finanzierung Mittelstand 2002—eine Empirische Untersuchung'; Institut für Mittelstandforschung, 'Mind-Mittelstand in Deutschland', 2000; Kreditanstalt für Wiederaufbau, *Unternehmensfinanzierung im umbruch—die Finanzierungs-perspektiven Deutscher Unternehmen im Zeichen von Finanzmarktwandel und Basel II*.
15   Dietsch, 'Financing Small Business in France', 115.
16   Padoa-Schioppa, 'Profili di diversitá nel sistema bancario Italiano'.
17   Ferri, Masciandaro, and Messori, 'Governo societario ed efficienza delle banche locali di fronte all'unificazione dei mercati finanziari'.
18   'SMEs Mind the Financing Gap', *The Banker*, 1 October 2002; Bank for International Settlements, *BIS Review*, 32 (2003).
19   For a comprehensive description of the changes that have taken place in the regulatory framework of British financial markets see Mayer, 'The Regulation of Financial Services: Lessons from the United Kingdom'.
20   *The Observer*, 14 October 2001.
21   The division was closed in 2004 to avoid replicating the activities of the Small Business Service unit at the Department of Trade and Industry, set up in 2000.
22   Bank of England, *Finance for Small Firms—A Tenth Report*, 16–17.
23   Bank of England, *Finance for Small Firms—An Eleventh Report*, 35–6.
24   See for example Davis, 'Bank Credit Risk'.
25   Federation of Small Businesses, *Lifting the Barriers to Growth in UK Small Businesses*, 52–8.

BIBLIOGRAPHY

Abraham, F. L. P., Abraham J. P., and Lacroix-Destree, Y. (1984). 'EMS, ECU and Commercial Banking', *Revue de la Banque*, 48, 5–35.

Ackrill, M. and Hannah, L. (2001). *Barclays: The Business of Banking, 1690–1996*. Cambridge: Cambridge University Press.

Acs, Z. J. and Audretsch, D. B. (eds.) (1993). *Small Firms and Entrepreneurship*. Cambridge: Cambridge University Press.

Adams, W. J. (1989). *Restructuring the French Economy*. Washington, DC: The Brookings Institution.

Albert, E. (1999). *Les Banques populaires en France au XXe siècle*. Paris: Economica.

Alhadeff, D. A. (1954). *Monopoly and Competition in Banking*. Berkeley: University of California Press.

Alifuoco, U. (1984). *Il sistema creditizio locale in un'economia periferica: ii caso del Veneto*. Milano: Franco Angeli.

Allen, F. and Gale, D. (1995). 'A Welfare Comparison of Intermediaries and Financial Markets in Germany and the US', *European Economic Review*, 39, 179–209.

Amatori, F. (1997) 'Italy: The Tormented Rise of Organisational Capabilities between Government and Families', in A. Chandler, F. Amatori, and T. Hikino (eds.), *Big Business and the Wealth of Nations*. Cambridge: Cambridge University Press.

—— (1997). 'Growth via Politics: Business Groups Italian Style', in Shimotani, M. and Shiba, T. (eds.), *Beyond the Firm*. Oxford: Oxford University Press.

—— Bigazzi, D., Giannetti, R., and Segreto, L. (eds.) (1999). *Annali della storia d' Italia: l'industria*. Torino: Einaudi.

—— and Colli, A. (1999). *Impresa e industria in Italia dall'unita' a oggi*, Bologna: Marsilio.

Amendola, M. and Gaffard, J. (1988). *The Innovative Choice*. Oxford: Basil Blackwell.

Aniello, V. and Le Gales, P. (2001). 'Between Large Firms and Marginal Local Economies: the Making of Systems of Local Governance in France', in C. Crouch, P. Le Gales, C. Trigilia, and H. Voelzkow, (eds.), *Local Production Systems in Europe*. Oxford: Oxford University Press.

Arnott, R. and Stiglitz, J. E. (1991). 'Moral Hazard and Non-market Institutions: Dysfunctional Crowding out or Peer Monitoring', *American Economic Review*, 81, 179–89.

Arrighetti, A. and Seravalli, G. (1997). 'Istituzioni e dualismo dimensionale dell'industria Italiana', in F. Barca, (ed.), *Storia del capitalismo Italiano dal dopoguerra a oggi*. Roma: Donzelli.

Associazione Bancaria Italiana (1963). 'L'intervento dell'avv. Siglienti ai lavori della commissione d'inchiesta sui limiti della concorrenza', *Bancaria*, 19, 10–15.

Bachi, R. (1923). *La Cassa di Risparmio delle Provincie Lombarde (1823–1923)*. Milano: Cariplo.

Bagella, M. (1986). *Gli Istituti di Credito Speciale e il mercato finanziario (1947–62)*. Milano: Franco Angeli.

Baglioni, G. (1974). *L'ideologia della borghesia industriale nell'Italia liberale*. Torino: Einaudi.

Bagnasco, A. (1995). *Le Tre Italie: la problematica territoriale dello sviluppo Italiano*. Bologna: Il Mulino.

—— and Sabel, C. (eds.) (1995). *Small and Medium Sized Enterprises*. London: Pinter.

Balderston, T. (1991). 'German Banking between the Wars: The Crisis of the Credit Banks', *Business History Review*, 65, 554–605.

Balducci, R. and Marconi, M. (1980). 'L'accumulazione del capitale nella visione del governo, della Banca d'Italia e della confindustria', in A. Lunghini (ed.), *Scelte politiche e teorie economiche in Italia (1945–78)*. Milano: Boringhieri.

Balogh, T. (1947). *Studies in Financial Organisation*. Cambridge: Cambridge University Press.

Banca d'Italia (1984). *Italian Credit Structures: Efficiency, Competition and Controls*. London: Euromonetary Publications.

—— (1958). *Relazione del governatore*. Roma: Banca d'Italia.

—— (1949). *Relazione 1948*. Roma: Banca d'Italia.

—— (1953). *Annual Report for 1952*, English version. Roma: Banca d'Italia.

—— (1957). *Relazione annuale 1956*. Roma: Banca d'Italia.

—— (1962). *Relazione annuale, 1961*. Roma: Banca d'Italia.

Banco di Roma (1974). *The Italian Banking System*, 3rd edn. Roma: Banco di Roma.

Bank of England (2003). *Finance for Small Firms—A Tenth Report*. London: Bank of England.

—— (2004). *Finance for Small Firms—An Eleventh Report*. London: Bank of England.

Bannock, G. and Albach, H. (1991). *Small Business Policy in Europe*. Anglo-German Foundation, London.

—— (1973). *The Juggernauts: The Age of the Big Corporation*. Harmondsworth: Penguin.

—— (1976). *The Smaller Business in Britain and Germany*. London: Wilton House Publications.

—— (1981). 'Finance for Small Firms', in Economist Advisory Group, *The British and German Banking System: A Comparative Study*. London: Anglo-German Foundation.

Barber, J., Metcalfe, J. F., and Porteous, M. (eds.) (1989). *The Barriers to Growth in Small Firms*. London: Routledge.

Barca, L. and Manghetti, G. (1976). *L'Italia delle banche*. Roma: Editori Riuniti.

—— (ed.) (1997). *Storia del capitalismo Italiano dal dopoguerra a oggi*. Roma: Donzelli.

Barcellona P. (ed.) (1980). *Casse di Risparmio: le istituzioni finaziarie del ceto medio*. Bari: Laterza.

Bates, J. (1971). *The Financing of Small Businesses*. London: Sweet & Maxwell.

Battilossi, S. (1996). *L'Italia nel sistema economico internazionale: Il Management dell'integrazione: finanza, industria ed istituzioni 1945–1955*. Milano: Franco Angeli.

—— (1999). 'Mercati e concentrazione', in F. Amatori, D. Bigazzi, R. Giannetti, and L. Segreto (eds.), *Annali della Storia d' Italia. L'Industria*. Torino: Einaudi.

Baum, W. C. (1958). *The French Economy and the State*. Princeton: Princeton University Press.

Beccattini, G. (1979). 'Dal "settore" industriale al "distretto" industriale: alcune riflessioni sull'unita' d'indagine dell'economia industriale', *Rivista di economia e politica industriale*, 1, 7–21.

Beckerman, T. (1980). *Das Handwerk in der Bundesrepublik Deutschland*. Berlin: Duncker & Humblot.

Beesley, M. E. and Hamilton, R. T. (1984). 'Small Firms' Seedbed Role and the Concept of Turbulence', *Journal of Industrial Economics*, 33, 217–31.

Bell, F. W. and Murphy, N. R. (1967). 'Economic Scale in Commercial Banking: the Measurement and Impact', *New England Business Review*, 11, 16–28.

Berghahn, V. (1986). *The Americanisation of Western Germany*. Cambridge: Cambridge University Press.

Berger, A. N. and Udell, G. (1995). 'Relationship Lending and Lines of Credit in Small Firm Finance', *Journal of Business*, 68, 3, 351–81.

——, Saunders, A., Scalise J. M., and Udell G. (1998). 'The Effects of Bank Mergers and Acquisitions on Small Business Lending', *Journal of Financial Economics*, 50, 187–229.

Berger, S. (1977). 'D'une Boutique à l'Autre: Change in the Organisation of the Traditional Middle Class from the Fourth to the Fifth Republic', *Comparative Politics*, 10, 121–36.

—— (1974). 'Uso politico e sopravvivenza dei ceti in declino, in F. L. Cavazza, and S. R. Graubard (eds.), *Il caso italiano*. Milano: Garzanti.

—— and Piore, M. (eds.) (1980). *Dualism and Discontent in Industrial Societies*. New York: Cambridge University Press.

Bergeron, L. (1978). *Les Capitalistes en France (1780–1914)*. Paris: Gallimard-Juillard.

Beyenburg-Weidenfeld, U. (1992). *Wettbewerbstheorie, Wirtschaftspolitik und Mittelstandsfoederung 1948–1963*. Stuttgart: Steiner.

Bigazzi, D. (1999). 'Modelli e pratiche organizzative', in F. Amatori, D. Bigazzi, R. Giannetti, and L. Segreto (eds.), *Annali della storia d' Italia: l'industria*. Torino: Einaudi.

Binks, M. R. (1979). 'Finance for Expansion in the Small Firm', *Lloyds Bank Review*, 134, 33–43.

—— and Ennew, C. T. (1997). 'The Relationship between UK Banks and their Small Business Customers', *Small Business Economics*, 9, 167–78.

Birch, D. L. (1979). *The Job Generation Process*. Cambridge, MA: MIT Programme on Neighbourhood and Regional Change.

Board of Trade (1949–63). *Bankruptcy: General Annual Reports*. London: HMSO.

Bonelli, F. (1975). *Lo sviluppo di una grande impresa in Italia: la terni dal 1884 al 1962*. Torino: Einaudi.

—— (1983). 'Alberto Beneduce, il credito industriale e l'origine dell'IRI', in Istituto per la Ricostruzione Industriale, *Alberto Beneduce e i problemi dell' economia italiana del suo tempo*. Roma: I.R.I.

Bonin, H. (1989). *L'Argent en France depuis 1880*. Paris: Masson.

Bordo, M. B. and Eichengreen, B. (1993). *A Retrospective on the Bretton Woods System*. Cambridge, MA: Chicago University Press.

Boswell, J. (1973). *The Rise and Decline of Small Firms*. London: Allen and Unwin.

Bouvier, J. (1973). *Un Siècle de Banque Francaise*. Paris: Hachette Littérature.

Brady, R. (1933). *The Rationalisation Movement in German Industry*. Berkeley: University of California Press.

Broadberry, S. N. and Crafts, N. F. R. (1996). 'British Economic Policy and Industrial Performance in the Early Post-War Period', *Business History*, 38, 65–91.

Brock, W. A. and Evans, D. S. (1986). *The Economics of Small Business*. New York: Holmes & Meier.

Brusco, S. and Paba, S. (1997). 'Per una storia dei distretti industriali italiani dal secondo dopoguerra agli anni novanta', in L. Barca (ed.), *Storia del capitalismo italiano dal dopoguerra a oggi*. Roma: Donzelli.

Bundesverband deutscher Banken (2002) *Neue Strukturen für die Zukunft—Wandel in der Deutschen Kreditwirtschaft*. Berlin: BdB.

Burn, D. (ed.) (1958). *The Structure of British Industry*. Cambridge: Cambridge University Press.

Cahen, L. (1954). 'La Concentration des établissements en France de 1896 à 1936', *Etudes et conjoncture*, 9.

Cailluet, L. (1998). 'Selective Adaptation of American Management Models', in M. Kipping, and O. Bjarnar (eds.) (1998). *The Americanisation of European Business*. London: Routledge.

Cain, P. J. and Hopkins, A. G. (1993). *British Imperialism: Innovation and Expansion, 1688–1914*. London: Longman.

Cameron, R. and Freedman, J. (1983). 'French Economic Growth: A Radical Revision', *Social Science History*, 7, 3–30.

Camilleri, A. S. (1966). *Industrial Medium-term Financial Institutions in Italy*. London: Macmillan.

Capie, F. (1995). 'Commercial Banking in Britain', in C. H. Feinstein (ed.), *Banking, Currency and Finance in Europe between the Wars*. Oxford: Clarendon Press.

—— and Rodrick-Bali, G. (1984). 'Concentration in British Banking 1830–1920', *Business History*, 24, 280–93.

——, Goodhart, C., and Fisher, S. (eds.) (1994). *The Future of Central Banking*. Cambridge: Cambridge University Press.

Capparelli, F. (1981). *Il ruolo della banca locale: il caso della Cassa di Risparmio di Prato*. Prato: Del Palazzo.

Carli, G. (1984). 'Trasformazioni reali e trasformazioni finanziarie', in F. A. Grassini (ed.), *Le banche e il capitale di rischio: speranze o illusioni?*. Bologna: Il Mulino.

Carnevali, F. (1995). 'Finance in the Regions: The Case of England after 1945', in Y. Cassis, D. G. Feldman, and V. Olsson (eds.), *The Evolution of Financial Institutions and Markets in 20th Century Europe*. Aldershot: Scolar Press.

—— (1996). 'Between Markets and Networks: Regional Banks in Italy', *Business History*, 38, 84–100.

—— (1997). 'British and Italian Banks and Small Firms: A Study of the Midlands and Piedmont 1945–1973', unpublished Ph.D. Thesis, London School of Economics and Political Science.

—— (2002). 'Did They Have it so Good? Small Firms and British Monetary Policy in the 1950s', *Journal of Industrial History*, 5, 15–34.

—— and Scott, P. (1999). 'The Treasury as a Venture Capitalist: DATAC Industrial Finance and the Macmillan Gap, 1945–60', *Financial History Review*, 6, 47–65.

Caron, F. (1979). *An Economic History of Modern France*. London: Methuen.

—— (1983). 'L'Évolution de la concentration des entreprises en France au XXème Siècle', in F. Caron (ed.), *Entreprise et entrepreneurs en France aux XIXème et XXème siècle*. Paris: Presses Universitaires de France.

—— and Bouvier, J. (1980). *Histoire économique et sociale de la France*, Part IV, vol. 2. Paris: Presses Universitaires de France.

Carré, J. J., Dubois, P., and Malinvaud, E. (1975). *French Economic Growth*. Stanford: Stanford University Press.

Cassese, S. (1988). *Come e' nata la legge bancaria*. Roma: Banca Nazionale del Lavoro.

Cassis, Y. (1985). 'Management and Strategy in the English Joint Stock Banks 1890–1914', *Business History*, 28, 301–16.

—— (1990). 'British Finance: Success and Controversy' in J. J. Van Helten and Y. Cassis (eds.), *Capitalism in a Mature Economy*. London: Gower.

—— (ed.) (1992). *Finance and Financiers in European History 1880–1960*. Cambridge: Cambridge University Press.

——, Feldman, G. D., and Olsson, U. (eds.) (1995). *The Evolution of Financial Institutions and Markets in 20th Century Europe*. Aldershot: Scolar Press.

Castronovo, V. (1980). *L'Industria italiana dall'ottocento a oggi*. Milano: Mondadori.

—— (1999). *La Fiat: un secolo di storia italiana, 1899–1999*. Milano: Rizzoli.

Cento Bull, A. (1993). *From Peasant to Entrepreneur: The Survival of the Family Economy in Italy*. Oxford: Berg.

Ceriani, L. (1962). 'The Commercial Banks and Financial Institutions', in R. S. Sayers (ed.), *Banking in Western Europe*. Oxford: Clarendon Press.

Cesarini, F., Ferri, G., and Giardino M. (eds.) (1997). *Credito e sviluppo: banche locali cooperative e imprese minori*. Bologna: Il Mulino.

Chadeaux, E. (1987). *L'Industrie aéronautique en France (1900–1950)*. Paris: Economica.

—— (1994). 'La Permanence des petites et moyennes enterprises en France au XXeme siècle' in M. Muller (ed.), *Structure and Strategy of Small and Medium-sized Enterprises since the Industrial Revolution*. Stuttgart: Franz Steiner Verlag.

Chandler, A. D. (1990). *Scale and Scope: The Dynamics of Industrial Capitalism*. Cambridge: Harvard University Press.

——, Amatori, F., and Hikino, T. (eds.) (1997). *Big Business and the Wealth of Nations*. Cambridge: Cambridge University Press.

Checkland, S. G. (1975). *Scottish Banking: A History 1695–1973*. Glasgow: Collins.

Ciampi, C. A. (1984). *La politica creditizia e l'innovazione finanziaria*. Milano: Franco Angeli.

Ciocca, P. and Toniolo, G. (1984). 'Industry and Finance in Italy 1918–1940', *Journal of European Economic History*, 13, 111–36.

Cohen, J. and Federico, G. (2001). *The Growth of the Italian Economy, 1820–1960*. Cambridge: Cambridge University Press.

Cohen, S. (1981). 'Twenty Years of the Gaullist Economy', in W. G. Andrews and S. Hoffman (eds.), *The Fifth Republic at Twenty*. Albany: State University of New York Press.

Colli, A. (2002). *I volti di proteo: storia della piccola impresa in Italia nel novecento*. Torino: Bollati Boringhieri.

Collins, M. (1988). *Money and Banking in the UK: A History*. London: Croom Helm.
—— (1991). *Banks and Industrial Finance in Britain 1800–1939*. London: Macmillan.
—— and Baker, M. (2003). *Commercial Banks and Industrial Finance in England and Wales, 1860–1913*. Oxford: Oxford University Press.
Competition Commission (2002). *Report on the Supply of Banking Services by Clearing Banks to Small and Medium-Sized Enterprises*. London: HMSO.
Conti, G. (1999). 'Le banche e il finanziamento industriale', in F. Amatori, D. Bigazzi, R. Giannetti, and L. Segreto (eds.), *Annali della storia d'Italia: l'industria*. Torino: Einaudi.
—— (2000). 'Processi di integrazione e reti locali: tipologie del credito e della finanza (1861–1936)' in G. Conti, and S. La Francesca (eds.), *Banche e reti di banche nell'Italia postunitaria*. Bologna: Il Mulino.
—— and Ferri, G. (1997). 'Banche locali e sviluppo economico decentrato', in L. Barca (ed.), *Storia del capitalismo italiano dal dopoguerra a oggi*. Roma: Donzelli.
——, Ferri, G., and Polsi, A. (2003). 'Banche cooperative e fascismo: performance e controllo durante le crisi finanziarie degli anni '20 e '30', *Credito popolare*, 1, 10–23.
Cooke, P. and Morgan, K. (2000). *The Associational Economy: Firms, Regions and Innovation*. Oxford: Oxford University Press.
Coopey, R. and Clarke, D. (1995). *3i: Fifty Years Investing in Industry*. Oxford: Oxford University Press.
Cottrell, P. L. (1979). *Industrial Finance 1830–1914*. London: Methuen.
—— (1997). 'Finance and the Germination of the British Corporate Economy', in P. L. Cottrell, A. Teichova, and T. Yuzawa (eds.), *Finance in the Age of the Corporate Economy*. Aldershot: Ashgate.
—— and Anderson B. L. (eds.) (1974). *Money and Banking in England*. Newton Abbott: David & Charles.
Cotula, F., Gelsomino, G. O., and Gigliobianco A. (eds.) (1997). *Donato Menichella: stabilità e sviluppo dell'economia italiana 1946–1960*, vol. 1, *Documenti e Discorsi*. Bari: Laterza.
Cova, A. and Galli, A. M. (1991). *Finanza e sviluppo locale: la Cassa di Risparmio delle provincie lombarde dalla fondazione al 1940*. Milano: Cariplo.
Cowling, K. and Stoneman, P. (1980). *Mergers and Economic Performance*. Cambridge: Cambridge University Press.
Crafts, N. F. R. (1995). ' "You've Never Had It So Good"?: British Economic Policy and Performance, 1945–60', in B. Eichengreen (ed.), *Europe's Post-War Recovery*. Cambridge: Cambridge University Press.
Crafts, N. and Toniolo, G. (1996). 'Postwar Growth: An Overview', in N. Crafts, and G. Toniolo. (eds.), *Economic Growth in Europe since 1945*. Cambridge: Cambridge University Press.
Crestanello, P. (1997). 'La trasformazione in 10 distretti industriali durante gli anni '80', in R. Varaldo and L. Ferrucci (eds.) (1997). *Il distretto industriale tra logiche di impresa e logiche di sistema*. Milano: Angeli.
Crick, W. F. and Wadsworth J. E. (1936). *A Hundred Years of Joint Stock Banking*. London: Hodder and Stoughton.
Croone, D. R. and Johnson, H. G. (eds.), (1970). *Money in Britain 1959–1969*. Oxford: Oxford University Press.

Crouzet, F. (1974). 'French Economic Growth in the 19th century Reconsidered', *History*, 59, 22–34.

—— (1982). *The Victorian Economy*. London: Methuen.

Curzio, Q. and Fortis M. (eds.) (2000). *Il Made in Italy oltre il 2000: innovazione e continuita' Locali*. Bologna: Il Mulino.

Daviet, J. P. (1988). 'Some Features of Concentration in France', in H. Pohl (ed.) *The Concentration Process in the Entrepreneurial Economy since the late 19th Century*. Steiner: Stuttgart.

Davis, E. P. (2003). 'Bank Credit Risk', Economics Division, Bank of England.

Dawson, P. (1926). *Germany's Industrial Revival*. New York: Macmillan.

De Cecco, M. (1997). 'Splendore e crisi del sistema Beneduce' in L. Barca (ed.), *Storia del capitalismo italiano dal dopoguerra a oggi*. Roma: Donzelli.

Deeg, R. (2002). *Finance Capitalism Unveiled: Banks and the German Political Economy*. Ann Arbor: University of Michigan Press.

Dei Ottati, G. (1995). *Tra mercato e comunita'*. Milano: Franco Angeli.

Della Peruta, F. (1987). *Milano: lavoro e fabbrica 1815–1914*. Milano: Franco Angeli.

De Marchi, G. (1952). 'Osservazioni critiche sull'attuale legislazione italiana per il medio-credito alle minori imprese industriali', *Moneta e Credito*, 4, 250–73.

Denton, G., Forsyth, M., and Maclennan, M. (1968). *Economic Planning and Policies in Britain, France and Germany*. London: PEP and George Allen.

Dietsch, M. (2003). 'Financing Small Business in France', *European Investment Bank Papers*, 8, 93–119.

Dixit, K. A. and Pindyck, R. S. (1994). *Investment under Uncertainty*. Princeton: Princeton University Press.

Djelic, M. L. (1998). *Exporting the American Model: The Postwar Transformation of European Business*. Oxford: Oxford University Press.

Donaubauer, K. A. (1982). *Die Konzentration im Deutschen Bankgewerbe 1848–1980*. Frankfurt am Main: Knapp.

Dow, J. C. R. (1970). *The Management of the British Economy 1945–60*. Cambridge: Cambridge University Press.

Driver, C. and Dunne P. (eds.) (1992). *Structural Change in the UK Economy*. Cambridge: Cambridge University Press.

Dunne, P. and Hughes, A. (1994). 'Age, Size, Growth and Survival: UK Companies in the 1980s', *Journal of Industrial Economics*, 42, 115–40.

Edwards, J. and Fischer, K. (1994). *Banks, Finance and Investment*. Cambridge: Cambridge University Press.

Ellwood, D. W. (1992). *Rebuilding Europe: Western Europe and Post-War Reconstruction*. Harlow: Longman.

Eschwege L. (1908). 'Hochfinanz und Mittelstand', *Die Bank* (May).

Eurostat (1996). *Enterprises in Europe, Fourth Report*. Bruxelles: Eurostat.

Faini, R., Galli, G. and Giannini, C. (1999). 'Finance and Development: The Case of Southern Italy', in A. Giovannini (ed.), *Finance and Development: Issues and Experience*. Cambridge: Cambridge University Press.

Falcone, F. (1975). 'Effetti dell'integrazione economica europea sulla struttura delle esportazioni italiane', *Rassegna economica*, 39, 1139–66.

Federation of Small Businesses (2004). *Lifting the Barriers to Growth in UK Small Businesses*. London: FSB.

Federico G. (ed.) (1994). *The Economic Development of Italy since 1870*. Aldershot: Elgar.

Feinstein, C. H. (ed.) (1995). *Banking, Currency and Finance in Europe between the Wars*. Oxford: Clarendon Press.

Feldenkirschen, W. (1987). 'Big Business in Interwar Germany: Organisational Innovation at Vereinigte Stahlwerke, I.G. Farben and Siemens', *Business History Review*, 61, 417–51.

—— (1988). 'Concentration in German Industry 1870–1939', in M. Pohl (ed.) *The Concentration Process in the Entrepreneurial Economy since the late 19th Century*. Stuttgart: Steiner.

Feldman, G. (1993). *The Great Disorder: Politics, Economics and Society in the German Inflation 1914–1924*. Oxford: Oxford University Press.

Fenoaltea, S. (1992). 'Il valore aggiunto dell'industria', in G. Rey (ed.), *I conti economici dell'Italia*, vol.II, *Una stima del valore aggiunto per rami di attivita per il 1911*. Bari: Laterza.

Ferri, G., Masciandaro, D., and Messori M. (2001). 'Governo societario ed efficienza delle banche locali di fronte all'unificazione dei mercati finanziari', in P. Alessandrini (ed.), *Il sistema finanziario italiano tra globalizzazione e localismo*. Bologna: Il Mulino.

Fischer, W. (1972). 'Das deutsche Handwerk im Strukturwandel des 20. Jahrhunderts', in W. Fischer (ed.), *Wirtschaft und Gesellschaft*. Göttingen: Vandenhoeck & Ruprecht.

Fohlen, C. (1956). *L'Industrie Textile au temps du Second Empire*. Paris: Plon.

—— (1965). 'Entrepreneurship and Manangement in France in the 19th Century', in H. J. Habbakkuk and M. Postan (eds.), *The Cambridge Economic History of Europe*, vol. 4. Cambridge: Cambridge University Press.

Foxwell, H. S. (1917). 'The Financing of Industry and Trade', *Economic Journal*, 27, 502–22.

Francke, H. H. and Hudson, M. (1982). *Banking and Finance in West Germany*. London: Croom Helm.

Frattiani, M. and Spinelli, F. (1997). *A Monetary History of Italy*. Cambridge: Cambridge University Press.

Frazer, P. and Vittas, D. (1984). *The Retail Banking Revolution*. London: Lafferty Publications.

Friedenson, P. (1972). *Histoire des usines Renault: naissance de la grande entreprise, 1898–1939*. Paris: Seuil.

Fritsch, M. (1993). 'The Role of Small Firms in West Germany', in Z. J. Acs and D. B. Audretsch (eds.), *Small Firms and Entrepreneurship*. Cambridge: Cambridge University Press.

Ganne, B. (1983). *Gens de cuir, gens du papier: transformations d'Annonay depuis les annees 1920*. Paris: Editions du centre national de la recherche scientifique.

—— (1988). 'La Mutation récente de PME Annonéennes' in B. Ganne et al., *Milieux industriels et systèmes industriels locaux: une comparaison France-Italie*. Lyon: Gruppe Lyonnais de Sociologie Industrielle.

—— (1995). 'France: Behind Small and Medium-size Enterprises Lies the State' in A. Bagnasco and C. Sabel (eds.), *Small and Medium Sized Enterprises*. London: Pinter.

Garside, W. R. and Greaves, J. I. (1996). 'The Bank of England and Industrial Intervention in Interwar Britain', *Financial History Review*, 3, 69–86.

Geroski, P. (1994). *Market Structure, Corporate Performance and Innovative Activity*. Oxford: Clarendon Press.

Gerschenkron, A. (1962). 'Notes on the Rate of Industrial Growth in Italy 1881–1913', in A. Gerschenkron (ed.), *Economic Backwardness in Historical Perspective*. Cambridge MA: Harvard University Press.

Giannetti, R., Federico, G., and Toninelli, P. A. (1994). 'Size and Strategy of Italian Enterprises (1907–1940): Empirical Evidence and some Conjectures', *Industrial and Corporate Change*, 3, 491–512.

—— (1998). *Tecnologia e Sviluppo Economico Italiano 1870–1990*. Bologna: Il Mulino.

Glyn, A., Hughes, A., Lipietz, A., and Singh, A. (1990). 'The Rise and Fall of the Golden Age' in S. A. Marglin and J. B. Schor (eds.), *The Golden Age of Capitalism: Reinterpreting the Post-War Experience*. Oxford: Oxford University Press.

Goodhart, C. A. F. (1972). *The Business of Banking 1891–1914*. London: Weidenfeld & Nicolson.

—— (1989). *Money, Information and Uncertainty*. London: Macmillan.

Gourvish, T. (1996). 'Beyond the Merger Mania', in R. Coopey and N. Woodward (eds.), *Britain in the 1970s*. London: UCL Press.

Grant, A. T. K. (1967). *A Study in the Capital Market in Britain from 1919–1936*, Second ed. London: Macmillan.

Graziani, A. (1972). *L'Economia italiana dal 1945 a oggi*. Bologna: Il Mulino.

Greenwald, B. C. and Stiglitz, J. E. (1990). 'Macroeconomic Models with Equity and Credit Rationing', in R. G. Hubbard (ed.), *Asymmetric Information, Corporate Finance and Investments*. Chicago: University of Chicago Press.

Guarino, G. and Toniolo, G. (1993). *La Banca d'Italia ed il sistema bancario 1919–1936*. Bari: Laterza.

Guerrieri, P. and Milana, C. (1990) *L'Italia e il commercio mondiale*. Bologna: Il Mulino.

Gueslin, A. (1982). *Le Crédit Mutuel: de la caisse rurale à la banque sociale*. Strasbourg: Editions Coprur.

—— (ed.) (1989). *Nouvelle histoire économique de la france contemporaine: l'économie ouverte, 1948–1990*, vol. 4. Paris: Éditions La Découverte.

—— (1992). 'Banks and State in France from the 1880s to the 1930s: The Impossible Advance of the Banks', in Y. Cassis (ed.), *Finance and Financiers in European History 1880–1960*. Cambridge: Cambridge University Press.

Hall, P. A. (1987). 'The State and Economic Decline' in B. Elbaum and W. Lazonick (eds.), *The Decline of the British Economy*. Oxford: Clarendon Press.

Hannah, L. (1976). *The Rise of the Corporate Economy*. London: Methuen.

Hansmann, K.-W. and Ringle, C. M. (2002). 'Finanzierung Mittelstand 2002—eine empirische Untersuchung', University of Hamburg, Institut für Industriebetriebslehre und Organisation, Working Paper no. 8.

Hardach, G. (1995) 'Banking in Germany' in C. H. Feinstein (ed.), *Banking, Currency and Finance in Europe between the Wars*. Oxford: Clarendon Press.

Hardach, G. (2004). 'Banques régionales et banques locales en Allemagne: un système bancaire polarisé', in M. Lescure and A. Plessis (eds.), *Banques locales et banques régionales en Europe au XXe siècle*. Paris: Albin Michel.

Harm, C. (1992). 'The Financing of Small Firms in Germany', *Policy Research Working Paper*, The World Bank, 1–35.

Harris, N. (1972). *Competition and the Corporate Society: British Conservatives, the State and Industry 1945–1964*. London: Methuen.

Hart, P. E. and Oulton, N. (1996). 'Growth and Size of Firms', *Economic Journal*, 106, 1242–52.

Heim, C. (1984). 'Limits to Intervention: The Bank of England and Industrial Diversification in the Depressed Areas', *Economic History Review*, 37 (4), 533–50.

Henze, W. (1987). *Grundriss für die Sparkassenarbeit: Grundzüge der Geschichte des Sparkassenwesen*. Stuttgart: Deutscher Sparkassenverlag.

Herrigel, G. (1994). 'Industry as a Form of Order: A Comparison of the Historical Development of the Machine Tool Industries in the United States and Germany', in J. R. Hollingsworth, P. C. Schmitter, and W. Streeck (eds.), *Governing Capitalist Economies*. Oxford: Oxford University Press.

—— (1996). *Industrial Constructions: The Sources of German Industrial Power*. Cambridge: Cambridge University Press.

Hertner, P. (1983). *Il capitale tedesco in Italia dall'unitá alla prima guerra mondiale*. Bologna: Il Mulino.

Hicks, J. R. (1935). 'Annual Survey of Economic Theory: The Theory of Monopoly', *Econometrica*, 3, 1–20.

Hilton, J. P. (1927). *Britain's First Municipal Savings Bank*. London: Blackfriars Press.

Hirst, P. and Zeitlin, J. (eds.) (1988). *Reversing Industrial Decline*. Oxford: Berg.

——, —— (1989). 'Flexible Specialisation and the Competitive Failure of UK Manufacturing', *Political Quarterly*, 60, 164–78.

Hoffman, S. (1963). *In Search of France*. Cambridge, MA: Harvard University Press.

Hollingsworth, J. R. and Boyer, R. (eds.) (1998). *Contemporary Capitalism: The Embeddedness of Institutions*. Cambridge: Cambridge University Press.

—— , Schmitter, P. C., and Streeck, W. (eds.) (1994). *Governing Capitalist Economies*. New York: Oxford University Press.

Holmes, A. R. and Green, E. (1986). *Midland: 150 years of Banking Business*. London: BT Batsford Ltd.

Hommel, U. and Schneider H. (2003) 'Financing the German Mittelstand', *European Investment Bank Papers*, no. 2, vol. 8, 73, 53–90.

Horne, H. O. (1947). *A History of Savings Banks*. Oxford: Oxford University Press.

Hughes, A. (1993). 'Industrial Concentration and Small Firms in the United Kingdom: the 1980s in Historical Perspective', Z. J. Acs, and D. B. Audretsch (eds.), *Small Firms and Entrepreneurship*. Cambridge: Cambridge University Press.

—— (1997). 'Finance for SMEs: A UK Perspective' *Small Business Economics*, 9, 151–66.

—— and Storey, D. J. (1994). *Finance and the Small Firm*. London: Routledge.

Institut für Mittelstandforschung (2000). 'Mind-Mittelstand in Deutschland'. Berlin: IfM.

James, H. (1986). *The German Slump*. Oxford: Clarendon Press.

Jewkes, J. (1958). *The Sources of Invention*. London: Macmillan.

Joseph, L. (1911). *Industrial Finance: A Comparison between Home and Foreign Development*. London: Institute of Electrical Engineers.

—— (1913). *The Evolution of German Banking*. London: C. E. Layton.

Killick, J. (1997). *The United States and European Reconstruction, 1945–1960*. Edinburgh: Keele University Press.

Kipping, M. (2000). 'A Slow and Difficult process: The Americanisation of the French Steel-producing and Using Industries after the SWW' in J. Zeitlin, and G. Herrigel (eds.), *Americanisation and its Limits*. Oxford: Oxford University Press.

—— and Bjarnar, O. (eds.) (1998). *The Americanisation of European Business*. London: Routledge.

Kluge, A. H. (1991). *Geschichte der Deutschen Bankgenossenschaffen*. Frankfurt-am-Main: Fritz Kapp Verlag.

Kocka, J. (1978). 'Entrepreneurs and Managers in German Industrialisation', in P. Mathias and M. M. Postan (eds.), *The Cambridge Economic History of Europe*, VII, part 1. Cambridge: Cambridge University Press.

—— (1980). 'The Rise of Modern Industrial Enterprise in Germany', in A. D. Chandler, and H. Daems (eds.), *Managerial Hierarchies: Comparative Perspectives on the Rise of the Modern Industrial Enterprise*. Cambridge MA: Harvard University Press.

Kreditanstalt für Wiederaufbau, *Unternehmensfinanzierung im umbruch—die Finanzierungs-perspektiven deutscher Unternehmen im Zeichen von Finanzmarktwandel und Basel II*. Berlin: KfW.

Kuisel, R. F. (1967). *Ernest Mercier, French Technocrat*. Berkeley: University of California Press.

—— (1981). *Capitalism and the State in Modern France*. Cambridge: Cambridge University Press.

Lamandin, M. (1998). *Le concentrazioni bancarie*. Bologna: Il Mulino.

Landes, D. S. (2003). *Unbound Prometheus: Technical Change and Industrial Development in Western Europe from 1750 to the Present*. Cambridge: Cambridge University Press.

Landi, A. (1990). *Dimensioni, costi e profitti delle banche italiane*. Bologna: Il Mulino.

Lescure, M. (1995). 'Banking in France in the Inter-war Period', in C. H. Feinstein (ed.), *Banking, Currency and Finance in Europe between the Wars*. Oxford: Clarendon Press.

—— (1996). *PME et croissance économique: l'expérience française des années 1920*. Paris: Economica.

—— (1999). 'SME in France, 1900–1975', in K. Odaka, and M. Sawai (eds.), *Small Firms, Large Concerns*. Oxford: Oxford University Press.

—— (2002). 'Entre ville et campagne: l'organisation bancaire des districts industriels: l'exemple du Choletais: 1900–1950', in M. Lescure and J. F. Eck (ed.) *Villes et districts industriels en Europe XVIIe–XXè siècle*. Tours: Presse de l'Université de Tours.

—— and Plessis, A. (eds.) (2004). *Banques locales et banques régionales en Europe au XXe siècle*. Paris: Albin Michel.

Lévy-Leboyer, M. (1964). *Les Banques européennes et l'industrialisation internationale dans la premiere moitié du XIX siècle*. Paris: PUF.

—— (1974). 'Le Patronat français, malthusien?', *Mouvement Social*, 88, 18–33.

Lévy-Leboyer, M. (1978). 'Capital Investment and Economic Growth in France, 1820–1930' in *Cambridge Economic History of Europe*, vol. II. Cambridge: Cambridge University Press.

—— (1980). 'The Large Corporation in Modern France', in A. D. Chandler, and H. Daems (eds.), *Managerial Hierarchies: Comparative Perspectives on the Rise of the Modern Industrial Enterprise*. Cambridge MA: Harvard University Press.

—— (ed.) (1996). *Histoire de la France industrielle*. Paris: Larousse.

—— and Lescure, M. (1991). 'France', in R. Sylla and G. Toniolo (eds.), *Patterns of European Industrialisation*. London: Routledge.

Lydall, H. F. (1957). 'The Impact of the Credit Squeeze on Small and Medium-sized Manufacturing Firms', *The Economic Journal*, 67, 415–31.

Loewenstein, A. (1912). *Geschichte des Württemberggischen Kreditbankwesens und seiner Beziehungen zu Handel und Industrie*. Tübingen: Mohr.

Lund, M. and Wright, M. (1999). 'The Financing of Small Firms in the United Kingdom', *Bank of England Quarterly Review*, 39, 73–8.

Lunghini, G. (ed.) (1981). *Scelte politiche e teorie economiche in Italia 1945–1978*. Einaudi: Torino.

Lutz, V. (1962). 'The Central Bank and the System of Credit Control', in R. S. Sayers (ed.) *Banking in Western Europe*. Oxford: Clarendon Press.

Macmillan, H. (1938). *The Middle Way: A Study of the Problem of Economic and Social Progress in a Free and Democratic Society*. London: Macmillan.

Malerba, F. (ed.) (1993). *Sistemi innovativi regionali a confronto*. Milano: Franco Angeli.

Marchesini, G. (1969). 'Gli effetti delle fusioni bancarie', *Moneta e Credito*, 1, 59–81.

Marshall, A. (1923). *Industry and Trade*, 1st edn 1993. London: Macmillan.

Matthias, P. (1983). *The First Industrial Nation: An Economic History of Britain 1700–1914*. London: Methuen.

Mattioli, R. (1961). *Relazione sull'esercizio della banca commerciale*. Milano: Banca Commerciale.

Mayer, C. (1993). 'The Regulation of Financial Services: Lessons from the United Kingdom', in J. Dermine (ed.), *European Banking in the 1990s*, 2nd edn. Oxford: Blackwell.

Meakin, W. (1928). *The New Industrial Revolution*. London: V. Gollancz Ltd.

Meeks, G. (1977). *Disappointing Marriage: A Study of the Gains from Merger*. Cambridge: Cambridge University Press.

Mengarelli, G. (1979). *Politica e teoria monetaria nello sviluppo italiano*. Torino: Einaudi.

—— (1979). 'La politica monetaria in Italia (1960–1975)', in G. Franco (ed.) *Sviluppo e crisi dell'economia italiana*. Milano: Bollati.

Menichella, D. (1950). 'Intervento al convegno nazionale delle casse rurali ed artigiane', *Cooperatione di credito*, August-September, 80–95.

—— (1955). 'Espansione economica in regime di stabilitá monetaria', *Bancaria*, 11, 101–12.

—— (1957). 'Il sistema creditizio fattore di stabilita' monetaria e di sviluppo economico', dichiarazioni fatte all'assemblea dell'associazione bancaria italiana, *Bancaria*, 13, 123–34.

—— (1967). *Scritti e discorsi. 1933–1966*. Roma: Banca d'Italia.

Mercer, H. (1995). *Constructing a Competitive Order: The Hidden History of British Antitrust Policies*. Cambridge: Cambridge University Press.

Middlemas, K. (1979). *Politics in Industrial Society*. London: André Deutsch.

Minguet, G. (1993). *Chefs d'Entreprise dans l'Ouest*. Paris: Presses Universitaires de France.

Ministero per la Costitutente (1946). *Rapporto della Commissione Economica presentato all'Assemblea Costitutente, Relazione su Credito e Assicurazione*. Roma: Poligrafico dello Stato.

—— (1947). *Rapporto della Commissione Economica presentato all'Assemblea Costituente. II: Industria, II, Appendice alla relazione (interrogatori)*. Roma: Poligrafico dello Stato.

Modigliani, F. and Miller, M. (1958). 'The Cost of Capital, Corporation Finance and the Theory of Investment', *American Economic Review*, 48, 261–7.

Monopolies Commission (1968). *Barclays Bank Ltd, Lloyds Bank Ltd, and Midlands Bank Ltd: A Report on the Proposed Merger*. London: HMSO.

Mosely, H. (1917). 'The German Method of Banking and How it is Designed to Help Commerce and Industry', *Journal of the Institute of Bankers*, 38, 64–82.

Nardozzi, G. (1983). *Tre sistemi creditizi a confronto: banche ed economia in Francia, Germania e Italia*. Mulino: Bologna.

National Board for Prices and Incomes (1967). *Report No. 34, Bank Charges*, Cmd 3292. London: HMSO.

Nelson, R. R. and Winter, S. G. (1982). *An Evolutionary Theory of Economic Change*. London: Belknap Press.

Nye, J. V. (1987). 'Firm Size and Economic Backwardness: A New Look at the French Industrialisation Debate', *Journal of Economic History*, 47, 649–70.

O'Brien, P. and Keyder, C. (1978). *Economic Growth in Britain and France, 1780–1914*. London: Allen and Unwin.

Ogilvie, S. and Overy, R. (eds.) (2003). *Germany: A New Social and Economic History*, vol. 3. London: Arnold.

Onado, M. (1980). *Il sistema finanziario italiano: i circuiti di distribuzione del credito: 1964–1978*. Bologna: Il Mulino.

Osti, G. L. and Ranieri, R. (1993). *L'Industria di stato dall'ascesa all'degrado*. Bologna: Il Mulino.

Owen Smith, E. (1994). *The German Economy*. London: Routledge.

Pace, C. and Morelli G. (eds.) (1984). *Origini e identita' del credito speciale*. Milano: Franco Angeli.

Padoa-Schioppa, T. (1993). *The Sheltered Economy: Structural Problems in the Italian Economy*. Oxford: Oxford University Press.

—— (1994). 'Profili di diversitá nel sistema bancario italiano', *Banca d'Italia bollettino economico*, 22, 234–45.

Pelly, D. R. (1992). *Loose Change*. Great Dunmow: D. R. Pelly.

Penrose, E. (1968). *The Theory of the Growth of the Firm*. Oxford: Basil Blackwell.

Piercy, Lord (1955). 'The MacMillan Gap and the Shortage of Risk capital', *Journal of the Royal Statistical Society*, 118, 4–8.

Piluso, G. (1999). 'Gli istituti di credito speciale', in F. Amatori, D. Bigazzi, R. Giannetti, and L. Segreto (eds.), *Annali della storia d' italia: l'industria*. Torino: Einaudi.

Piluso, G. (2000). 'Il mercato del credito a milano dopo l'unita', in G. Conti, and S. La Francesca (eds.), *Banche e reti di banche nell'italia postunitaria*. Bologna: Il Mulino.

Piore, M. and Sabel, C. (1994). *The Second Industrial Divide*. New York: Basic Books.

Pizzorno, A. (1974). 'I ceti medi nel meccanismo del consenso', in F. L. Cavazza and S. R. Graubard (eds.), *Il caso italiano*. Milano: Garzanti.

Plessis, A. (1987). 'Le "Retard français": la faute á la banque? Banques locales, succursales de la Banque de France et financement de l'économie sous le Second Empire', in P. Friedenson and A. Strauss (eds.), *Le Capitalisme français, 19e–20e siècles: blocages et dynamismes d'une croissance*. Paris: Fayard.

—— (1991). 'Les Banques, le crédit et l'économie' in M. Lévy-Leboyer and J. C. Casanova (eds.), *Entre l'état et le marché: l'économie française des années 1880 à nos jours*. Paris: Gallimard.

Polanyi, K. (1957). *The Great Transformation: The Political and Economic Origins of our Time*, 1st edn 1944. Boston: Beacon Press.

Polsi, A. (2000). 'L'articolazione territoriale del sistema bancario italiano fra scelte di mercato e intervento delle autorità monetarie (1900–1936)', in G. Conti and S. La Francesca (eds.), *Banche e reti di banche nell'italia postunitaria*. Bologna: Il Mulino.

Prais, S. J. (1974). 'A New Look at the Growth of Industrial Concentration', *Oxford Economic Papers*, 26, 273–88.

Ritschel, D. (1997). *The Politics of Planning: The Debate on Economic Planning in Britain in the 1930s*. Oxford: Oxford University Press.

Robson, M. T. (1998). 'Self-employment in the UK Regions', *Applied Economics*, 30, 313–22.

Ross, D. M. (1990). 'The Clearing Banks and the Finance of Industry: New Perspectives for the Interwar Years', in J. J. van Helten and Y. Cassis (eds.), *Capitalism in a Mature Economy*. Aldershot: Elgar.

—— (1992). 'British Monetary Policy and the Banking System in the 1950s', *Business and Economic History*, 21, 199–208.

—— (1996). 'The Unsatisfied Fringe in Britain, 1930s–80s', *Business History*, 38, 11–26.

—— (1997). 'The "Macmillan Gap" and the British Credit Market in the 1930s', in P. L. Cottrell, A. Teichova, and T. Yuzawa (eds.), *Finance in the Age of the Corporate Economy*. Aldershot: Ashgate.

Rossi, N. and Toniolo, G. (1992). 'Catching Up or Falling Behind? Italy's Economic Growth, 1890–1947', *The Economic History Review*, 45, 537–63.

——, —— (1995). 'Italy', in N. Crafts and G. Toniolo (eds.), *Economic Growth in Europe since 1945*. Cambridge: Cambridge University Press.

Rothwell, R. and Zegveld, W. (1983). *Innovation and the Small and Medium-Sized Firm*. London: Frances Pinter.

Rouse, H. (1950). 'Midland Bank Ltd.', in G. E. Milward (ed.), *Large Scale Organisation*. London: MacDonald & Evans.

Sabbatucci Severini, P. (2002). 'Circuiti creditizi per la manifattura e le piccole imprese', in G. Conti and T. Fanfani (eds.), *Regole e mercati: fiducia, concorrenza e innovazioni finanziarie nella storia creditizia italiana*. Pisa: Edizioni Plus.

Sabel, C. and Zeitlin, J. (1985). 'Historical Alternatives to Mass Production: Politics, Markets and Technology in Nineteenth Century Industrialisation', *Past and Present*, 108, 133–76.

——, —— (1997). *World of Possibilities: Flexibility and Mass Production in Western Industrialisation*. Cambridge: Cambridge University Press.

Sapelli, G. and Carnevali, F. (1993). *Uno sviluppo fra politica e strategia: ENI (1953–1985)*. Milano: Franco Angeli.

—— (1958). *Storia economica dell'Italia contemporanea*. Milano: Boringhieri.

Saraceno, P. (1958). 'Riesame del piano Vanoni al fine 1957', *Moneta e credito*, 1, 15–27.

Saville, R. (1996). *Bank of Scotland: A History, 1695–1995*. Edinburgh: Edinburgh University Press.

Sauer, W. (1984). 'Small Firms and the German Economic Miracle', in C. Levicki (ed.), *Small Business. Theory and Policy*. London: Acton Society Trust.

Schneiger, I. and Moole, J. (1961). 'Chicago Banking: The Structure of Banks and Related Financial Institutions in Chicago and Other Areas', *Journal of Business*, 34, 203–366.

Segreto, L. (1996). 'Americanizzare o modernizzare l'economia? Progetti americani e risposte italiane negli anni cinquanta e sessanta', *Passato e presente*, 14, 55–83.

—— (1999). 'Storia d'italia e storia dell'industria' in F. Amatori, D. Bigazzi, R. Giannetti, and L. Segreto (eds.), *Annali della storia d'italia: l'industria*. Torino: Einaudi.

Servan-Schreiber, J. J. (1967). *Le Défi américain*. Paris: Denöel.

Shonfield, A. (1965). *Modern Capitalism: The Changing Balance of Public and Private Power*. Oxford: Oxford University Press.

Small Business Research Trust (1999). 'Business Finance', *NatWest SBRT Quarterly Survey of Small Business in Britain*, 15, 17–22.

Spadavecchia, A. (2003). 'State Subsidies and the Sources of Company Finance in Italian Industrial Districts, 1951–1991'. Unpublished PhD thesis, University of London.

—— (2005). 'Financing Industrial Districts in Italy, 1971–91: A Private Venture?', *Business History*, forthcoming.

Stewart, A. (1916). *British and German Industrial Conditions*. London: Odhams.

Stiglitz, J. E. and Weiss, A. (1981). 'Credit Rationing in Markets with Imperfect Competition', *American Economic Review*, 71, 393–416.

Storey, D. J. and Johnson, S. (1987). *Job Generation and Labour Market Changes*. London: Routledge.

—— (1994). *Understanding the Small Business Sector*. London: Routledge.

Streeck, W. (1984). *Industrial Relations in West Germany: A Case Study of the Car Industry*. London: Heinemann.

—— (1991). 'On the Institutional Conditions of Diversified Quality Production' in E. Matzner, and W. Streeck (eds.), *Beyond Keynesianism: The Socio-economics of Production and Full Employment*. Aldershot: Edward Elgar.

—— (1997). 'German Capitalism: Does it Exist? Can it Survive?' in C. Crouch and W. Streeck (eds.), *The Political Economy of Modern Capitalism*. London: Sage.

Strong, N. and Waterson, M. (1987). 'Principles, Agents and Information', in R. Clarke and T. McGuiness (eds.), *The Economics of the Firm*. Oxford: Oxford University Press.

Tew, B. and Henderson, R. F. (1959). *Studies in Company Finance*. Cambridge: Cambridge University Press.

Thomas, W. A. (1978). *The Finance of British Industry 1918–1976*. London: Methuen.

Thomes, P. (1995). 'German Savings Banks as Instruments of Regional Development up to the Second World War' in Y. Cassis, G. D. Feldman, and U. Olsson (eds.), *The Evolution of Financial Institutions and Markets in 20th century Europe*. Leicester: Scolar Press.

Thompson, J. (1963). 'Chairman's Address', *Annual Statement to Barclays Bank Ltd Shareholders*. London.

Tilly, R. (1966). *Financial Institutions and Industrialisation in the Rhineland 1815–1870*. Madison: University of Wisconsin Press.

—— (1986). 'German Banking 1850–1914: Development Assistance for the Strong', *Journal of European Economic History*, 15, 113–81.

—— (1991). 'Germany', in R. Sylla and G. Toniolo (eds.), *Patterns of European Industrialisation*. London: Routledge.

—— (1999). 'Policy, Capital and Industrial Finance in Germany' in R. Silla, R. Tilly, and G. Tortella (eds.) *The State, the Financial System and Economic Modernisation*. Cambridge: Cambridge University Press.

Tiratsoo, N. and Tomlinson, J. (1993). *Industrial Efficiency and State Intervention: Labour 1939–51*. London: Routledge.

Tolliday, S. (1987). 'Steel and Rationalisation Policies, 1918–1950', in B. Elbaum and W. Lazonick (eds.), *The Decline of the British Economy*. Clarendon Press: Oxford.

—— (1987). *Business, Banking and Politics: A Case Study of British Steel, 1918–1936*. Cambridge MA: Harvard University Press.

Tomlinson, J. (1980). 'Socialist Politics and the "Small Business"', *Politics and Power*, 1, 165–74.

—— (1990). *Public Policy and the Economy since 1900*. Oxford: Clarendon Press.

—— (1997). 'Conservative Modernisation, 1960–1964: Too Little, Too Late?', *Contemporary British History*, 11, 18–38.

—— and Tiratsoo, N. (1998). 'Americanisation Beyond the Mass Production Paradigm' in M. Kipping and O. Bjarnar (eds.), *The Americanisation of European Business*. London: Routledge.

——,—— (1998). *The Conservatives and Industrial Efficiency 1951–64: Thirteen Wasted Years?*: London: Routledge.

Toniolo, G. (1993). *'Il profilo economico': la Banca d'Italia e il sistema bacario 1919–1936*. Bari: Laterza.

Trentman, F. (2001). 'Bread, Milk and Democracy: Consumption and Citizenship in 20th Century Britain', in M. Daunton and M. Hilton (eds.), *The Politics of Consumption: Citizenship in Europe and America*. Oxford: Berg.

Trigilia C. and Voelzkow, H. (2001). *Local Production Systems in Europe: Rise or Demise?* Oxford: Oxford University Press.

Truptil, R. J. (1936). *British Banks and the London Money Market*. London: Jonathan Cape.

Tuke, A. W. (1972). *Barclays Bank Ltd. 1926–1969*. London: Barclays Bank.

'Un Tout Petit Boum' (1998). *Euromoney*, January, 95–9.

Van Helten, J. J. and Cassis, Y. (eds.) (1990). *Capitalism in a Mature Economy*. Aldershot: Elgar.

Verdier, D. (2002). *Moving Money*. Cambridge: Cambridge University Press.

Vinen R. (1996). *France 1934–1970*. London: Macmillan.

Warriner, D. (1931). *Combines and Rationalisation in Germany 1924–1928*. London: King & Son Ltd.

Weiss, L. (1984). 'The Italian State and Small Firms', *Archives européennes de sociologie*, 25, 223–37.

—— (1988). *Creating Capitalism: The State and Small Business since 1945*. London: Basil Blackwell.

Wellhöner, V. and Wixforth, H. (2003). 'Finance and Industry', in S. Ogilvie and R. Overy (eds.), *Germany: A New Social and Economic History*, vol. 3. London: Arnold.

Wengenroth, U. (1999). 'Small-scale Business in Germany', in K. Odaka and M. Sawai (eds.), *Small Firms, Large Concerns*. Oxford: Oxford University Press.

Williamson, O. (1979). 'Transaction Cost Economics: The Governance of Contractual Economies', *Journal of Law and Economics*, 22, 233–61.

Willis, H. P. and Beckhart, B. H. (eds.) (1929). *Foreign Banking Systems*. London: I. Pitman & Sons.

Wilson, J. S. G. (1957). *French Banking Structure and Credit Policy*. London: Bell & Sons.

Winkler, H. A. (1976). 'From Social Protectionism to National Socialism: The German Small Business Movement in Comparative Perspective', *Journal of Modern History*, 48, 1–18.

Winter, S. G. (1984). 'Schumpeterian Competition In Alternative Technological Regimes', *Journal of Economic Behaviour and Organisation*, 5, 287–320.

Wood, J. H. (1975). *Commercial Bank Loans and Investment Behavior*. London: Wiley.

Worswick, G. D. N. and Ady P. H. (eds.) (1962). *The British Economy in the 1950s*. Oxford: Clarendon Press.

Zamagni, V. (1990). *Dalla periferia al centro: la seconda rinascita economica dell'italia, 1861–1990*. Bologna: Il Mulino; English translation 1993, *An Economic History of Italy, 1860–1999*. Oxford: Oxford University Press.

Zeitlin, J. (2000). 'Americanizing British Engineering? Strategic Debate, Selective Adaptation and Hybrid Innovation in Post-War Reconstruction, 1945–1960' in J. Zeitlin and G. Herrigel (eds.), *Americanization and its Limits: Reworking US Technology and Management in Post-War Europe and Japan*. Oxford: Oxford University Press.

Ziegler, D. (1990). *Central Bank, Peripheral Industry: The Bank of England in the Provinces, 1826–1913*. Leicester: Scolar Press.

—— (1997). 'The Origins of the Macmillan Gap: Comparing Britain and Germany in the Early 20th Century', in P. L. Cottrell, A. Teichova, and T. Yuzawa, *Finance in the Age of the Corporate Economy*. Aldershot: Ashgate.

Zysman, J. (1983). *Governments, Markets and Growth: Financial Systems and the Politics of Industrial Change*. Oxford: Martin Robertson.

INDEX